DISCARD

World University Library

The World University Library is an international
series of books, each of which has been specially
commissioned. The authors are leading scientists
and scholars from all over the world who, in an age of
increasing specialisation, see the need for a
broad, up-to-date presentation of their subject.
The aim is to provide authoritative introductory
books for university students which will be of
interest also to the general reader.
The series is published in Britain, France, Germany,
Holland, Italy, Spain, Sweden and the United States

Frontispiece: Units of the Chinese People's Liberation Army
advance through a curtain of smoke to seize Lanchau in 1949.

Robert C. North

Chinese Communism

World University Library

McGraw-Hill Book Company
New York Toronto

Library of Congress Catalog Card Number: 64–66180
Filmset by BAS Printers Limited, Wallop, Hampshire, England
Printed by Officine Grafiche Arnoldo Mondadori, Verona, Italy

Contents

Ch'en Tu-hsiu, scholar and one of the founders of the
Chinese Communist movement (1879–1942). As dean of the department of literature
at Peking National University and also as editor of the magazine
New Youth, Ch'en had a powerful influence upon Chinese revolutionary
thought even before his conversion to Communism – demanding the
introduction of Western ideas and opposing Chinese traditions.

1 China and the challenge of the West

Commissioner Lin's myopia

Communist China is struggling to transform itself from an agrarian to an industrial state – from bullock cart to atomic reactor – in something less than a generation. This in itself is no mean task, but the political and psychological challenges are no less spectacular. For the Peking leadership seeks also to regain in an age of nuclear energy, automation and space exploration, the power, prestige, and cultural eminence which the ancient Chinese empire once enjoyed – but lost with the rise of Western commerce, finance, science and technology.

Before about 1850 the Chinese Empire had viewed itself as the center of the universe, the greatest power on earth, and the only civilization in the world that really mattered. People living around the periphery were considered barbarians and their states were looked down upon as tributaries to Chinese suzerainty. In Chinese diplomacy there was no concept of equality between the Empire and other nations, and the outsider, including the European, was accorded minimal status. 'The laws of China recognize the duty of pity to foreigners in distress,' a Western 'barbarian' reported, 'such as shipwrecked seamen, or needy traders who require the necessities of life for their starving native countries. But in any other light the law views them as rivals and enemies, to be distrusted and guarded against.[1] Imperial edicts, 'fulminated by the government' were usually intended, Westerners felt, 'to answer the double purpose of holding up foreigners to the contempt of the people and of oppressing them, under cover of old regulations,' whenever it was convenient to do so.

With the close of the eighteenth century and the beginning of the nineteenth, Great Britain and other expanding European nations addressed the Chinese Emperor on a variety of occasions and often sent him presents. What they did not at first realize was that even these small courtesies were interpreted by the Chinese Son of Heaven as obeisances and tributes from sovereigns lesser than himself.

7

China

The approach of the Emperor of China to his tent in Tartary to receive the British Ambassador, the Earl of Macartney, in 1793. As the Chinese saw it, the paying of tribute and also 'the performance of the kowtow, the three kneelings and nine prostrations' – to which British and other European envoys objected – were acknowledgments of the Emperor's supremacy as mediator between Heaven and Earth.

When the Earl of Macartney headed a British Embassy to the Chinese Court in 1793, he was viewed as a bearer of tribute, and the Emperor made it clear to King George III that there was no need for trade with him or other barbarians. 'As your Ambassador can see for himself, we possess all things. I set no value on objects strange or ingenious, and have no use for your country's manufactures.'[2]

But the first Anglo-Chinese War – the so-called Opium War of 1839 – dissolved Chinese seclusion and undermined her self-assured dignity. More and more the situation was reversed: China became an economic and political tributary to Western suzerainty.

A Gillray print of the Macartney embassy to the Chinese court, 1793. For generations the Chinese emperors had been receiving tribute from various neighbouring peoples and bestowing in return a seal somewhat comparable to the investiture of a vassal in medieval Europe. Undoubtedly, many of the ambassadors had intended the goods they bore as gifts rather than as tributes.

In 1644 a foreign, Manchu dynasty, the Ch'ing, had established its rule over China. During early decades of the nineteenth century the Ch'ing government found itself less and less competent to cope with problems arising in the country. The government bureaucracy had lost its vigor, and the leadership was corrupt and effete. From the middle of the previous century the Chinese population had been expanding rapidly, and peasants on the countryside were suffering more and more distress. The dynasty had made itself vulnerable, moreover, by trying to preserve segregation between Manchus and Chinese. Disproportionate numbers of Manchus were appointed to administrative positions. Indeed, there were separate governmental examinations for Manchu candidates. The Manchu banner system dominated army organization and military affairs. Marriage was officially forbidden between Manchus and Chinese. And Chinese were forced to wear the queue as a sign of their subservience – 'a long tail behind, thus causing the Chinese to become animals.'[3] Manchu rulers never allowed the Chinese to forget that the Ch'ing was a foreign dynasty.

Unfortunately for the Manchus, it was almost precisely at this juncture that the challenge of Western political, military and economic penetration became increasingly acute.

Like other Western maritime nations seeking to open China for commerce, Great Britain had found itself blocked at almost every turn by the Ch'ing government. In order to establish its trade on a sound financial basis, therefore, the British began smuggling opium into Chinese ports. British merchants soon developed an enormous clientele, however illicit, and the enterprise proved extraordinarily profitable.

Chinese efforts to halt this trade, coupled with British resentment of Chinese attitudes towards even legitimate foreign commerce, led to the so-called Opium War of 1839.

Lin Tse-hsü, Imperial High Commissioner and a director of the Emperor's War Board, wrote Queen Victoria at this time protesting the opium trade. 'When your majesty receives this document,' he urged, 'let us have a speedy communication in reply . . . Do not . . . evade or procrastinate.'[4]

The High Commissioner chided the Queen for allowing the opium trade to flourish. '. . . we have heard that in your honorable barbarian country the people are not permitted to inhale the drug. If it is admittedly so deleterious, how can to seek profit by exposing others to its malific power be reconciled with the decrees of Heaven?'[5]

Commissioner Lin made perfectly clear how he viewed the British monarch. 'You, queen of your honorable nation, sit upon a throne occupied through successive generations by predecessors all of whom have been styled respectful and obedient.' Over the years,

Capture of Ting-hai, Chusan during the First Anglo-Chinese War, 1839–42. The Chinese had kept themselves isolated from the rest of the world so long that they thought the British warships were ineffectual because of their deep draft, and that British soldiers were unable to maneuver on land because of their tight trousers.

China's Heavenly dynasty had 'nourished and cherished' the British people and had made it possible for remote England to 'become the rich and flourishing country' it was said to be.

In this myopic and self-centered view the Emperor was clearly not to be trifled with. 'Our celestial empire rules over ten thousand kingdoms,' Lin Tse-hsü warned. 'Most surely do we possess a measure of god-like majesty which ye cannot fathom. Still, we cannot bear to stay or exterminate without previous warning.'

The High Commissioner could afford to be generous with the far-off queen, for the British appeared to have been grossly over-rated. 'Now here is why the people are dazzled by the name of

Signing of the Anglo-Chinese Treaty of Nanking in
August 1842 as an outcome of the so-called Opium War
in which the Chinese were repeatedly defeated. This treaty
ceded the island of Hong Kong to Great Britain and opened five major
Chinese ports to foreign commerce and residence,
thus bringing China's splendid isolation to an end.

England,' Lin informed the Emperor. 'Because her vessels are
sturdy and her cannons fierce, they call her powerful. But the warships of the said Barbarians are very heavy, taking water to the
depth of tens of feet . . . If we refrain from fighting with them on the
sea, they have no opportunity to take advantage of their skill. Once
in harbour their vessels become unwieldy . . . '

With respect to British soldiers – they lacked skill in using fists
and swords like proper fighters. 'Also, their legs are firmly bound
with cloth, and in consequence it is very inconvenient for them to
stretch. Should they land it is apparent that they can do little harm.
and therefore, what is called their power can be controlled without
difficulty.'[6]

In due course British and Chinese naval units found themselves
engaged in combat. 'Their guns and powder must have been good
from the distance they carried,' a British eyewitness reported, 'but
not being fitted for elevation or depression, all their shot were too

high to have any effect, except on the spars and rigging . . . Their wretched gunnery hurt no one.'[7]

The battle was over in less than an hour, and it was then the High Commissioner's painful duty to break this news to his Emperor. Prudently, Lin Tse-hsü proceeded as high-ranking officers in similar predicaments had proceeded before and have proceeded since: he reported the defeat as a glorious victory. The Emperor, being enormously pleased that his ships had overcome the Barbarian fleet, issued a Vermilion Decree commending the admiral in command and bestowing upon him a commensurate decoration.

Rise and fall of the Heavenly Younger Brother

For over half a century the Ch'ing Dynasty managed to live on – self-centered, threatened from all sides, and pathetically out of touch with the rest of the world that was changing so rapidly. Meanwhile, the Western merchant, the Western missionary, the Western diplomat and eventually the Western intellectual chipped and hacked and battered at the foundations of China's age-old 'world order'.

At the same time, moreover, the Empire was increasingly threatened domestically. The population was steadily increasing, there was peasant unrest, and Chinese of differing interests considered the Ch'ing administration incompetent as well as arrogant. In the south of China, particularly, Ch'ing officials found their authority challenged by the activities of secret societies that were dedicated to overthrowing the dynasty. Even before the Opium War these societies had made their influence felt in Kiangsi, Kwangsi, Kwangtung, Hunan, Taiwan and especially in Fukien. By 1850 the societies were fomenting open rebellion in some of these provinces, and in Hunan, Kwangsi and Yunnan local authorities were finding it impossible to maintain order.

One of these local disorders in Kwangsi set in motion a vast movement in 1851 which lasted for more than a decade and became known as the Taiping Rebellion. Hung Hsiu-ch'üan, the titular head of this movement, had been ambitious to win a government post but could not pass the pre-requisite examinations. With his third failure, Hung began reading with great care a number of Christian evangelical tracts which persuaded him that in a series of earlier visions – during a prolonged nervous collapse – he had come face to face with God, the Heavenly Father, in the form of a 'venerable old man', and also with Jesus Christ, who had appeared as the Elder Brother. Hung now became convinced that God had recognized him as the Second Son, the Heavenly Younger Brother, and was commissioning him to destroy idols and demons and lead China back to worship of the Heavenly Father.

After this essentially religious beginning, Hung's movement began attracting large numbers of followers, with the consequence that government authorities became increasingly concerned. Conflicts developed, and the activities and aims of the movement grew more and more political. This change in purpose soon attracted rapidly growing numbers of people who had little else in common other than a desire to overthrow the government. The movement developed an army, which successfully repulsed a Manchu assault in December 1850. During a public celebration of the victory Hung proclaimed himself Heavenly King of the T'ai-p'ing t'ien-kuo, or Heavenly Kingdom of Great Peace.

Over succeeding years Hung's fast-growing army fought its way through Hunan to the Yangtze, then proceeded eastward by land and water, captured Nanking in March 1853, and made preparations for a 'Northern Expedition' against Peking itself. Collateral Taiping armies attacked cities which the 'Northern Expedition' by-passed, or which had been re-captured by Manchu forces.

Taiping troops never succeeded in capturing Peking, however, and after 1856 their tide began slowly to ebb. In this change of fortune the attitude of Westerners in China was a crucial factor. In opposing the Ch'ing government, the Taiping rebels and the British and other foreign powers with footholds in China were fighting a common enemy. But to the Westerners it became more and more evident that their trade was ruined wherever Taiping

forces took over. First came Western decisions to defend their treaty ports from Taiping forces; then the policy of tactical alliance with the Empire. The British lent Charles George – 'Chinese' – Gordon to the Manchu government, which placed him in command of the 'Ever-victorious Army' – a contingent of foreign adventurers serving under an American, Frederick T. Ward. Thereafter the Ch'ing régime, supported by various foreign contingents, pressed the rebel forces with almost constant attack. Hung Hsiuch'üan, the Heavenly King, died, and on 19 July 1864 Imperial troops captured Nanking, the Taiping capital – though not until the city walls had been undermined and the defences stormed. Thousands of rebels were slaughtered by the victorious Ch'ing forces, but none surrendered. Two-thirds of the Empire had been ravaged and an estimated 10,000,000 lives lost. The rebel forces, moreover, had tried to institute a land system including the classification of land, its redistribution and administration, and a 'collective' plan of living for the peasants – which in many respects foreshadowed Communist plans one hundred years later.

At last the rebellion had come to an end. Taiping troops in other parts of China were now rapidly exterminated – the relatively few who were captured being promptly executed. The foreign powers were now free to extend their various interests by means that were less spectacular, perhaps, but in the long run more effective.

Collapse of an Empire, the rise of nationalism and some dilemmas of Sun Yat-sen

With succeeding years the Western impact gathered increasing force. In the past China had often granted concessions as a means of accommodating – and controlling – foreigners. But now the system began to get out of hand as Westerners secured concessions or settlements in Shanghai, Canton, Hankow, Tientsin and in other cities – enclaves over which the Chinese government retained no administrative jurisdiction. More extensive control was exercised by means of leases over whole areas: Dairen and Port Arthur to

Russia for twenty-five years; Kiaochow to Germany for ninety-nine years; Weihaiwei, Mirs Bay and Deep Bay to Great Britain; Kwangchowan to France for ninety-nine years; and so forth.

In their competition for economic and political advantages in China, Great Britain, France, Germany and other nations approached by sea and then moved from treaty ports into the interior. Britain also advanced from India into Tibet. Tsarist Russia proceeded overland, trying to check British influence along frontiers from Turkey to Korea, to secure warm-water ports on the Pacific coast, and to protect its Far Eastern flank against a rapidly rising Japan.

Shortly after the middle of the nineteenth century Tsarist Russia established the city of Khabarovsk and strengthened its military power in the Far East as conflicts inspired by the Crimean War spread into the Pacific. Subsequently, through the Convention of Peking (1860), St Petersburg secured title, at Chinese expense, to the whole coast of Manchuria east of the Ussuri River and south to the Korean border. With this new sphere and with an ocean outlet through Vladivostok, Russia in 1895 completed construction of a first stage in the Trans-Siberian Railway. Then in order to avoid a loop around Manchuria, the Russian government secured a right of way across Chinese territory for the Chinese Eastern Railway which was to be jointly operated for eighty years thereafter. A year and a half later the Russians obtained from China the twenty-five year lease of the Port Arthur and Dairen area for a naval base, and concessions for a spur system, the Chan Chung, or South Manchurian Railway, in order to connect Dairen with the main Trans-Siberian line.

Imperial Russia also made important incursions into Sinkiang, or Chinese Turkestan, which China claimed to have held for more than 2,000 years. In 1871 St Petersburg moved troops into the territory of Ili in order to safeguard trade routes. Though assurances were made that the occupation was temporary, the Treaty of Livadavia (1879) ceded to Russia the western and richer part of Ili, together with strategic mountain passes in the Tien Shan ranges.

The storming of Pai-how Forts by French forces during the Anglo-Franco-Chinese War of 1860. As Europeans consolidated their positions in China through treaties which the Chinese considered unequal, East–West antagonisms multiplied, and new wars broke out. Momentarily repulsed at Taku, British and French forces fought their way through Tientsin, captured Peking and put the emperor to flight.

Subsequently, through the Treaty of St Petersburg (1881), parts of this territory were re-acquired by China.

The Tsarist Government pressed its encroachment on Chinese territory almost to the eve of the Bolshevik revolution. In 1911 Outer Mongolia proclaimed its independence from China. During World War I, however, St Petersburg concluded the Kiakhta Agreement (1915) with China which labeled the region a Chinese vassal state, but actually transformed it into a Tsarist protectorate.

The extension of foreign commercial and political interests led to the division of China into spheres of interest. Imperial Russia

Siberian Railways, December 1911. During the Anglo-French occupation of Peking in 1860 the Russians, acting as intermediaries, promised to 'secure' a withdrawal from China which they knew the British had already decided upon. As a consequence, Russia obtained the whole coast of Manchuria south to the Korean border. They completed construction of a first link in the Trans-Siberian Railway in 1895.

claimed Manchuria as such a sphere, and Germany claimed similar prerogatives in Shantung. With possession of a coastal leasehold, the Western powers (and later Japan) tended to assume presumptive claims to much larger areas in the hinterland. Increasingly, foreign syndicates strengthened their positions by obtaining railroad rights of way and also rights over large areas for exploitation of mineral and other natural wealth. Moreover, foreign loans to the Chinese government were often secured by payments from maritime customs revenue, or the salt tax, the inland customs tax (*likin*), or other internal revenues.

During the latter half of the nineteenth century and the early years of the twentieth, Empire leaders sharply disagreed over the most effective way to meet the Western economic, political and technological onslaught. Some Chinese believed that stubborn isolation and the eradication of foreign influences offered the only feasible course. Others called for reinvigorating those customs, values and institutions that had made the Empire great, but which were thought to have fallen into disuse. A third group argued for the carefully controlled incorporation into the system of selected techniques and institutions from the West. And finally, there were leaders who stood for repudiation of the old system and thorough-going westernization as the only possible solution.

Unfortunately, Imperial leadership, torn by these divided councils, lost the capacity to act. Any admission that a major institution was inadequate tended to be viewed as a criticism of the whole system and, more immediately, as a threat to the dynasty. By the turn of the century the Empire was caught in quicksand: the harder it struggled to preserve itself, the deeper it sank.

Among those who wanted to rebuild China by westernization was the revolutionist, Sun Yat-sen. A physician by training, Sun had ambitious dreams for his country, but few practical notions about how to achieve them. Primarily, he hoped to secure advice, technical assistance and funds from Great Britain and the United States, but he had no success. Other than a few visionaries, no one in these countries could see reason, or hope, for building a parliamentary democracy and a modern economy in far-off China.

In 1905 Sun Yat-sen had organized his followers into the Alliance Society, the T'ung-meng Hui, forerunner of the Kuomintang, to overthrow the Manchus, regenerate China, establish a republic, and equalize land ownership. The membership was drawn from overseas Chinese, students studying abroad, and secret societies which had existed for years, especially in provinces south of the Yangtze. Most came from scholar-official or gentry families. Those who had studied or lived abroad had notions of transforming China into a modern state, though again they lacked any practical plans. Those from the secret societies, on the other hand, were generally ignorant, indifferent or even hostile to republicanism, democracy and other Western ideas. Their revolutionary purposes were largely anti-dynastic, especially anti-Manchu, and as the years passed, Sun Yat-sen found it more and more difficult to recruit them behind even the vague program which he himself had in mind.

Discontent was growing among young intellectuals educated abroad, or by foreign schools in China, and also among soldiers trained by Western military officers and drill masters. Yet many of the popular dissatisfactions were directed against these and other Western 'barbarians' and 'foreign devils' rather than against the dynasty itself. On the other hand, the Empire was rapidly approaching a functional impasse where adjustments to changing domestic and foreign environments could not be accomplished without dislocating the whole system. The 'revolution', when it came, was really a collapse, the breakdown of a system which could not cope with the penetrations of a superior technology. The real revolution was to come later.

An incident in Wuchang, one of the so-called Wuhan cities in Hupeh Province, was what toppled the Ch'ing superstructure. In those days Wuchang had about half a million inhabitants. A great walled city on the southern bank of the Yangtze, it stood almost precisely in the center of China's eighteen provinces. Opposite, on the north bank, were Hankow and Hanyang, the latter famous for its arsenal and iron and steel works which, a decade and a half later, were to provide worker-soldiers for the nucleus of Mao Tse-tung's Red Army.

A small group of Chinese revolutionaries had established their headquarters in the Tsarist Russian concession, where they were manufacturing bombs. Suddenly, on the afternoon of 9 October 1911 an explosion occurred. Imperial authorities searched the premises and found explosives, revolutionary pamphlets, flags, insurrectionary plans and maps, and lists naming many of those associated with the movement.

Sun Yat-sen (1866–1925), founder of the Kuomintang and frequently called the 'Father of the Chinese Revolution'. After being implicated in preparations for a revolution in Canton (1895), Sun was forced to flee, and during many years of exile lived in Hawaii, the United States, England and Japan. His program was based on the three principles of nationalism, democracy, and the people's livelihood.

That night the revolutionists made contact with soldiers in the Empire's foreign-trained Model Army. These units, drilled in Western military discipline and inspired by Western military concepts, had been organized by the Empire as part of its convulsive efforts toward modernization. The next morning a contingent of Engineers rose in revolt. There was brief resistance from other regiments encamped outside the city, but most of the action was half-hearted. Loyal troops took refuge in flight while the rest joined the revolutionaries who totalled about two thousand men. The Imperial Viceroy fled the city, his palace in flames, and numbers of Manchu officers and their families were slaughtered.

The rebellion spread, and when dissident forces seized Nanking, the city was proclaimed the seat of a new Provisional Government.

'At date of writing,' a missionary journal reported in November, 'the Yangtze valley from Ichang in the west to Wuhu is in the hands of the "People's Army" . . . and the people are so overwhelmingly and so enthusiastically in favour of the new régime that, with the possible exception of Peking, a corporal's guard could capture almost any city in the Empire.'

'To accomplish these sweeping results,' the journal pointed out, 'one or two skirmishes have taken place, and probably two hundred soldiers have laid down their lives.'[8]

Sun Yat-sen, who had been seeking American funds in Denver, Colorado, when the rebellion broke out, characterized the whole episode as a 'sheer accident'. Upon his return to China, Sun assumed the office of Provisional President.

As the revolution proceeded, Yüan Shih-k'ai, commanding Imperial forces, learned that the rebels were short of funds and open to negotiation. In mid-January 1912 Sun Yat-sen, lacking an army he could rely upon, wired Yüan an offer of the presidency if he would support the Republic and persuade the Ch'ing Government to abdicate. The terms were accepted, the Manchus abdicated, and Yüan Shih-k'ai assumed power. After his own resignation, Sun urged the republican assembly convened in Nanking to elect the erstwhile commander of Imperial forces as Provisional President.

Yüan Shih-k'ai lacked sufficient military power to control the independent bodies of troops raised by local landlords for their own protection, and also funds sufficient to buy them off in customary fashion. Falling back on a third traditional alternative, therefore, he legalized the position of local militia commanders by giving them the official rank of Governor in their respective provinces. In this way the twentieth century 'warlord' era began in China, reinforcing provincial political loyalties dating from the Taiping Rebellion. For the next three decades – until Mao Tse-tung seized power over the Chinese mainland in 1949 – no government was able to maintain itself except with the support of a warlord coalition in one combination or another.

In fact, the 1911 revolution had overthrown nothing but the

central power of the Empire. Thereafter, a considerable part of the sovereignty which had resided in Peking was distributed, so to speak, amongst the provincial 'Governors'. At one point Yüan Shih-k'ai tried to re-establish the monarchy with himself as Emperor, but he failed and in mid-1916 his death, while extinguishing his personal ambitions, gave rise to a tiresome succession of struggles for central power by the various warlord factions and in due course by the Kuomintang and the Chinese Communists.

Meanwhile, with the overthrow of the Manchu Dynasty a new kind of young Chinese became conspicuous. Since the end of the nineteenth century larger and larger numbers of students had been going abroad to study. Many of them became teachers upon their return, spreading foreign ideas among their own students, often in 'Western style' schools. Hypnotized by the almost magical touch of foreign ideas, these youngsters trooped into new reform movements, established revolutionary societies, and proclaimed their opposition to everything associated with Confucianism and the ancient way of life. They organized a 'family revolution', an 'equality for women revolution', a 'birth control revolution', a 'freedom and equality between father and son revolution', and even a 'funeral practices revolution'. Scarcely a traditional institution remained that was not under attack, and the Chinese extended family was denounced as the greatest source of evil.

Only one positive value was widely shared: *nationalism*, the building of a new China. It was the single goal upon which large numbers of Chinese could agree.

Many of these youngsters joined Sun Yat-sen's nationalist movement, but increasing numbers had become even more deeply disillusioned with Western democracy than had Sun Yat-sen. With the apparent success of the 1917 Bolshevik Revolution in Russia. many of them were intrigued by the possibilities of a different solution. Contributing to this tendency were the difficulties Sun Yat-sen faced domestically, as well as abroad, and the growing belief that not only the old government, but the total society needed to be rebuilt after a wholly different pattern.

Nine revolutionaries in a girls' school

During the latter days of July 1921 nine men appeared as uninvited guests in a private school for girls in Pubalu Street of the French Concession of Shanghai – 'where Chinese law did not reach' – and settled on the top storey. The building was otherwise deserted except for a cook on the gound floor who served also as watchman to see that no outsiders disturbed the new guests. The young ladies and their teachers had left for the summer holidays.

Who were these mysterious men and what were they after?

They were young intellectuals representing various Marxist study groups in China who had gathered in Shanghai in order to organize an official Communist Party. Soon they were joined by three more comrades already living in the city, and by two foreigners. One of the Chinese present – Chou Fu-hai – represented a group of students who had returned from studying in Japan. Another was Mao Tse-tung, the son of a Hunanese peasant, who had become interested in Marxism while studying at the University of Peking. Also attending the Congress was a Hollander, Henricus Sneevliet (known as Maring), who represented the Communist International in Moscow, and probably a Russian named Nikorusky.

Ch'en Tu-hsiu, virtually the father of the Chinese Communist movement, had been expected, but he was detained in Canton by circumstances that are still not clear.

The organization of the meeting on Pubalu Street, known subsequently as the First Congress of the Chinese Communist Party, was simple: Chang Kuo-t'ao – who led one of the columns of the Long March in 1934–5 and competed with Mao for leadership – was elected chairman and Mao himself and Chou Fu-hai secretaries. The meetings lasted four days and considered such questions as the current political situation, the basic tasks of the Party, the drafting of statutes, and the details of organization.

Serious disagreements soon arose among the representatives. Li Han-chün, who was executed by counter-revolutionary forces in 1923, argued that the Chinese proletariat was too young to be effective and required a lengthy period of instruction and training. The movement was premature for the establishment of a real working class party, and hence it would be better to start with a middle class democracy.

Liu Jen-ch'ing – denounced a decade later as a Trotskyite – took the other extreme, insisting that establishment of a proletarian dictatorship ought to be the immediate aim of the struggle. He opposed all legal organizational forms. The intelligentsia were essentially bourgeois, he argued, and as a rule should not be accepted into the Party. Pao Hui-sheng, who later defected to the Kuomintang, supported this ultra leftist viewpoint.

A majority of the delegates opposed both extremes and settled upon a general policy. The Party must struggle for the eventual achievement of a working class dictatorship, but must also be prepared to operate during a crucial transition period. The middle classes should not be rejected during this phase. On the contrary, the Party must call upon the working class to take part in and lead the bourgeois democratic movement. This task, combined with the organization of the Chinese trade union movement, would require a well organized, militant and highly disciplined Party capable of both legal and illegal operations according to circumstance. Toward these ends the delegates agreed to make full use of the experience and example of the Communist Party of the Soviet Union.

The Party statutes were to be endorsed on the fourth day of the Congress. But shortly after supper, as the delegates gathered in Li Han-chün's apartment, a 'suspicious person in a long coat' appeared in an adjoining room. Li went to investigate. 'This person replied that he was seeking for the chairman of the Association of Social Organizations, Wan by name', Ch'en T'an-ch'iu recalled many years later, 'and then said he was mistaken and speedily left.'[9]

Such an organization maintained offices only three houses distant, but it had no chairman nor anyone named Wan associated with it. 'The appearance of this person appeared suspicious to us, and so we quickly gathered together our documents and disappeared. Only Li Han-chün and Ch'en Kung-po stayed behind, and it was a fact that before ten minutes had passed after our departure, nine spies and policemen turned up at Li Han-chün's apartment to institute a search. Apart from legal Marxist literature, they found nothing there, and were therefore unable to arrest anybody.'

To return to the young ladies' school was now out of the question. Later they reconvened the Congress on a small lake some 100 miles from Shanghai. There they rented a large boat, bought food and wine and continued with their work under the guise of nature lovers enjoying an outing on the lake.

A new debate developed concerning the proper attitude of the Party toward Sun Yat-sen and his Nationalist movement. Pao Hui-sheng maintained that the Communist Party and the Kuomintang represented diametrically opposed classes and that there could be no compromises between them. Therefore, the Chinese Communists ought to maintain the same hostile attitude toward Sun Yat-sen as toward the northern militarists who played musical chairs with the official seat of government in Peking and depended upon foreign gold and foreign arms for their power and influence. Indeed, the Communists ought to be even more deeply hostile toward Sun lest he 'confuse the masses by his demagogy'. But the delegates rejected this concept. While criticizing and exposing the false teachings of Sun Yat-sen, the Communist Party should support his various practical and progressive activities through various modes of unofficial, non-Party collaboration. 'The adoption of this principle,' according to Chen Pan-tsu, 'laid the basis for further collaboration between the Communist Party and the Kuomintang and for the development of the anti-militarist and anti-imperialist movement.'

2 The great empires and their disintegration

Conflict among the giants

China was not the only country facing dilemmas and upheaval. If many Chinese were trying to dismantle their traditional order, there were also men and women in Europe and elsewhere who were working to unhinge the political, economic and social systems of the West and over much of the world. What was happening in Hankow and Wuchang and Shanghai and Canton – ideas igniting, conspiracies hatching, movements mobilizing, old institutions collapsing – was to some degree a microcosm of what was happening, or about to happen, over a large part of the earth.

For generations a majority of mankind had been governed by a few great empires – the British, French, German, Austro-Hungarian, Russian, Dutch, Belgian, Chinese, Portuguese, Ottoman – which held many millions of diverse races and religions under their imperial order. Maps and globes of the time show their pinks and greens and yellows and browns spread over extended areas of the earth's surface.

The empires of the time fell into two general groups: the Austro-Hungarian, Chinese and Ottoman orders – the 'infirm old men' of the world system – which were in obvious decay, and the more vigorous new imperiums of Great Britain, France, Germany and other powers of Western Europe. The Chinese imperial order had already been overthrown by the outbreak of World War I, while the Ottoman, German and Austro-Hungarian failed to survive the conflict.

The British Empire had come to represent a model which other European powers sought to emulate. It was widely assumed that the British had become strong and great in consequence of their colonial possessions, and their example served to inspire other countries to build similar empires of their own. Both leaders and citizens of these aspiring nations sometimes saw greater value in the extent and might of the British Empire than did the British themselves.

By the early twentieth century Germany had an empire stretching into Africa and the Far East, but to many Germans this imperium looked inadequate compared with that of the British, and there was a strong impulse to overtake Great Britain. 'We do not want to put anyone in the shade,' Prince von Bülow told the Reichstag on 6 December 1897, 'but we demand for ourselves a place in the sun.'[1]

Working against the great empires were the emerging nationalisms – and also the ambitions of the empire builders themselves who, in seeking power and aggrandizement and national prosperity and self-preservation, were, in fact, preparing their own destruction.

For generations the Western merchant, the Western soldier, the Western missionary, the Western technician and the Western intellectual, rough-shod, had been carrying into far-flung places a new order of concepts and ways of doing things. For generations they had been altering the tastes and preferences and hopes and expectations of distant peoples and – in the long run – sowing discontent and eventual revolution.

Though they seldom perceived it, the builders of empire faced an inescapable dilemma. The more the subject peoples were educated and the more their circumstances were improved, the sooner their eyes were opened to the possibilities of independence and the sooner an intellectual class emerged to lead a nationalist movement. If, on the other hand, the subject peoples were kept in subordination and poverty and ignorance, the deeper was likely to be the shock when Western influences were brought in – as eventually they were – by other carriers, and the more bloody was likely to be the revolt. Even in training local armies to secure their footholds and enforce their sovereignty the builders of empire were preparing the lethal instruments that might one day be turned against them.

The empires were ensuring their demise in another way. For the European 'balance of power' had begun to depend more and more upon the 'balance of empire' rather than upon the distribution of capabilities on the European continent. Obscure conflicts in Central Africa or the Middle East or Oceania disturbed the politics of London, Berlin, and Paris, and rising nationalisms added elements of power or potential power which Western statesmen scarcely fathomed or even recognized.

By eroding the Ottoman Empire and weakening it, militant nationalism disturbed the European 'balance', and the growing dissatisfaction of minority groups in the Austro-Hungarian Empire had much to do with the outbreak of World War I. Once this great conflict had begun, moreover, the two rival alliances tried to disrupt each other's empires by arousing the nationalist movements within them.

Great Britain organized Arab groups against the tottering Ottoman Empire, while the Imperial Germans subsidized nationalist revolutionary movements in the colonies and spheres of influence belonging to the British and other opposing powers.[2] The Kaiser could not bear being second to England. ' . . . our consuls in Turkey and India, agents, etc.,' he scribbled in his revealing marginal note of 30 July 1914, 'must fire the whole Mohammedan world to fierce rebellion against this hated, lying, conscienceless nation of shopkeepers . . .'[3]

During the war Great Britain proclaimed throughout the world that British troops were fighting for the right of self-determination, the freedom of small nations, and the prevention of imperialist aggression. Woodrow Wilson seized upon the concept and developed it further. The German war dream, as Wilson saw it, ' . . . contemplated binding together racial and political units which could be kept together only by force – Czechs, Magyars, Croats, Serbs, Rumanians, Turks, Armenians – the proud states of Bohemia and Hungary, the stout little commonwealths of the Balkans, the indomitable Turks, the subtle people of the East. These people did not wish to be united. They ardently desired to direct their own affairs, would be satisfied only by undisputed independence. They could be kept quiet only by the presence of the constant threat of armed men.'[4] Wilson wanted the war – and the subsequent peace – to unbind what the empires had bound together.

But the British Empire was itself a tying together of racial and political units by force, and the Imperial Germans recognized this vulnerability. The Kaiser's government began subsidizing nationalist revolutionary movements over much of the globe.

It was not long before the leaders of these nationalist movements became bitterly disenchanted with Kaiser Wilhelm as a 'liberator' of the colonies and 'oppressed peoples'. But at this precise juncture (during the latter months of 1917) a new revolutionary champion appeared on the horizon like a knight in shining armor. This man, V. I. Lenin, had made a near science of revolution and knew far better than the Kaiser how to 'gather up' the hostilities of dissatisfied and angry people, how to harness this dynamic against the old order. Numbers of the Indians, Chinese, Japanese and others – first recruited under the aegis of Imperial Germany – looked to this man for inspiration.[5]

To some degree the Kaiser had facilitated the rise of his energetic 'revolutionary successor'.

While financing nationalist movements in various parts of the world and bringing the leaders into touch with one another, the Imperial Germans had not overlooked the various Russian revolutionaries who were bent on unseating the Tsar. Particularly, the Kaiser's government had provided funds for the Bolsheviks and had facilitated Lenin's return to Russia in the spring of 1917. By these acts the Kaiser – quite unwittingly – was instigating one more thrust not only against the vast British Empire, but also against the old imperial order of which Germany was itself a part. Subsequently it was the convergence of these two powerfully rebellious forces – nationalist dissatisfactions and Bolshevik organization, ideology and discipline – which overwhelmed the old empires already so mortally weakened by their own conflicts.

Chinese disillusionment with the West

China had begun to feel the impact of World War I soon after its outbreak. Japan lost no time in taking possession of German holdings in Tsingtao and Kiaochow, and in 1915 she presented the Twenty-one Demands – imposing further political and economic encroachments – which China was forced to accept. As a student in the First Normal School in Changsa, Hunan Province, Mao Tse-tung followed developments carefully.

There was a special study hall for students, and Mao went there often in the evenings when it was ablaze with lights. Newspapers held a special fascination for him, and he read them studiously. He absorbed information quickly and could explain 'in a clear and analytical manner' the situation facing China and all the world, which he knew, according to a fellow student, 'like the back of his hand'. Other students frequently came to listen as though Mao were presenting a formal lecture. 'He went into everything: how the Crown Prince of the Austrian-Hungarian Empire was assassinated at Sarajevo; how Kaiser Wilhelm II mobilized his army; how war was declared between Germany and Russia, between Germany and France, and between Germany and England; how a pitched battle was fought at Verdun; how Japan seized the opportunity to impose the Twenty-one Demands, designed to subjugate China, and so on and so forth.'[6]

These were days before Mao Tse-tung had become a Communist. Like so many other young Chinese intellectuals of the time, his ideas were a confused blend of Western democratic liberalism and utopian socialism. Concretely he knew only that he was against the warlords, against foreign encroachments and for the building of a new and more powerful China.

About this time Mao began reading a magazine known as *La Jeunesse* and published by Ch'en Tu-hsiu, a newly returned student who had been appointed Dean in the National University in Peking. 'Oh, young men of China!' wrote Ch'en Tu-hsiu. 'Will you be able to understand me? Five out of every ten I see are young in age, but old in spirit . . . Where this happens to a body, the body is dying. When it happens to a society, the society is perishing . . . We must have youth if we are to survive, we must have youth if we are to get rid of corruption. Here lies the only hope of our society.'[7]

The new movement of Chinese youth was bitter in its attacks on the old social structure, its customs and institutions. 'In order to support Mr Democracy,' Ch'en Tu-hsiu wrote before he had been converted to Communism, 'we are obliged to oppose Confucianism, the code of rituals, chastity, traditional ethics, old politics; and in order to support Mr Science, we are compelled to oppose traditional arts, traditional religion; and in order to support Mr Democracy and Mr Science, we just have to oppose the so-called national heritage and old literature . . .'

With the close of World War I the Chinese Renaissance with its uncritical enthusiasm for the West began to encounter a succession of rude and embittering shocks. For many Chinese students and intellectuals Woodrow Wilson had sounded like a prophet of liberation when he condemned secret covenants and coercive treaties, and when he called for self-determination of peoples and peace over the earth. In the new era, many Chinese told themselves, less powerful nations like China could develop their industries, cultures and national welfare, and join the great nations in warm sun.

Chinese expectations remained high during Armistice negotiations, but the Versailles Conference brushed aside a Chinese request for the cancellation of Japan's Twenty-one Demands. Western statesmen seemed to feel that the issue lay outside the area of considerations which the Conference had decided upon. Yet Japan – having taken advantage of the war, many Chinese thought, in order to rob China of territory – was nevertheless permitted to retain special rights which Imperial Germany had previously enjoyed in Shantung.

Chinese disillusionment grew. '. . . when the news of the Paris Peace Conference finally reached us,' a Peking University student wrote in *The Renaissance*, 'we were greatly shocked. We at once awoke to the fact that foreign nations were still selfish and militaristic and that they were all great liars . . . We came to the conclusion that a greater world war would be coming sooner or later, and that this great war would be fought in the East. We had nothing to do with our Government, that we knew very well, and at the same time we could no longer depend upon the principle of any so-called great leader like Woodrow Wilson, for example. Looking at our people and at the pitiful ignorant masses, we couldn't help but feel that we should struggle.'[8]

On 4 May 1919 five thousand students and older Chinese demonstrated in Peking. Advancing into the legation quarter to demand the intercession of American and European diplomats against the aggressive attitudes of Japan, they shouted angry slogans: 'Cancel the Twenty-one Demands . . . Down with Japan . . . Down with power politics . . . .'

Police began rounding up the students, but disorders continued. The whole country seemed electrified by the incident. And more and more, now, the implications of the Russian Revolution were beginning to dawn on many Chinese intellectuals. Men like Ch'en Tu-hsiu and Li Ta-chao hailed the event as the beginning of a 'New Tide'. The real victory had not been won by Woodrow Wilson, they concluded, but by Lenin, Trotsky and Marx. 'It was at the summons of this revolutionary upheaval, of the Russian revolution, and at the call of Lenin,' Mao Tse-tung wrote years later in his *New Democracy*, 'that the "May 4th" movement actually took place.'[9]

Lenin harnesses the dynamics of discontent

During the summer of 1920 revolutionaries from all over the world began beating their way toward Soviet Russia where the Second Congress of the Communist International was scheduled to convene. Dressed in firemen's overalls and seamen's caps an Englishman and an American negotiated their way on to the docks of Stettin, boarded a ship and stowed away. Members of the ship's crew bundled them into a chain locker and told them to stay there until the vessel was safely out to sea. From Mexico City, by way of Berlin, came M.N.Roy, an Indian revolutionist who had already served on the Kaiser's secret payroll for a number of years. Recently converted to Communism from his earlier militant nationalism, Roy wanted to put his new ideas to work in underdeveloped countries of Asia.

There were many others from the countries of Europe and the East. Some bore false passports, and others had no identification at all, but they made their way somehow, stowing away on ships, riding freight car buffers, slipping across inhospitable borders in the darkness of night, converging toward Petrograd and Moscow, where their hopes were focused. For Russia, with the victory of the Bolshevik revolution, had become more than another, more radical nation state. It had become already the staff headquarters and logistical base for the world Communist movement, the thrust point for disrupting the old order.

The Russian air seemed to crackle with expectation and excitement. 'At last our slow-moving train reached Leningrad,' the stowaway Englishman wrote many years later after his disillusioned withdrawal from the Communist movement. 'And what did I see? Drabness? Yes, drabness. Ruined buildings and shops closed? Yes, ruined buildings, shops closed, streets torn up and the famous Nevsky Prospect in the shabbiest raiments it had ever worn. Yes, I saw all that and more. I saw battalions of the New Red Army marching down that famous highway. Some had German uniforms, some had British, some had French, some American; some had fur hats, some caps, a few had boots. Most had their feet wrapped up in rags and tied up in straw matting. Never had I seen such a shabbily clothed army. But also I saw there a light in their eyes such as I had never seen in the eyes of soldiers on the march. Perhaps I, too, had that light in my eyes for I saw in this marching ragged army a new force rising from the ruins of the old order, a new creation which cradled the future in its hands.'[10]

These foreign revolutionaries had journeyed to Soviet Russia with a dedicated purpose. Lenin and his colleagues had already perceived a three-fold challenge: to strengthen their own Soviet system; to hasten the disintegration of the colonial empires; and, in the long run, to unite the whole of mankind in an entirely new kind of world order. By the summer of 1920 Lenin saw possibilities for achieving these objectives.

Immediately after World War I the Russian Communist leader-

M. N. Roy, Indian revo-
lutionary nationalist and
Comintern theoretician
(*c.* 1886–1954), at the time
of his 1927 mission to
China. Roy rose to leadership in terrorist circles while
still a student and participated in anti-British plots
and *dacoities.* During
World War I he figured in
unsuccessful attempts,
financed by the German
government, to foment
rebellion against British
rule in India.

ship had assumed that widespread revolts in central Europe would
fuse into a general revolution over the whole continent. But newly-
formed workers' and soldiers' soviets in Germany, Hungary and
Austria had met early defeat, and by the opening of the Second
Congress Lenin and his colleagues were shifting their plans in
another direction. The number of delegates from Asia offered a
clue to what this new orientation was.

Only delegates and spectators with special tickets could gain
admittance to the old Smolny Institute when the Congress opened.

Formerly a school for daughters of the nobility, the Institute now provided offices for the various commissars, and it was there that the convocation ceremonies were held. Shortly the auditorium was packed with people sitting on the floor and jamming every passageway and corner. Near the front sat M.N. Roy, and not far from him were delegates from China, Korea, the Dutch East Indies, Persia, Turkey, and more than thirty other states and colonial dependencies.

The Congress was formally opened with cheers from the delegates and the singing of the *International*. Then all stood for a few moments in silent tribute to those who had already given their lives in the revolutionary struggle.

Finally, Lenin himself rose to speak, addressing himself to the deep contradictions and divisions which he saw disrupting the imperial order. By the outbreak of World War I, he said, more than 600,000,000 people in Asia, Africa and elsewhere had fallen subject to the colonial rule of major European empires, while another 400,000,000 in Persia, Turkey and China had been reduced to semi-colonial status. 'The imperialist war of 1914–1918 grew inevitably from this division of the whole world,' Lenin charged, 'from this domination of capitalist monopoly, from this unlimited power of a mere handful of the biggest banks, say, two to five in each country.' From the Communist viewpoint this war had been waged over the question of the division of the whole world. 'It was waged over the question as to which of two groups of the biggest states – the British or the German – should secure the opportunity and the right of robbing, crushing and exploiting the entire world. And you know that the war settled this in favor of the British group.'[11] It was Lenin's basic premise that the major capitalist powers owed their continuing survival to the exploitation of raw materials, cheap labor and mass markets in the colonies and semi-colonies.

The war had also served to draw into the arena of history various dependent nations and their masses of dissatisfied peoples who increasingly challenged the old empires, Lenin said, and threatened to pull them apart.

The British bourgeoisie had tried to make Hindu soldiers believe that it was their duty to protect Britain against Germany. And similarly, the French ruling class had tried to convince soldiers from the colonies that it was the duty of colored people to defend France. In each case the imperial powers had educated their colonials in the art of war. 'This is an extremely useful acquirement,' Lenin declared, 'for which we might be very grateful to the bourgeoisie – grateful in the name of all the Russian workers and peasants and particularly in the name of the Russian Red Army.'

These dependent nations of the world – both colonies, such as India, and semi-colonies, such as China – embraced the enormous mass of the population of the earth. Now the victors, through the Versailles Treaty, were reducing new millions of human beings to colonial submission. Even 'advanced peoples' in Germany and elsewhere were finding themselves in the 'position of colonial dependents, of misery, starvation, and ruin, deprived of all rights' because they had become bound by the treaty for generations and placed under conditions which no civilized nation had previously suffered.

While seeking to draw more and more millions of Chinese and other peoples into colonial servitude, Lenin declared, the imperialist leaders were encouraging false visions of 'self-determination' and 'federation' under the so-called League of Nations. There was a bitter history behind this, he warned, and in effect the empires were setting a snare.

Both sides in the 'imperialist' war of 1914–18 had invoked 'false slogans' of the liberation of peoples and the right of nations for self-determination. Subsequently, the three major victors – Japan Great Britain and the United States – had used the peace treaties, quite 'unceremoniously', to determine national boundaries in conformity with their own bourgeois economic interests. '"National" boundaries are, to the bourgeoisie, nothing but market commodities,' Lenin charged. 'The so-called "League of Nations" is nothing but an insurance policy in which the victors mutually guarantee each other their prey.'[12]

'This League of Nations agreement furnishes the best agitation for Bolshevism every day of its existence,' Lenin asserted, 'for the mighty adherents of the capitalist "order" show how they put stumbling blocks in each other's way upon every question.' In particular, Japan, England, France and the United States were engaged in a 'mad fight' over the division of China, Turkey, Mesopotamia and Russia itself.

The Communists had a different concept of 'self-determination' and an alternative form of federation. Lenin saw self-determination as a means of furthering 'disunion for the purpose of union', that is, the dissolution of the various empires and capitalist states as a first step toward a new, communist unification.

To some degree the reunion of nationalities 'artificially torn apart' coincided with the interests of the working class. But 'real national freedom and unity' could be achieved only by the proletariat through revolutionary struggle and the overthrow of the bourgeoisie – in no circumstances by the bourgeoisie itself or through the League and other essentially capitalistic schemes and institutions.

Self-determination signified the right of colonial and semi-colonial peoples to throw off the imperialist yoke. But the right was temporary and particular. For after the proletarian class had begun its own organization of peoples, the achievement of a single, centralized indivisible order must take clear precedence over divisions and secessionist tendencies. And federation, within the proletarian context, was a transitional stage in the movement toward this complete union and integration of 'the toilers of all nations' and the eventual emergence of a classless society.

Lenin saw the militant nationalism of colonial and semi-colonial peoples as a powerful force that was challenging the old empires and threatening to tear them apart. Despite what he perceived as the bourgeois inclinations of these revolutionary nationalists, he thought that the dynamic of their discontent and bitterness could be harnessed by the Communists. 'The Communist International must be ready to establish temporary relationships and even alliances with the bourgeois democracy of the colonies and back-ward countries,' he declared in a set of theses presented to the Second Congress. The major responsibility for rendering revolutionary support to the oppressed peoples of the colonies and semi-colonies, he thought, should be borne by the workers of these countries upon which a subject nation such as India or China was dependent 'in a colonial or financial way.'[13]

Essentially, Lenin envisaged the Communists as supporting bourgeois nationalists 'from above' – helping them to disrupt the old order, to drive out imperialist influences, and to establish their own republics in which the workers and peasants would 'cooperate'. Gradually, then, the revolutionary vanguard – the Communist Party – would expand its influence within the new order as the political representative of the toiling masses.

During subsequent sessions of the Second Congress, held in Alexander Palace of the Kremlin in Moscow, the Indian delegate M. N. Roy challenged certain aspects of Lenin's analysis. Perhaps it was because of his own background as a nationalist revolutionary and the recency of his own conversion to Communism that Roy was now inclined toward the masses and distrustful of the middle class, however revolutionary they seemed to be. 'Two distinct movements which grow farther apart each day are to be found in the dependent countries,' he told the Congress. 'One is the bourgeois democratic nationalist movement, with a program of political independence under the bourgeois order. The other is the mass struggle of the poor and ignorant peasants and workers for their liberation from all forms of exploitation.'[14]

Roy thought it would be useful to cooperate with bourgeois nationalist revolutionaries in China and elsewhere – but only during initial stages and with caution. The primary task was to form Communist parties which would organize the workers and peasants and inspire them to revolution 'from below', so to speak, and to the establishment of soviet republics.

Roy further contended that the revolutionary movement in Europe was dependent upon the course of revolution in Asia.

Super-profit extracted from the colonies and semi-colonies such as China was the mainstay of world capitalism. 'Without control of the extensive markets and vast areas for exploitation in the colonies,' he argued, 'the capitalist powers of Europe could not maintain their existence even for a short time.'

After spirited debate, the Second Congress sought to resolve the argument by approving both theses. Communist leaders – while collaborating with middle class nationalists in the colonies and semi-colonies – were expected to make every effort to arouse and organize the masses and to penetrate and achieve leadership over existing revolutionary movements. Revolution, in short, must pursue a subtle balance of 'tactics from above' and 'tactics from below'.

3 The Communist-Nationalist collaboration

The bloc of four classes

During the early 1920s at least three major leadership groups in China were negotiating in one way or another with the Russian Bolsheviks. In Peking the legal but somewhat unstable government of warlords received A. A. Joffe, L. M. Karakhan and other Soviet emissaries and entered into seemingly endless discussions about the proper basis for diplomatic relations between the two countries. At the same time Sun Yat-sen, who hoped to overthrow the Peking government, was seeking Soviet military aid and advice in pursuit of his own revolutionary aims. And while the Kuomintang re-organized itself after Soviet Russian political models, the Chinese Communist Party negotiated with Sun Yat-sen, joined his party, and conspired with Soviet colleagues toward the eventual displace-ment of the Nationalists and their own achievement of power.

After the death of Yüan Shih-k'ai in 1916, a prolonged struggle had broken out between two main factions of northern warlords. On achieving power in Peking one group, the Anfu Clique, ob-tained a series of substantial loans from sources in Japan and thus gained a pro-Japanese orientation. Against the background of the Twenty-one Demands this orientation gave rise to much popular dissatisfaction which culminated in the May Fourth Movement of 1919 with its outburst of demonstrations.

The Anfu Clique was overthrown, and in due course a warlord coalition centering on Wu P'ei-fu achieved power in Peking. With Japanese encouragement, however, the warlord Chang Tso-lin succeeded in declaring the 'independence' of Manchuria while awaiting a favorable opportunity for re-establishing himself in Peking.

As early as 25 July 1919 the Soviet government had dispatched a declaration to the governments at Peking and Canton and to the Chinese people proposing the establishment of diplomatic relations. As an inducement, the Soviet government offered to abrogate all previous Russian treaties limiting Chinese sovereignty and to abolish Russian concessions and special privileges in China. The

Photograph taken in the firing line during the fighting between Chekiang and Kiangsi provinces, 1922. The figure on the elevation is the Chekiang artillery commander who stood directing fire for half an hour. The fall of the Empire in 1911 left what was often only nominal power in Peking and released a Pandora's box of regional conflicts between provincial governors and other local warlords.

document was signed by L. M. Karakhan of the People's Commissariat of Foreign Affairs. When it reached the Chinese officials in Peking, the translated text included a paragraph with abrogations which Moscow later insisted had not been present in the original Russian text.

In August 1922 the Soviet government sent A. A. Joffe, one of its leading diplomats, to negotiate treaty relations with the Peking régime. But difficulties arose almost immediately regarding Chinese sovereignty over Mongolia, Soviet claims to the Chinese Eastern Railway, which had been built under Tsarist Russian auspices, and other issues. A series of frustrating negotiations ensued before diplomatic relations were established in 1924 and an agreement reached that was minimally acceptable to both governments. It was obvious that China had not gained all that Moscow had seemingly promised a few years earlier. Soviet Russia still held vast territories that had once been a part of the Chinese Empire; the Russians continued to control a considerable sphere of Chinese Eastern Railway activities; and Soviet consulates in China were being used for a variety of propaganda and subversive purposes. Within less than a year, moreover, Moscow concluded an agreement with Japan which recognized the Treaty of Portsmouth (1905) as a basis for Russo-Japanese relations and thus prejudiced Chinese rights and interests in Manchuria.

Taken as a whole, however, and compared with treaties which other powers had imposed upon China, the Sino-Russian Agreement of 1924 did not seem unfavorable to the interests of the Peking government.

At the same time lesser warlords were contending for local advantage in various parts of China: Ch'en Ch'iung-ming and Li Chi-shen in Kwantung; Sun Ch'uan-fang in the eastern provinces with Shanghai as a major base; Feng Yü-hsiang, the so-called 'Christian General' in Honan and Shensi; T'ang Sheng-chih in Hunan; Yen Hsi-shan in Shansi; and so forth.

These men had their own separate ambitions – and armies at their backs. To maintain their forces, however, they needed arms, ammunition, supplies, advisers and money, and for these indispensables they were often compelled to look toward outside sources. Increasingly, during the 1920s, several of them discovered that the Soviet Union was a ready supply-base – provided one approached Communist negotiations with revolutionary slogans and a comradely mien. Some went directly to Soviet agents, while others betook themselves and their armies into the Kuomintang.

In the meantime, Sun Yat-sen and his colleagues pursued their own negotiations. Repeatedly, since 1911, Sun had found himself caught in a familiar Chinese dilemma: How could he rebuild China and resist foreign encroachments without financial and technological assistance from the West? And how could he achieve and maintain political power without military support either from the foreigner, whom he wanted to drive out, or from the warlord, whom he sought to eradicate?

For Sun – as for many uprooted and alienated younger Chinese – the ideas of Western statesmen, philosophers, economists and political scientists had offered tantalizing visions of what China *could be* and *ought to be*. Men like John Dewey, Bertrand Russell and Woodrow Wilson were regarded as prophets of a new freedom, a new order and a new enlightenment.

But increasingly it seemed that the West had no program or plan, whereas the Communists had devised a belief system, a road map, a tool kit, and a 'how-to-do-it' instruction book rolled into one. Neither Sun nor most of his colleagues wanted the whole packet, but parts of it looked useful, even indispensable. This was particularly true of Soviet arms, ammunition, money and organizational techniques.

In fact, however, the Communists were not as omniscient nor as shrewdly effective as they themselves, their admirers and even their bitterest enemies frequently assumed. On the contrary, the comrades both in China and in Moscow planning sessions were in a dilemma not unlike that of Sun Yat-sen's *vis-à-vis* the Chinese revolution – though they seem to have been slow to perceive it. Chinese Communist membership was small and made up largely of intellectuals who were generally out of touch with the expanding labor movement. Obviously, they were even more remote from the peasantry. The Party had minimal influence politically, and no military force whatsoever. Under these circumstances it seemed to make sense for the Chinese Communists, individually, to join the Kuomintang, influence Sun Yat-sen's revolutionary policies, and use the Nationalist organizational structure for developing Bolshevik propaganda and contact with the masses. It was not foreseen how utterly this maneuver put the Communist movement at the mercy of the Kuomintang and its supporting warlord armies.

The Lenin–Roy debates before the Second Congress of the Communist International had laid the theoretical groundwork for just this procedure.

The Second Congress had tried to resolve the disagreement between Lenin and Roy by essentially combining the two emphases of revolution 'from above' and revolution 'from below'. *While supporting middle class nationalists, Communist leaders would make every effort to arouse and organize the peasant and proletarian masses and penetrate and gain leadership over existing revolutionary and potentially revolutionary movements.*

According to Marxist–Leninist theory there were three major, irreconcilable contradictions in the world: the antagonisms between and among imperialist powers competing for a re-division of the earth; the antagonism between the highly developed imperialist powers and the 'under-developed' colonies and semi-colonies; and the basic antagonism between the capitalist oppressor and the exploited masses everywhere. Throughout the world, cutting across all political boundaries, the proletariat – under the leadership of the various Communist parties and with the support and guidance of the Soviet Union – was inevitably aligned, according to Bolshevik theory, with the toiling masses. But special problems arose because of the different levels of economic development in various parts of the world, with the accompanying differences in class structure.

As early as the mid-1920s the Communists leadership began predicting a second world war emerging from antagonisms among the imperialists. Much of the conflict would be fought in Asia, the Communists asserted, with Great Britain and the United States probably aligned on one side and Japan on the other. It was within this broad and strongly determinative context that the Chinese revolution needed to be viewed.

In the colonies and semi-colonies the basic class structure was perceived like this:

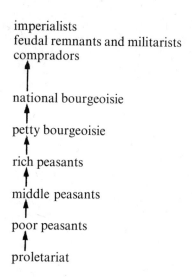

imperialists
feudal remnants and militarists
compradors

↑

national bourgeoisie

↑

petty bourgeoisie

↑

rich peasants

↑

middle peasants

↑

poor peasants

↑

proletariat

The correct procedure for the Communists was to form first of all a bloc of four classes – the national bourgeoisie, the petty bourgeoisie, the peasants and the proletariat – against the imperialists and reactionary indigenous classes. This was defined as the bourgeoisie democratic stage of the revolution. Later, as this bloc gained strength the proletariat, under Communist leadership, should put forward further revolutionary demands such as the confiscation and re-allocation of land. Inevitably, these demands would antagonize large sections of the bourgeoisie, who would then 'go over to the imperialists', but not, presumably, until the three remaining classes – the petty bourgeoisie, the peasantry, and the proletariat – had sufficiently consolidated their strength.

During subsequent revolutionary stages parts of the petty bourgeoisie would also 'go over to the imperialists', but others would find their interests increasingly similar to those of the peasants and proletariat.

So it was that Marxist–Leninist–Royist theory – whatever its own internal contradictions – stood receptive, at least initially, to the needs of both Sun Yat-sen and the newly formed Chinese Communist Party.

The local warlord, Ch'en Ch'iung-ming, occupied Canton and in 1920 made himself governor of Kwangtung Province. He then invited Sun Yat-sen to establish his Nationalist government there. The Kuomintang leader, in turn, reaffirmed his benefactor's governorship. Compared with many militarists, Ch'en was outstanding for his attempts at reform, but he made no effort to abolish the landlord system. In the meantime, Sun Yat-sen was already making tentative inquiries of the Soviet Russians.

In August 1921, Sun sent a letter to the People's Commissar of Foreign Affairs in Moscow, G. V. Chicherin. ' . . . I would like to enter into personal contact with you and my friends in Moscow,' he wrote in part. 'I am extremely interested in your work, and particularly in the organization of your soviets, your army, and educational system.'

At about the same time Sun, headquartering in Kweilin, made preparations for an attack upon the northern militarists through Hunan. But meanwhile, in August or September 1921, he met Henricus Sneevliet, also known as Maring, who was serving as Comintern delegate to the Chinese Communist Party. The discussions were indecisive but friendly, and led to further negotiations.

The danger of relying too heavily on warlord forces was soon amply demonstrated to Sun Yat-sen.

During the early morning hours of 16 June 1922 Ch'en Ch'iung-ming had turned against Sun Yat-sen in a sudden *coup*. Finding his Canton residence surrounded by troops, Sun barely made his escape by taking refuge on a gunboat where he and his principal colleagues remained for fifty-six days. The Kuomintang leaders finally disembarked in Shanghai on 14 August – just two days after Joffe's arrival in Peking for negotiations with the legal government there. On the side, Joffe discussed revolutionary collaboration with Sun, and a joint statement was soon drafted.

China makes war on bandits, July 1923. Many parts of
the country sank into a kind of chaos where warlords,
revolutionists and common bandits struggled for their own diverse purposes.
Until Russian Communists sent Michael Borodin to train a Nationalist army,
Sun Yat-sen was dependent upon whatever provincial or warlord forces
could be persuaded to support the Kuomintang cause.

This Sun-Joffe manifesto established Soviet willingness to support the Kuomintang struggle for national unification and independence. Plans were made for reorganizing the Kuomintang
and establishing a military academy. The Kuomintang also appointed a delegation to study conditions in Soviet Russia. In
Moscow the ECCI (Executive Committee of the Communist International) passed a resolution 12 January 1923 which identified the

A Chinese general in command of local troops engaged
in fighting bandits, July 1923. In the chaotic
conditions throughout many parts of China,
banditry was a real and ubiquitous phenomenon.
However, Chinese leaders of whatever faction tended to
identify opponents as 'bandits' to justify their extermination.

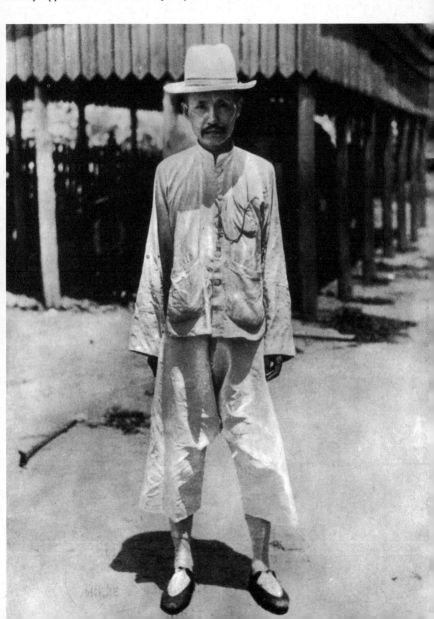

Chiang Kai-shek and Sun Yat-sen *circa* 1924. As an outcome of
his meetings with Soviet representatives and of his correspondence with
Soviet leaders, Sun sent Chiang, then a young Kuomintang military
officer, to Russia in 1923 for a few months' study of
the Red Army. Chiang was appointed commandant of the Whampoa
Military Academy, which had been established under Soviet supervision.

Kuomintang as a national revolutionary party representing different classes and which urged Chinese Communist cooperation with it.

In China the policy of dual membership was officially approved at the Third Congress of the CCP the following summer. 'The working class has not yet become great and powerful,' the Congress asserted in a set of resolutions. 'Hence, it is impossible to create a powerful Communist Party – a Party of the great masses to meet the immediate needs of the Revolution. The Executive Committee of the Comintern and the Central Committee of the Chinese Communist Party have therefore resolved that the Chinese Communist Party should cooperate with the Kuomintang and that Communist members should enter the Kuomintang. We enter the Kuomintang, but preserve still our own organization.'[1] It was agreed that the Communist Party should make every effort toward absorbing Kuomintang members with left wing tendencies as well as proletarians under Sun's influence.

In the sphere of foreign policy the ECCI urged the Chinese Communists to oppose Kuomintang attempts to 'court the capitalist powers and their agents, i.e. the Chinese military governors who are hostile to proletarian Russia.' At the same time, the Chinese Communists were to spare no efforts in influencing the Kuomintang toward unifying its efforts with the Soviet struggle against 'European, American, and Japanese imperialism'. Especially, the ECCI warned the Chinese Communist Party against merging with the Kuomintang or 'folding up its own banner'.[2]

Several more months were to pass before Soviet advisers and supplies began reaching China, but in the meantime, on 21 February 1923 Sun Yat-sen – with the aid of three rival militarists – recovered Canton from Ch'en Ch'iung-ming and re-established Kuomintang power in the city. During the next summer Sun sent a young Kuomintang military officer, Chiang Kai-shek, to Soviet Russia for a brief study of the Red Army. Not long after this Karakhan, arriving in Peking to replace Joffe, wired greetings to Sun, who answered in friendly terms and asked for a Comintern representative in Canton for organizational and advisory purposes.

The arrival of Michael Borodin

The man selected by Moscow to advise Sun Yat-sen was none other than Michael Borodin, who had played chess with M.N.Roy in Mexico City immediately after World War I and had converted the Indian revolutionist to Communism. Known also as Gruzenberg, Borodin had been released most recently from a six months' prison term for revolutionary activities in Glasgow. Born in Russia and

educated in Latvia, Borodin had lived for some time in Chicago, but
returned to Moscow after the Bolshevik revolution. Within the next
few years Borodin and Roy would be at odds over the correct
policy for advancing the revolution in China.

Officially, Borodin set out for Canton – via Vladivostok and
Shanghai – as an agent of the Rosta news service, but in fact he
represented the Communist International and carried a letter of
introduction to Sun Yat-sen bearing Karakhan's signature.

To avoid stopping at British-controlled Hong Kong, Borodin
left Shanghai on a small ship bound straight for Canton with a
cargo of sheep. During the voyage a typhoon struck and the
animals perished. But the vessel itself completed the voyage in
safety, reaching Canton 6 October 1923. 'Sun Yat-sen welcomed me
very warmly,' Borodin recalled later, 'made me sit with him and
looked at me fixedly for several seconds.'[3]

Sun asked probing questions about the Russian revolution. 'It
was evident that he was greatly interested in the question of how the
struggle in South China, which had just been liberated from
counter-revolutionary troops in Canton, could be joined with the
struggle of faraway Russia.'

The Comintern representative conveyed to Sun Yat-sen greetings
from his superiors in Moscow and added that Karakhan was looking forward to conversations on the first favorable occasion. 'Then
I shortly explained to him the aim of my coming to Canton and
asked him several questions about the situation in the country and
particularly in Kwangtung . . .'

Within a few weeks of his arrival Borodin was appointed by Sun
as special advisor to the Kuomintang.

In Moscow the ECCI had already specified the limits of Communist participation in Sun Yat-sen's party. Collaboration with the
Kuomintang was necessary, but membership should under no
circumstances be purchased 'at the price of the effacement of the
political characteristics of the Chinese Communist Party.' The
education and organization of the working class in China and the
development of trade unions as a foundation for an effective

Communist Party were primary tasks. In cooperating with the Nationalists, moreover, the Communist Party must be careful to maintain and strengthen its own organization and highly centralized apparatus.

In subsequent months Borodin developed a considerable staff of Russian political and military specialists and began effecting a complete overhaul of Sun Yat-sen's party and government.

In late January 1924 the First Congress of the Kuomintang, under Borodin's influence, reinterpreted Sun Yat-sen's Three People's Principles – Nationalism, Democracy, and the People's Livelihood – and set forth a program of strict party discipline, intense propaganda, extensive social legislation, the 'equalization' (but not the nationalization) of land, the state control of capital and monopolistic enterprises, and the building of an army to drive out 'imperialism'. Under reinterpretation, Sun's concept of Nationalism was equated with anti-imperialism, and the People's Livelihood was expanded to encompass the role of the masses – the workers and poor peasants – in the National Revolution.[4] Borodin himself wrote the new Kuomintang constitution, which was then checked by Sun Yat-sen and translated from English into Chinese.

In elections to the first Central Executive Committee, three of the twenty-four seats were won by Communists.

In May 1924 Borodin and General Galen (V. K. Blücher) supervised the establishment of the Whampoa Military Academy. The first commandant was Chiang Kai-shek, who had visited Moscow the previous summer. The chief of the academy's political department was Chou En-lai. It should be kept in mind, however, that the academy focused on the training of young cadet officers; for higher ranking military leadership and for troops, the Kuomintang remained largely dependent upon local warlords and their separate, virtually private armies.

The first shipment of Soviet supplies reached Canton on 7 October 1924 – a year after Borodin's arrival. The acquisition of these materials was most propitious, since the Kuomintang was threatened just then by the Merchant Corps, a private militia

maintained by Cantonese merchants and supported – Sun Yat-sen
believed – by the local British consul. During the night of 14
October Chiang Kai-shek himself led an attack on the Merchant
Corps and routed them successfully.

Death of Sun and the rise of Chiang Kai-shek

Michael Borodin's arrival in Canton undoubtedly augmented the
growth of Chinese Communist membership and political vigor.
Already young Party members were spreading Marxist–Leninist
doctrine among the youth, helping labor to organize, and playing
significant roles in strikes and demonstrations. A young Communist named Li Li-san had been active within the Seamen's Union,
while Mao Tse-tung and others were organizing railway workers,
municipal workers, printers and other labor groups in Hunan.

As early as 1921 Mao had helped to establish a workers' club
among miners in the Anyang, Hanyang and other mines of the
Hanyehp'ing area near Hankow, and Li Li-san founded a school
for mine workers. Thrown out of work a few years later, thousands
of these men – and others from the Toyeh mines – were to join the
first units of the Chinese Red Army under Yeh T'ing and Mao Tse-
tung. Now, in view of Borodin's presence, these and other young
Communists became more and more active in the Kuomintang and
increasingly able to affect its policies. Borodin's influence – and
Comintern reliance on the Kuomintang as a revolutionary vehicle –
also tended to obscure Communist Party activities somewhat.
Meanwhile, events were also shaped in other ways by Sun Yat-
sen's continuing relations with various warlords – and deeply influenced by his death.

An armed struggle broke out on 16 September 1924 between the
Manchurian warlord, Chang Tso-lin, and the coalition of warlords
– centering on Wu P'ei-fu – which held power in Peking. Two days
later Sun Yat-sen announced his support of Chang Tso-lin and
launched an expedition against the Peking coalition. The intent was
not only to overthrow the Peking government as it was – for the

moment – constituted, but also, Sun declared, to eliminate imperialism upon which Chinese warlordism depended. How he could eliminate imperialism through an alliance with Chang Tso-lin – to say nothing of eliminating warlordism – was not made explicit.

As matters turned out, Sun did not live long enough to accomplish the search for an answer. On 12 March 1925 the Nationalist leader died in Peking – an occurrence which laid bare a number of conflicts which had been developing for some time within the Nationalist party and government.

In a document commonly referred to as Sun Yat-sen's will, Sun Yat-sen charged the Kuomintang with responsibility for awakening the masses and continuing the revolutionary struggle. On his deathbed Sun had also addressed a letter to the Soviet Russian leadership in Moscow. 'I leave behind me a party which, as I always hoped, will be allied with you in its historical task of liberating China and other suppressed peoples from the yoke of imperialism. My charge to the Kuomintang party before all is that it shall continue to promote the course of the national revolutionary movement for the emancipation of China, which has been degraded by imperialism into a semi-colonial country. I therefore charge my party to maintain permanent contact with you . . .' Sun concluded with the charge that a 'free and strong China' would proceed as an ally with Russia 'in the great fight for the emancipation of the oppressed of the whole world.'[5]

In subsequent years both Russian and Chinese Communist writers tended to emphasize Sun's political practices which they viewed as relatively leftist, but to discount his theoretical pronouncements.

As early as 18 June 1924 five members of the Kuomintang Central Supervisory Committee had submitted a petition for impeachment of the Communists. The majority of Kuomintang organizers sent out to various localities were actually Communists, they charged, who were taking advantage of their positions to organize peasant associations for Communist purposes. Communists within the Kuomintang were forcing their policies onto the

The Yangtze Valley

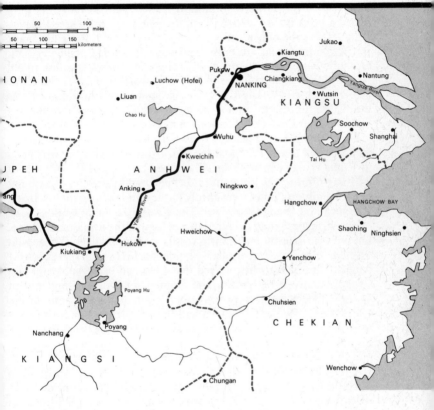

Nationalist party and seeking to destroy it through criticism, propaganda, and the furtherance of a 'party within a party'. Despite these dissatisfactions, however, the Second Plenum of the Kuomintang Central Executive Committee which convened 15 August 1924 provided a decisive victory for those who supported the admission of Communists.

After Sun's death, however, the basic conflict took on new

dimensions. A veteran Kuomintang leader, Tai Chi-t'ao, had published a book in July which identified Sun Yat-sen's Three People's Principles as the only correct values of the National Revolution and the Kuomintang as its only legitimate party. He challenged the Communists, if they did not really believe in Sun's Principles, to put forward their true beliefs publicly and work openly in the name of their own party. The Kuomintang, he warned, should not allow the Communists to maintain a parasitic existence within the Nationalist framework. Tensions increased within the Kuomintang.

Liao Chung-k'ai, a leader of the Left, was mysteriously assassinated on 20 August 1925 and his death was immediately attributed to Right Wing elements allegedly bribed by the British. A series of anti-Right measures were put into effect, and by the end of September Kuomintang power was firmly in the hands of two men, Chiang Kai-shek and Wang Ching-wei. There was no issue of Communism in this struggle, Wang declared in a eulogy of the assassinated Liao, but only the issue of imperialism versus anti-imperialism. Those who wanted to oppose imperialism should go Left. In a speech on 31 August Chiang Kai-shek agreed that Liao had been the victim of a struggle between revolution and counter-revolution – and not of any so-called struggle between Communism and anti-Communism.

Previously, Wang Ching-wei had been relatively unimportant as a Kuomintang leader, and now Right Wing quarters tended to see his emergence as an outcome of the growing influence of Borodin and of Communists within the Nationalist movement.

The influence of Chiang Kai-shek, Wang Ching-wei and Michael Borodin was steadily enhanced, with Soviet supplies continuing to reach Canton through Vladivostok. By 1 December 1925 the total value of these materials was estimated by the Russians at $2,000,000. But even these stores were insufficient for the needs of the Kuomintang's rapidly expanding military establishment. By mid-December the National Revolutionary Army had achieved control of the whole of Kwantung Province with the exception of Hainan Island, which was to be under attack by the end of the month.

In a report to the Military Attaché of the Soviet Embassy in Peking a leading Soviet advisor to the Kuomintang wrote, 'We have already secured good positions in the various departments of the National Revolutionary Army.' It was not possible 'to penetrate further to obtain complete control', however, because of the shortage of advisers and the non-availability of Russian–Chinese interpreters. Major commands still remained with local Chinese militarists. Inevitably, these activities of Russian advisers and of their Chinese Communist colleagues roused opposition. On 23 November 1925 fifteen Kuomintang leaders with Right Wing inclinations gathered before Sun Yat-sen's tomb in the western hills of Peking. In a special manifesto the group denounced the Communists for using the Kuomintang to enhance their own influence and to further Soviet Russian interests. The conference had therefore decided to annul the Kuomintang membership of all Communists within the Nationalist movement. Both the Kuomintang and the Chinese Communist Party shared a dedication to the National Revolution, but China and Russia had different historical backgrounds, social conditions and national interests.

Thereafter, the Kuomintang was increasingly split between the Left Wing, which supported Sun's decision on the Communist issue, and the Right Wing, which opposed it.

The gunboat *coup*

On 18 March 1926 the Kuomintang gunboat *Chung-shan* lay at anchor in the river near Canton where members of Chiang Kai-shek's Russian advisory group were planning to inspect it the following day. But during the night an officer of the Kuomintang Navy Bureau – a member of the Chinese Communist Party – received orders for moving the vessel to Whampoa, where the military academy was located. Without checking the source of his instructions, the officer proceeded to comply.

At Whampoa the local Russian advisers expressed astonishment: clearly, there had been a mistake. The *Chung-shan's* orders were

South China

Changsha

Fuchow

Shaowu

K I A N G S I

Kian

Kwangchang

Yungsin

Yen

Yutu

Juichen

Changting

HUNAN

Chenhsien

Shangyiu

Kanhsien

Tingchow

Hweichang

F U K I E N

Tayu

Wuping

Namyung

Kukong

Lungnan

Tingnan

Meihsien

Changchow

Linping

Changpu

Yingtak

Lungmoon

Hoyun

Chaochow

Kityang

Macau

K W A N G T U N G

CANTON

Sheklung

Swatow

Waiyeng

Kitchioh

SOUTH CHINA SEA

Macau

Kowloon
Victoria

HONG KONG

0   50   100
Miles

0   50   100   150
Kilometers

reversed, and the gunboat returned to Canton where it dropped anchor around midnight. From shore it was apparent that the vessel remained under full steam and ready for precipitate action.

What did the *Chung-shan*'s maneuvers mean? No one seemed to know, at first, but by the morning of 20 March Chiang Kai-shek had interpreted them as an attempt by Chinese Communists, in league with the Russians, to assassinate him and usurp his power.

The Kuomintang leader lost no time in retaliating. First, he ordered the arrest of Communists aboard the *Chung-shan*, and then he sent troops to surround the residences of Soviet advisers and to disarm the guards. In the city, meanwhile, his forces also surrounded labor union headquarters, railway stations and the Central Bank.

Borodin himself was away from Canton at the time, negotiating with Feng Yü-hsiang. But a Russian adviser to Chiang Kai-shek admitted in a report to his Soviet superiors that the *coup* had come 'as a lightning shock'. Upon his return on 29 April, Borodin evidenced some doubts about possibilities for further collaboration. And yet neither he nor Stalin and his colleagues in Moscow could bring themselves to take decisive action against Chiang, his party, or his government. The Soviet policy of 'revolution from above' required tactical cooperation with the Nationalists during 'bourgeois-democratic' phases of the revolution, and the Chinese Communists were dependent upon the armies which Chiang Kai-shek was putting together and also upon the Kuomintang as a vehicle for reaching the masses.

The ECCI in Moscow – and the Russian advisers in Canton – took the view that preservation of the Kuomintang–Communist entente was paramount. According to the 'Resolutions on the China Question' adopted by the ECCI's Sixth Plenum just one week before Chiang's *coup*, the Canton government constituted a model for a future revolutionary democratic order. It was the duty of the Chinese Communists to 'democratize' China through the Kuomintang and a single national revolutionary front of workers, peasants and bourgeoisie.

The correct course was neither too far Left nor too far Right. More specifically, Moscow warned the Chinese Communist Party against 'Right Wing liquidationism', a deviation which overlooked the independent class tasks of the proletariat in China and led thus to a 'formless merging with the general democratic national movement', and also against 'Left moods which try to skip over the revolutionary-democratic stage of the movement straight to the tasks of proletarian dictatorship and Soviet power, forgetting all about the peasantry, which is the most important and decisive factor of the Chinese national-liberation movement.'[6]

What did Chiang intend?

'There are two different conclusions,' a Soviet adviser reported shortly after the *coup*. 'One is that Chiang intends sincerely to temper the incident of 20 March and to cooperate with the Left for the cause of the National Revolution. If this should be the case, it would be very profitable to us. The second conclusion is that Chiang's actions are intended to deceive his opponents in preparation for a second move.'[7]

To the Russians there seemed to be only one choice. 'No one can guarantee that Chiang will always be one of us,' the adviser concluded in his report, 'but we must utilize him for the cause of the National Revolution.'[8]

Chiang, in pursuit of his ambitions, was perceived as 'wavering between the Right and the Communists'. It therefore made sense to some of his Russian advisers to appoint him Commander-in-Chief in order to 'satisfy his lust for position and power'.

The Russians thought they could force Chiang's further cooperation by 'satisfying his desire for glory' and helping him to achieve even greater power. They recognized him as a man of determination, endurance, intelligence and ambition who used money to further his purposes, but not 'to enrich his own pocket'. It would be unfortunate if he sought further opportunities for attacking the Left, but such a course, leading Russian advisers believed, would lead to his extermination, and they thought that his recent *coup* had somehow taught him this lesson.

Chiang Kai-shek (fourth from left) with Soviet Russian advisers during the period of Soviet–Kuomintang collaboration (1924–7). General Galen is seated at Chiang's immediate right, while Borodin is at the extreme left. The Soviet advisers respected Chiang's ability and integrity, but thought he could be controlled as long as the Soviet Union provided funds, weapons and advisers.

In either case, according to an influential Russian adviser, the fundamental policy was to cooperate with Chiang Kai-shek 'to the very end possible'.

Actually, Chiang's attitudes and intentions after the *coup* were by no means clear. The responsibility for moving the *Chung-shan* was not fully established, he asserted publicly, and it was not certain but that an individual Communist – the Navy Bureau official – might be guilty rather than the Chinese Communist Party itself. Chiang – while taking emergency measures against the Communists – ostentatiously accepted official responsibility for the whole incident, and later he even praised the Communists for their spirit. When asked by the Russian advisers how they should proceed, moreover, he assured them that they should continue as before.

Support for the Kuomintang Left

Having decided to accommodate themselves to Chiang Kai-shek's demands, both Borodin and the Chinese Communist leadership found themselves increasingly at the mercy of Kuomintang politics and the whims and ambitions of various warlords. It is true that as Chiang Kai-shek's influence increased, the Communists became more and more apprehensive of what they perceived as his Right Wing tendencies. But none could see clearly what to do about it. In general, continuing dependence upon Chiang and various warlords forced the Communists to suppress many revolutionary tendencies – especially among the peasantry – as rapidly as they succeeded in stimulating them.

During subsequent months the Chinese Communists identified Chiang Kai-shek's increasing power with the emergence of what they called a New Right, which was distinguished from the 'reactionary Right'. The non-revolutionary tendencies of the New Right were undeniable, the Party conceded, but it was still necessary to cooperate.

In April 1926 the ECCI had instructed the Chinese Communist Party to bend every effort toward compelling the Kuomintang Right Wing to withdraw or, if these efforts failed, to expel it from the nationalist party. At the same time the Chinese comrades were exhorted to strengthen the Kuomintang Left Wing as their central task. Thus, Communist policy within the Kuomintang was like the policy toward various classes country-wide: to unite with the Left and force the Center to attack the reactionary Right.

In fact, however, with Chiang Kai-shek's *coup* and the withdrawal of Wang Ching-wei – who had retired 'for reasons of health' – the Kuomintang Left Wing lacked both leadership and mass following. In Canton the Kwangtung Regional Committee of the Chinese Communist Party – in contrast to the Central Committee – 'argued that the Kuomintang Left Wing was illusory and, for practical purposes, did not exist.

By the summer of 1926 two opposition groups had developed

within the Chinese Communist Party, one favoring immediate withdrawal from the Kuomintang, the other urging a struggle to seize Kuomintang leadership. Both viewpoints were condemned by the Central Committee: the withdrawal proposal betrayed a misunderstanding of long-range trends of the Chinese revolution; the proposal for seizing leadership was in error because it would reduce the Kuomintang to a narrow organization with a narrow base and excessively concentrated power.

In the cross-fire between Chiang and T'ang

In late May the National Government had dispatched a unit of the Kuomintang Seventh Army to Hunan in support of the warlord T'ang Sheng-chih, with whom it had been negotiating an alliance. It was then decided to gain control of the Wuhan cities (Wuchang, Hankow, Hanyang), pacify the rest of Hunan, and join with Feng Yü-hsiang in unifying the whole country. But these plans soon brought the Communists into a cross-fire of rivalry between T'ang Sheng-chih and Chiang Kai-shek.

The Russians recognized T'ang as ambitious, but hoped to play him off against Chiang. 'T'ang-chih himself is lively, resolute and radical in speech,' a Soviet adviser reported. 'He acts with great determination. Since he himself does not smoke, he forbids others to smoke. However, he must be hypocritical about this, because two fingers on his right hand are stained as dark as smoked sausages. It is reported that he used to smoke opium.'[9]

The operation in support of T'ang thus took shape as the first campaign of a new Northern Expedition. Chiang Kai-shek was formally appointed Commander-in-Chief shortly thereafter, and on 6 July he was elected chairman of the Standing Committee of the Kuomintang, CEC. By now he enjoyed full control of his party's military and political organs. By the end of July the eight armies of the National Revolutionary Army totalled about 100,000 men. By December, after a victorious sweep northward into Hunan, the same forces would be increased to 260,000 men.

Chiang Kai-shek as Commander-in-Chief of victorious Nationalist forces in the mid-twenties. Despite the development of his own nationalist armies, Chiang was forced to preside over shifting coalitions in order to maintain cohesion. This precarious balance was repeatedly challenged by ambitious militarists, Kuomintang dissidents, Japanese invaders and the Chinese Communists.

The Northern Expedition met with considerable opposition from leading Chinese Communists, ostensibly because Wu P'ei-fu had undertaken his own 'southern expedition' and because Nationalist power in Kwangtung was being threatened by anti-Red forces. A deeper cause for Communist anxiety was probably a growing fear of Chiang Kai-shek and the power of the New Right Wing. But the Chinese Communist leadership also feared the possibility of a split within their own ranks over the issue, and it was therefore decided to support the undertaking. In the meantime, the Communists were to work toward expanding and strengthening the Kuomintang Left.

Chiang Kai-shek reached Changsha, Hunan on 11 August 1926, and there he conferred with T'ang Sheng-chih. Each man viewed the other with uneasiness and suspicion, but the Russians still thought they could make good use of both.

As the Russians saw it, T'ang wanted to overthrow Chiang Kai-shek and replace him as Commander-in-Chief. It was necessary, therefore, to strengthen Chiang, but without rejecting T'ang. 'I have been working together with Chiang Kai-shek,' reported a senior Soviet adviser, 'and simultaneously manipulating T'ang.'[10] Undoubtedly, the Hunanese warlord was an 'opportunist' and 'not in full accord with the revolution'. But this did not mean that the Russians should sever all relations with him. On the contrary, '. . . . I have given T'ang moral support and shown good will toward him.'

Pursuing their northern sweep with considerable *élan*, Chiang Kai-shek's Nationalist troops seized the Wuhan cities (Wuchang, Hankow, Hanyang) in early October, 1926. A few weeks later – almost at the same time as the opening of the Comintern's Seventh Plenum in Moscow – the Kuomintang transferred its headquarters to Hankow. Responsibility for law and order in Kwangtung Province fell to the commander of the Fourth Army, Li Chi-shen, who soon seized Canton in an old-style militarist coup.

4 The Communist-Nationalist split

Peasant revolution – through the Kuomintang

Stalin and his colleagues were already beginning to foresee a new world war which was expected to break out among the major nations. 'Three imperialist powers stand face to face in the Pacific,' D. Z. Manuilsky asserted in late 1926, 'the United States, Japan and Great Britain . . . . The armed clash which may break out there in the near future will be of unimaginable violence and serious consequences.'[1] The Communists predicted a conflict of two phases: first, a struggle between Japan on one side and Great Britain and the United States on the other; and a subsequent phase in which the American and British victors would parcel out Asia and all its spoils.

Only two developments could change this course of events, according to Manuilsky: a decisive proletarian revolution in the United States or Great Britain, or a victorious revolution in China. So it was that Communist strategists saw the pursuit of the Chinese revolution as a major factor in world affairs and a possible key to the avoidance of 'imperialist war' and the maintenance of peace.

China was a vast reservoir of raw materials for Japan and a major field for Japanese exports. 'For Japan,' according to Manuilsky, 'it is a matter of – to be or not to be.' That explained why Japan, tightly crowded, was pushing toward the Philippines, the Malay Archipelago, and the islands of the Pacific. It explained also why Great Britain was installing guns of higher calibre in Singapore, and why American economic penetration of China and other parts of Asia was antagonizing the Japanese who, nevertheless, badly needed American credits and American markets.

Yet all these vicious competitions for markets and raw materials depended upon one condition, according to the Communist viewpoint, namely, a disunited and pitifully weak China. If a major war broke out in the Pacific before China had been unified, Japan, waging a preventative war against Great Britain and the United States, could drive through Manchuria and occupy China with all its vital arteries for commerce and defense. Because of these possibilities, Stalin and his colleagues perceived the unification of China – and *not* the social and agrarian revolutions – as the foremost priority. A strong Communist–Kuomintang alliance was the first step, but there were two further tasks: the exclusion of foreign capital from China, and the building of a vast peasant army.

Stalin saw the Peking militarists as agents, primarily, of foreign imperialism. 'We are apt to understand under intervention a condition in which foreign troops march into Chinese territory,' he told the Seventh Plenum of the Communist International, 'and if this does not take place there is no intervention. This is a serious error, comrades ... In the present circumstances, imperialism prefers to intervene against the revolution by organizing civil war within a dependent country, by financing the counter-revolutionary forces against the revolution, by moral and financial support of its Chinese agents ...'[2]

Wu P'ei-fu, Sun Ch'uan-fang and other northern militarists could not oppose the revolutionary forces in China, according to Stalin, if the imperialist powers had not inspired them and supplied them with arms, money, instructors, advisers and other support. 'Intervention by using other people,' the Soviet leader asserted, 'that is the kernel of imperialist intervention at present.'

What was Stalin's response to the imperialist powers and their counter-revolutionary instruments, the northern warlords? The plan was to support with Soviet arms, money, instructors and advisers, not only Chiang Kai-shek, but also whichever local warlords were willing to oppose Peking.

Over the next few months Stalin tried – and failed – to banish foreign influence *first*, before the building of a Communist-controlled peasant army. In subsequent years Mao Tse-tung reversed procedures, building a peasant army first, and eventually achieved success.

Stalin's approach to the Chinese revolution was embodied in theses adopted by the Seventh Plenum in late November and early December 1926 – though N. I. Bukharin, M. N. Roy, and other Comintern theoreticians had a hand in the drafting. The Plenum urged peasant revolt in China, but at the same time insisted on Communist support of the Kuomintang.

'If the proletariat does not put forward a radical agrarian program,' the theses of the Plenum asserted, 'it will fail to attract the peasantry into the revolutionary struggle and will lose hegemony in the national revolutionary movement.' But the peasant revolution must be accomplished within the Kuomintang, many of whose more or less rightist members 'would continue to march with the revolution for a time'. It was assumed that the Nationalist party and government – at least temporarily – would provide sufficient channels for reaching and dealing with the peasantry. In the somewhat longer run Communist members of the Kuomintang could transform it 'into a real people's party – a solid revolutionary bloc of the proletariat, peasantry, the urban petty bourgeoisie, and other oppressed and exploited strata.'[3]

In China, meanwhile, Kuomintang forces were pursuing their northward sweep. The troops of the northern warlord, Wu P'ei-fu, were falling back, and local commanders in many areas were defecting to the Nationalists. Particularly, Borodin apparently continued to assume that the Communist–Kuomintang alliance could count upon the Hunan militarist T'ang Sheng-chih and increasingly upon Feng Yü-hsiang, who had returned to north-western China recently from a visit to Moscow – sounding more pro-Soviet now than 'Christian'. Yet the drive was by no means over. Chang Tso-lin and Wu P'ei-fu still controlled the approach to Peking. Sun Ch'uan-fang occupied the eastern provinces and especially the city of Shanghai. Chang Tsung-ch'ang held Shantung. Lesser militarists vacillated, waiting to make certain which side was likely to win.

Nanchang versus Wuhan

The Kuomintang advance had rapidly brought the Chinese Communists in touch with the rural masses. Indeed, Communist propagandists were effectively penetrating territories just in advance of Kuomintang armies and bringing the peasantry over in considerable numbers. But their success in these endeavors soon presented the Communists with their long-standing dilemma: preservation of the Communist–Kuomintang *entente* might lead to neglect of the masses. On the other hand, Communist stimulation of radical demands and slogans on the part of the masses might damage the united front.

The Chinese countryside itself was on the verge of widespread peasant revolt. Before the Northern Expedition, according to the veteran Communist Ts'ai Ho-shen, 'we had sufficiently trained workers only in Shanghai, Kwangtung and Hunan'. With Chiang Kai-shek's northward advance, however, the peasants began rising by the hundreds of thousands until the number, according to subsequent estimates by Ts'ai Ho-shen, reached, in the spring of 1927, 'not less than 15,000,000' in Kiangsi, Kwangtung, Hunan, Hupeh and other provinces.

Yet it was recognized by Communist leaders that this peasant groundswell might threaten their alliance with the Kuomintang. In October the Kremlin wired the Chinese Communists to restrain the peasantry in order not to antagonize Nationalist generals and their local warlord collaborators, many of whom were landowners. Months later Stalin, under attack from Trotsky, was to admit that these instructions had been a 'mistake'.

In cautioning against precipitate action on the countryside, the Central Committee linked the peasant problem with the *min-t'uan*, or People's Corps, which were viewed as essentially private militia used by 'the landlords, bad gentry and local bullies' to oppress the peasantry. The Central Committee's objective, as put forward in the summer and autumn of 1926, was not to destroy the *min-t'uan*, but to replace the 'bad gentry' leaders with 'honest gentry'. Under these circumstances the Central Committee was reluctant to encourage militant action on the part of the peasantry.

Meanwhile, tensions were beginning to mount between the Communists and Chiang Kai-shek.

On paper the policy of the Soviet Union and of the Chinese

Communists was to shift support toward the Kuomintang Left Wing under Wang Ching-wei. But Chiang Kai-shek was too strong to be ignored. The Nationalist leader had become increasingly critical of the Communists, and care must be observed if the *entente* were to survive. The Communists were beginning to find themselves in a difficult dilemma. 'We must safeguard the interests of the peasantry,' T'an P'ing-shan told the Seventh Plenum in Moscow, 'but on the other hand we must maintain and solidify the united front of the national revolutionary movement. In so contradictory a situation it is far from easy to maintain a correct tactical line.'[4]

It was only a short time after this that Mao, who was still a relatively obscure member of the Central Committee, began his now-famous investigation of the peasant movement in Hunan. According to his subsequent report, some 2,000,000 peasants were already organizing in that province alone. All in all, the peasant associations in Hunan probably influenced the lives of over 10,000,000 persons.

Yet relations still remained cordial between Chiang Kai-shek and his Soviet advisers, who considered it important to support him against the ambitions of his rival, T'ang Sheng-chih. On 7 November Chiang wired congratulations to Stalin on the ninth anniversary of the Bolshevik Revolution and reiterated his hopes for a continued Sino-Soviet alliance in the World Revolution.

From this point forward, however, Chiang Kai-shek became more and more aware of Communist opposition to him – even though the Soviet Union and the Chinese Communist Party were proceeding also upon the essentially antagonistic assumption that the alliance with Chiang could still be maintained. In December the Central Committee even sent a letter assuring Chiang of support and insisting that the recall of Wang Ching-wei should not be interpreted as in any sense an attempt to overthrow him.

There were other complications.

The Nationalist drive had consistently defeated the forces of the northern warlord Wu P'ei-fu, and increasing numbers of local commanders were going over to the revolutionary armies. Both the Communists and leaders of the Kuomintang Left felt more secure in their newly-established Hankow headquarters because of labor strength in the Wuhan cities. But despite this gain – and despite their covert support of Chiang against his rival T'ang Sheng-chih – Borodin and his Soviet colleagues continued to count on T'ang's Hunanese troops, as well as the armies of Feng and other militarists. The Communists were not just trying to play both ends against the middle; they were trying to play everyone against everyone else. The countryside teemed with warlord forces – some more or less loyal to the legal government in Peking, some disposed toward the Kuomintang, some wholly unreliable. How many of them could be influenced by Soviet weapons, supplies and advisers?

The Russian advisers tried to find out, but in the meantime new disagreements emerged between Chiang and the Left Wing. There seemed to be three major issues: the problem of army supplies and funds; the location of the Kuomintang party and governmental headquarters; and a proposed south-eastern campaign.

In a series of telegrams toward the end of the year Chiang complained that funds and supplies were grievously insufficient and that troops of the Seventh Army had mutinied for lack of pay. He implied that the delay in providing him with funds was deliberate.

On the question of the location of Kuomintang party and government headquarters, Chiang argued in favor of Nanchang, whereas Borodin and the Left Wing leaders insisted on Wuhan. On 11 January Chiang made a special trip to Wuhan in an effort to win support for his view, but Left Wing leaders were adamant and he returned shortly to Nanchang where his own staff was still headquartered.

In the meantime, Chiang had convened at Nanchang a conference of army commanders in order to propose a strategy of attacking south-eastward in the direction of Nanking and Shanghai. Galen and the other Russian advisers – and also T'ang Sheng-chih – remained strongly in favour of a continuing northern drive on Peking.

Chiang strikes at the Communists

By the first weeks of January 1927 the issues were multiplying between Chiang Kai-shek in Nanchang and the Kuomintang Left in Wuhan; between Chiang and his chief adviser, Borodin; between Borodin and the Comintern representative H. N. Voitinsky; and among various small cliques of Communists, both Russian and Chinese. Particularly critical of unfolding events were three young Communists – Nassonov, Fokine and Albrecht – reporting back to Moscow what they saw from Shanghai.

Chiang proposed now to attack south-eastward from Nanchang in the direction of Nanking and Shanghai – rather than push on against Peking. Borodin, Galen, the Chinese Communist Central Committee, T'ang Sheng-chih and various leaders of the Kuomintang Left in Wuhan were opposed to Chiang's proposal.

Communist circles, meanwhile, were riven by their long-standing debate: the continuing controversy over how much weight should be assigned to the Communist–Kuomintang *entente* and how much to peasant rebellion.

On 11 January Chiang made a special trip to Wuhan in an attempt to gain support for his own position. During this visit Borodin delivered a banquet speech in which he denounced personal dictatorships and – implicitly – criticized Chiang Kai-shek. Meanwhile, under Borodin's influence, the Kuomintang Left Wing was consolidating whatever forces were available to it and firmly opposing Chiang's insistence on transferring the capital to Nanchang.

Borodin's determination and the hopes of the Left Wing were probably strengthened by the Hankow incident of the previous week when crowds of angry Chinese staged a demonstration and seized the British Concession at Hankow. The 'revolutionizing effect' of the incident was perceived as strengthening Borodin and the Kuomintang Left against Chiang's point of view.

On the other hand, these events in Hankow further uncovered the difference of viewpoint between Borodin, on the one hand, and

Voitinsky and the Chinese Communist Central Committee on the other. According to Nassonov, the CC 'did not want to react at all' to the incident, whereas Borodin was sensitive to its revolutionary implications.

'Why should we clamber over it,' Ch'en Tu-hsiu was reported to have asked, 'and what kind of agitation should we develop when the aggressors were not the English but the Chinese?'[5]

Subsequently, it appeared that Ch'en Tu-hsiu was not the only apprehensive revolutionist. After the banquet with Chiang, according to Communist critics, Borodin 'recoiled in fright' from his own bold position and confessed to Fokine, 'I am afraid I made a mistake. My standing up against Chiang Kai-shek was provoked by the pressure of public opinion, and I do not know if I acted correctly.'[6]

In the eyes of several of the leading Chinese Communists, according to Nassonov, the workers and peasants were 'a dull, dumb mass, unconscious and inactive' which the Communists must lead by the hand. 'The party leadership declares, for example, that the peasants do not want land.'

The petty bourgeoisie had become a bogy to the Chinese Communist leadership. 'No peasants' power can be organized,' Nassonov complained, 'for it will frighten away the petty bourgeoisie. No demands must be raised for the workers for they will scare away the petty bourgeoisie.' The Communist leadership also appeared reluctant to use what strength they had in Kuomintang armies.

By the end of 1926 there were dozens of company commanders, battalion commanders and even a few regimental commanders in the Kuomintang forces who were Communist Party members. 'But out of fear of revolutionizing the army which pervades some party leaders, the various comrades working in the army become detached from the party, are transformed into "individual" Communist commanders, and, as one of the Russian comrades in charge of military work in the CC declared: "they probably refuse to take workers into their sections of the army, because the workers constitute a turbulent element".'[7]

Militarily, the Central Committee staked everything on the 'old staff' which consisted largely of warlords and other landholding officers. Virtually no provisions were made for raising officers from the ranks. 'With the aid of all sorts of combinations, oppositions, etc., our comrades hoped to maintain a balance of forces in the army,' Nassonov complained, 'but it never occurred to them to capture it.'

Returning to Nanchang, Chiang Kai-shek soon opened a verbal attack upon the Communists. Every loyal Kuomintang member must be a faithful believer in the doctrines of Sun Yat-sen, he asserted, 'and nothing else'.[8]

On 7 March Chiang Kai-shek again issued a public criticism of Borodin and other Soviet advisers, but reaffirmed Kuomintang friendship for the Soviet Union. It was not Soviet policy to 'tyrannize over us,' he declared, 'though her representatives have acted otherwise, insulting our every movement. I am convinced that it has naught to do with Russia, but [is] the individual actions of these representatives.' The Kuomintang must unite with the Soviet Union and 'fight against all countries with imperialist tendencies'.[9]

With time the various Communist leaders and advisers became more and more uncertain and divided on the issue of Chiang Kai-shek's advance. According to Nassonov and his comrades, Borodin and certain other Russian advisers 'were of the opinion that it would not hurt for Chiang Kai-shek to break his neck on Shanghai and Chekiang, and they egged him on; Comrade Galen was of the opinion that the march on Shanghai was a hopeless military undertaking and did not participate in it.'

A second group representing the 'Right Wing of the CC and the Shanghai Committee' were in favor of supporting the march on Shanghai unconditionally. 'Whether consciously or not,' as Nassonov and his associates saw it, 'these comrades consented to hand over power to Chiang Kai-shek in Shanghai, that is, to help the bourgeoisie entrench itself there.'

A third group, which included Nassonov, Fokine, Albrecht,

'and a part of the Chinese comrades' wanted to support with all available means 'the capture of Shanghai by the people's revolutionary army, and, on the other hand, by the unleashing of a mass movement in Shanghai as a counterpoise to the Right Wing, of creating a democratic people's power so that the democratic factor would predominate over the military factor and the occupation of Shanghai would simultaneously result in the victory of the national revolution, of the anti-imperialist movement, and in the defeat of Chiang Kai-shek as the representative of the bourgeois Right Wing of the Kuomintang.'

In Moscow, however, the Stalinist leadership was convinced that Chiang would not dare break with the Communists at this point.

'The revolutionary pressure from below is so strong,' a *Pravda* editorial asserted on 17 March, 'that in the present stage of the [revolutionary] development Chiang Kai-shek is compelled to maneuver, to swear allegiance to principles of revolutionary loyalty, of Sun Yat-sen's teaching of socialism, and to submit himself to the leadership of the mass party of the Kuomintang.'

Stalin himself was outspoken. 'Why drive away the Right when we have the majority and when the Right listens to us?' a Yugoslav Communist quoted the Soviet leader as explaining to 3,000 local Communist Party functionaries in Moscow. 'The peasant needs an old worn-out jade as long as she is necessary. He does not drive her away. So it is with us.'[10]

Meanwhile Nationalist troops moved unhurriedly eastward against the local warlord Sun Ch'uan-fang. In late February a massive general strike was called in Shanghai, but the Communist leadership vacillated in their policy, uncertain whether to develop the demonstrations into an insurrection, or to hold back. The conflict became insurrectionary almost in spite of Communist leadership.

As the situation in Shanghai became 'red hot', according to Nassonov, the Chinese Communist Central Committee had difficulty deciding 'whether the uprising should be made or not' – at the very moment when the uprising was already taking place.

Execution squads armed with broadswords patrolled the streets, decapitating whoever looked to them like a revolutionist. Yet the insurrection continued to develop.

'Many Chinese left Shanghai for their native villages, which they regarded as safer,' wrote the American correspondent, George Sokolsky. 'The foreigners were nervous, tense, irritable. A fear psychology possessed us. We were all to be murdered by our own servants.'[11]

'The Canton advance guard is twenty-five to thirty miles from Shanghai,' Nassonov wrote. 'The troops of Sun Ch'uan-fang, absolutely demoralized, began pillaging and dispersing homewards. In the city, sections of the military forces waver, the fleet comes over to our side. Three hundred thousand workers go out on strike and pass over to armed struggle. The military commander executes dozens of workers.'[12]

The strike and insurrection were soon put down by the local garrison commander, Li Pao-chang, a northerner who was rumored to have made a special agreement with Chiang – and who, indeed, accepted command of the Eighth Nationalist Army only a few weeks later.

Nationalist troops moved closer to Shanghai while the public dialogue continued between Chiang Kai-shek and the Communists. 'I have never taken the view that I cannot cooperate with the Communists,' Chiang asserted on 17 March. 'As a matter of fact, I may rightly claim the credit for bringing the Communists into the fold of the Kuomintang. But I have also made it clear that while I was opposed to the oppression of the Communists, I would check their influence as soon as they grew too powerful.'[13]

Communist controlled labor unions – having organized their February strike and insurrection in premature anticipation of the Nationalist advance – were concluding preparations for a second strike to be coordinated with Chiang's entry into Shanghai.

Shanghai was captured by Nationalists on 22 March, and over the next few days Chiang Kai-shek himself proceeded toward the city at an unhurried pace. Rumor had it that the Communists were

A 'famine ticket' circulated in Shanghai early in 1927.
Allegedly the Chinese Communists printed and distributed these cards to
hold the British responsible for starvation in China and to
increase Chinese hatred for foreigners. Famine and starvation have been
persistent in China for generations, and it has been traditional for
the Chinese people to hold the ruler responsible for the consequent misery.

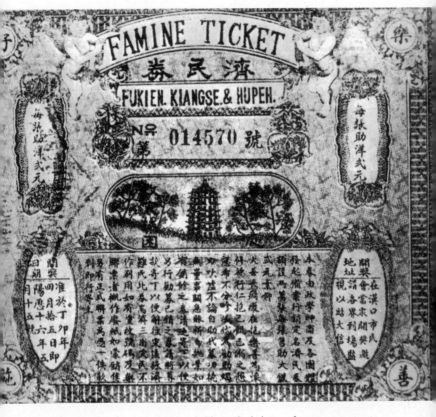

planning to make a shambles of Shanghai in order to prevent
Chiang from establishing himself there. Yet as Chiang approached,
the Communists were impotent. By order of the Comintern they
had laid aside whatever plans they may have devised, and had
carefully buried their weapons.

Chiang finally arrived aboard a gunboat – unannounced – on
26 March. He was allowed to walk ashore without opposition.

In Shanghai, Ch'en Tu-hsiu issued a joint statement with Wang Ching-wei, who had just returned from France: an alliance between the Kuomintang and the Chinese Communist Party was necessary. 'At the present time China needs a democratic dictatorship of all oppressed classes to suppress the counter-revolution ...' But counter-revolutionaries inside and outside China were spreading false reports in order to bring the two parties into opposition with each other. 'Some say that the Communist Party is preparing to form a workers' government, to overthrow the Kuomintang and to recover the concessions by force of arms. Others say that the leaders of the Kuomintang intend to make war on the Communist Party, to suppress the labor unions and to dissolve the workers' defense organizations ... *there is no basis whatever for these malicious rumors.*'[14]

Nor did Chiang display hostility toward the Kuomintang Left. 'Wang Ching-wei is my teacher and friend ...' *Pravda* of 6 April quoted him as declaring. 'All military, political and civil problems, the problems of finance and foreign policy must be settled under the guidance of Chairman Wang Ching-wei.' Reassurance statements of this kind were seized upon by the Moscow leadership.

Soon after his arrival, however, the Nationalist leader began soliciting support from a number of strikingly unrevolutionary sources. 'Bankers and merchants flocked to his standard,' wrote George Sokolsky. 'The Shanghai Chinese Bankers' Association, the representatives of the Chinese modern banks, arranged for an immediate 3,000,000 dollar loan ... Arrangements were made with the Green and Red Societies', secret organizations with which Chiang was asserted by his critics to have had years of association.

By now Stalin and his associates were being deluged with conflicting information about events in China. Nassonov felt that Voitinsky was at fault for much of the confusion and misinformation. 'He sent Moscow bastardized information, held back material, and concealed the real situation ...'[15] It was not only necessary to relieve Voitinsky of his duties, Nassonov asserted at a time when Roy was already *en route*, but also to send 'a much stronger worker who is capable at the same time of representing the ECCI and of directing Borodin.'

Early morning darkness still lay over Shanghai when, on 12 April, squads of armed men – variously described as merchant volunteers, Kuomintang workers, Nationalist troops, and Red and Green Society men posing as 'white' laborers – began organizing into patrols. Just before dawn an order was passed, and they began rounding up Communist labor pickets, seizing whatever weapons were found, and executing whoever resisted. Within a few days Communist strength in Shanghai was shattered.

The peasants rebel – and are restrained by the Communists

Meanwhile, in an effort to resolve these various conflicts among revolutionary leaders in China, Stalin had dispatched a special Comintern delegation headed by M. N. Roy. There were particular reasons, in addition to his many years of revolutionary experience, why Roy seemed a logical choice for the mission.

During the Seventh Plenum in November 1926 Roy had been elected to the Presidium of the Comintern and to the Chinese Commission, and he felt secure in his personal relations with Stalin. 'We see things alike,' Stalin had told him once. 'We are both Asiatics.'

In Wuhan Roy was received by his old friend from Mexico City days, Michael Borodin, though within a few weeks they were to find themselves in stubborn disagreement. Borodin had a big house at his disposal, and he invited Roy to share it with him.

By the latter half of April 1927, Chiang Kai-shek seemed to rival the Peking warlords as Number 1 Enemy of the Chinese Communist Party and the Kuomintang Left. The Central Committee of the Chinese Communist Party issued a special Declaration welcoming Wuhan's decision 'to remove Chiang Kai-shek from command of the national-revolutionary armies, to expel him from the party, and to issue an order for his arrest.' What the Declaration seemed to overlook was the fact that Chiang had an army and a part of the Kuomintang political hierarchy with him in Nanchang. There was also the same old dilemma emerging from the contradiction between land-holding Nationalists and the exploding revolution of the peasantry.

In a resolution of 16 April the Central Committee of the Chinese Communist Party urged that the campaign against Peking warlords be deferred in order to build a strong revolutionary base and to 'defeat Chiang Kai-shek and the bourgeoisie which is attempting to split the revolutionary movement.' Under pressure from the Kuomintang Left, however, the Central Committee reversed itself two days later and supported a Wuhan decision on the immediate dispatch of troops to the north.

The dilemma became a major issue during the Fifth Congress of the Chinese Communist Party, and also in Moscow.

A few days before the convening of the Congress, the Central Executive Committee of the Kuomintang Left held a two-week conference on the issue of land confiscation and distribution to the peasantry. In addition to influential members of the Kuomintang Left, the meetings were attended by Ch'en Tu-hsiu, T'an P'ing-shan, Mao Tse-tung, Borodin, Roy, and two peasant leaders from Hunan and Hupeh respectively. During the discussions there was considerable disagreement. In general, the military men opposed land confiscation outright or insisted that the lands of 'revolutionary military men' must be safeguarded. Wang Ching-wei was 'evasive', but suggested that only owners of 50 *mou* or more – about 7·5 acres – should be subject to confiscation. Among the Communists, T'an P'ing-shan seemed to vacillate, but in the end he supported Borodin and Ch'en Tu-hsiu in a proposal for 'political confiscation' to be directed against the property of counter-revolutionaries only. The Hunanese delegates, some of the Russians present, and presumably Roy argued for the confiscation of all land held by landlords.

The issue, far from settled, was carried over into the Fifth Congress of the Chinese Communist Party.

The Congress opened 27 April in Hankow and continued for two weeks. Among the eighty delegates were representatives from the Communist International, and leaders from the Kuomintang Left attended at least some of the sessions. Debate centered on support for T'ang Sheng-chih and other 'revolutionary' warlord generals; on a plan put forward by Ch'en Tu-hsiu 'to retire to the northwest provinces'; and on the issues of agrarian revolution and the confiscation of land.

Borodin and Ch'en Tu-hsiu argued in favor of support for T'ang Sheng-chih during the northern campaign, Roy and T'an P'ing-shan against. To rely on warlord generals like T'ang Sheng-chih and on other so-called Left militarists was illusory and dangerous, Roy insisted. Such military forces could never be properly controlled or won over or transformed into revolutionary troops. 'The task of the revolution is to demoralize and destroy them.' On the other hand, it made sense to use them as long as feasible – but not at the expense of the revolution: the important thing was to get control of their troops. 'There is only one way,' Roy asserted, 'of really winning the soldiers of the warlords' armies over to the side of the revolutionary army: it is by way of an agrarian revolution.'[16]

Yet the inescapable fact remained that T'ang Sheng-chih and his army – and other essentially warlord contingents – constituted a large part of the armed forces remaining to Wuhan, and the views of Borodin and Ch'en Tu-hsiu prevailed.

At the same time, however, Ch'en Tu-hsiu put forward a proposal that was remarkably similar to a decision which Mao Tse-tung and his colleagues were to implement some years later. The Chinese revolution could not develop in Canton, Shanghai, Tientsin, Hankow or other regions where industry was most developed, Ch'en reasoned, because imperialism and the Chinese bourgeoisie were too strong there. The only solution for the Communists was 'to retire to the northwest provinces where the influence of imperialism was weaker and where the revolution could more easily concentrate its forces for a later attack on imperialist strongholds.'[17]

The Fifth Congress rejected this proposal.

Endorsing a rigorous agrarian program in principle, Ch'en Tu-hsiu warned that the Communists must make temporary concessions to the petty bourgeoisie in order to ensure its support. Military action must therefore come first, the confiscation of large and middle land holdings later. 'The only correct solution,' Ch'en asserted, 'is to deepen the revolution after it has first been spread.'

Roy took sharp issue – though in the long run he failed to press his argument hard enough. The central task was to augment the class struggle, and this meant facilitating the agrarian revolution. The militarists must be demoralized and destroyed and the rank and file of soldiers – mostly landless peasants – turned against their land-holding officers. Essentially, the army must be captured from within – and also the political apparatus of the Kuomintang Left. 'The Communist Party,' he said, 'must create in various organs of the Kuomintang and of the government Communist factions under the political leadership of the Central Committee so that every decision of the national government will be adopted with the consent and under the influence of the proletariat and the peasantry.'

Roy urged further development of the agrarian revolution, the establishment of peasant power in the villages, and the creation of a reliable revolutionary army that would serve directly under the Communists and Kuomintang Left and would not be the mere creation of warlords and other landowning generals. The way to recruit this army, he believed, was to encourage the agrarian revolution by organizing the dissatisfied peasantry into troops ready to fight for the ownership of lands they themselves tilled but which belonged to someone else.

Wuhan could be defended by a concentration of revolutionary troops along the border between Hupeh and Honan. The agrarian revolution could be encouraged in Hupeh and Hunan, which were controlled by the Wuhan government, and at the same time a political penetration of Kiangsi and Kwangtung could be reinforced by military action. Gradually, step by step, Kiangsi, Fukien, Kwangtung and Kwangsi could be brought under control of Wuhan, and from this base it would then be feasible to attack Peking.

The priorities seemed clear: *first*, to stimulate existing peasant discontent; *second*, to provide the peasants generally with arms; *third*, to encourage rural self-government; *fourth*, to create a state machinery through which a 'democratic dictatorship' could develop; *fifth*, the achievement of a truly revolutionary army – not by transforming warlords and landholders – but by seizing control 'upward' from the revolutionary masses.

During a debate with Wang Ching-wei, however, Roy – wittingly or unwittingly – made a crucial capitulation. After arguing persistently for agrarian revolution – including the confiscation of land – he assured the Kuomintang Left leader that 'inasmuch as the revolution, in its present stage, will be led by a coalition of classes – and the proletariat is prepared to lead the revolution in collaboration with other classes – the proletariat can not put forward a program for the immediate abolition of private property.'

Clearly, at this point, the tactics of revolution 'from below' and revolution 'from above' had collided head on. One or the other had to be recognized as subordinate. Even Roy had backed down. Subsequently there were further discussions of confining confiscations to 'large' holdings and exempting property belonging to Kuomintang officers, but Roy, according to Ts'ai Ho-shen, 'did not object' to these suggestions and even 'severely criticized' the counterproposal of some Russian advisers. And in a speech welcoming the new Central Committee which the Fifth Congress had elected, he seemed to express an approval highly inconsistent with his earlier arguments. 'This Congress was Bolshevist,' he declared. 'It showed that the Chinese Communist Party is on the way to becoming a genuine Bolshevik party.'[18]

The Fifth Congress closed, but Communist troubles were only beginning. On 18 May one of the generals allied with the Wuhan government, the commander of the Fourteenth Division, Hsia Tou-yin, suddenly rebelled against the Kuomintang Left, seeking to overthrow it. The Wuhan government itself was next to helpless, the bulk of available troops having been dispatched toward Peking with the Northern Expedition. But the local garrison commander was the Communist general Yeh T'ing who, acting on his own initiative, scraped together an irregular force of about 1,500 men – including several hundred cadets from the local military school.

Hsia Tou-yin's revolt was put down, but then – during the night of 21 May – General Hsü K'e-hsiang and other Nationalist officers in command of troops stationed in Changsha staged a *coup d'état*. The Hunan provincial government was overthrown, local committees of the Kuomintang Left dissolved, and repressive measures taken against Communist organizations in the area. 'The insurgents,' Roy charged, 'were direct subordinates of the Commander-in-Chief of the [Wuhan] Nationalist Army, T'ang Sheng-chih. From the front he remained in telegraphic communication with them.'[19]

In Changsha the Communists and members of local Kuomintang Left organizations prepared a counter-attack against Hsü K'e-hsiang and his forces. The intent was to retake the city and thus 'save the revolution'. More than twenty thousand peasants were mobilized and led against Changsha from all directions. Then the attack was suddenly called off. 'Nearly at the gates of the city,' Roy remembered later, 'they were ordered to go back and dissolve their military formations. The instructions came from the Communist headquarters at Wuhan.'[20] As chairman of the National Peasant Federation, Mao Tse-tung, who had championed the agrarian revolution in his report on the peasantry of Hunan, now found himself compelled by Party discipline to play a major role in discouraging peasant revolt in his own province.

Retreating in chaos, the peasant troops fell into skirmishes with insurgent forces. Wild stories circulated in Wuhan about 'peasant excesses', and word of spontaneous agrarian uprisings reached Moscow while the Comintern's Eighth Plenum was in session.

The Communist defeat

The problem of Communist policies in China was discussed at length by Comintern leaders in Moscow. Should the agrarian movement be curbed in order to appease the Kuomintang Left?

Some leaders argued 'yes': by curbing the insurgent peasants, the Chinese Communists would enlarge their influence in the Kuomintang, and as they gained in influence they could then press forward beyond their more hesitant and conservative allies. Others argued 'no': the issue was to choose now between the insurgent peasants and the Kuomintang Left.

Stalin argued for curbing the agrarian revolution lest the Kuomintang Left turn against the Communists. 'The armed Chinese are largely mercenaries,' he said, 'and we do not dispose of enough financial resources to have them on our side.'[21] Only by containing the peasantry could the Communists maintain the support of the Kuomintang Left.

But the so-called 'mercenaries' were themselves largely ruined peasants, according to Stalin's opposition in Moscow, who would desert the Kuomintang Left for the Communists if an agrarian program were put forward. 'We must fight,' asserted a leader of the opposition.

'To fight means certain defeat,' Stalin countered. But the Communists could maneuver, he thought, without sacrificing anything.

Stalin produced a telegram from Borodin which declared that the Kuomintang Left would oppose agrarian revolution even if it meant a break with the Communists. The Kuomintang Left was still too powerful, Stalin asserted. 'Its armies will not disband in the twinkle of an eye, and we will then be defeated in a civil war before the insurgent agrarians are able to connect with the proletarian insurrection.'

The issue soon became entangled in the power struggle between Stalin and Trotsky – and it was Stalin who had the greater strength. In a telegram which reached Hankow on 1 June he put forward the course he had in mind. The agrarian revolution was indispensable, but peasant 'excesses' must be combatted – through the peasant unions, however, and not with troops. Many Kuomintang leaders were vacillating, compromising and afraid. They must be replaced by new peasant and working class leaders. The structure of the

Kuomintang must be changed, and an end put to the dependence on unreliable generals: 'Mobilize about 20,000 Communists and about 50,000 revolutionary workers from Hunan and Hupeh, form several new army corps, utilize the students of the school for commanders, and organize your own reliable army before it is too late.'[22]

In his telegram Stalin ordered also the organization of a revolutionary tribunal headed by prominent non-Communist members of the Kuomintang in order to punish officers who maintained contact with Chiang Kai-shek or who set soldiers against the people generally, or the workers and peasants.

The receipt of this telegram by Comintern agents and Chinese Communists in Wuhan opened a Pandora's box of further disagreements, vacillations and futile conflicts. Should the Communists depend on Wang Ching-wei? On T'ang Sheng-chih? On Feng Yü-hsiang, who was already moving his Russian-trained and Russian-equipped troops south-eastward? No one had a clear plan. On the contrary, Roy, Borodin, Ch'en Tu-hsiu and other Chinese Communists and Soviet advisers seemed to be arguing in circles.

In the confusion, Roy showed Stalin's telegram to Wang Ching-wei on the assumption that Wang would perceive it as a 're-assurance' of Soviet support for the Kuomintang Left. But Wang's response was quite the opposite: he saw the telegram as a Russian attempt to control the Kuomintang and, in the long run, to seize control of the revolution. He lost no time, therefore, in communicating with other non-Communist members of the Wuhan government, with T'ang Sheng-chih, and with other army commanders 'about the contemplated *coup d'état* of the Communist Party'.

As for Roy, Borodin, and the Chinese Communist leaders, each managed to believe that there was still a way out – that T'ang Sheng-chih, Feng Yü-hsiang or some other leader could be relied upon and exploited. In later years a Chinese Communist recalled how 'Comrade B used to say: "There is still food in our box; he [i.e., T'ang Sheng-chih] is hungry, and therefore he will not run away".'[23]

In fact, T'ang Sheng-chih was already completing an investigation for the Wuhan government which 'confirmed the existence of a Communist conspiracy against the Kuomintang'. And Feng Yü-hsiang, negotiating in a somewhat different quarter, was rapidly deciding 'to join hands with Chiang [Kai-shek]'. The house of illusions built by the Communists was rapidly falling apart.

On 30 June the Chinese Communist leaders received new words of warning and wisdom from Moscow: 'Trust in your own forces alone! Do not trust the generals and officers! Organize your own troops.' Only Wang Ching-wei was perceived in Moscow as 'firmer than the others'.[24]

But even Wang had made up his mind differently.

The Chinese Communist Party decided during early July to withdraw from the Wuhan government, but to remain within the party of the Kuomintang Left, carrying on 'all its work jointly with the truly revolutionary elements of the Kuomintang and together with the Kuomintang masses.' At the same time the Communists would 'mercilessly denounce all quasi-Kuomintangists who are misusing the great name of Sun Wen [Sun Yat-sen] in order to betray the revolution.'

At about this time, however, the Wuhan government claimed to have found documents revealing these decisions and instructing Communist Party members to establish secret cells within the Kuomintang and to seize every opportunity 'to incite disorders to discredit and destroy the [Kuomintang] Party'. The Central Executive Committee of the Kuomintang Left instructed Communists within the Nationalist armed forces and the Wuhan government to renounce their Communist affiliation forthwith or 'be dismissed from their offices immediately'. Meantime, execution squads had already swung into action, and Chinese Communists who survived the first raids lost no time in disappearing from the city.

On 27 July a group of Kuomintang Left leaders gathered at the Hankow railway station to speed their 'honored guest', Michael Borodin, on his journey. Executions were taking place in the streets even as the formal farewells were tendered. Nominally, the Comintern agent was leaving to confer with Feng Yü-hsiang, but it was understood by everyone that in fact he was setting out on a long journey across the north-western provinces of China to the Soviet frontier.

Within a few days Roy was on his way also. Three large touring cars had been equipped by the Comintern with special heavy-duty springs and gasoline cans lashed to the running boards. The drivers were GPU agents. From Wuhan the caravan proceeded north-west, crossed the Mongolian deserts, and entered the Soviet Union by way of Urga.

Roy was depending heavily on his prestige as a veteran revolutionist and on his personal relations with Stalin to see him through. However, during the Ninth Plenum of the Comintern held in Moscow during February 1928, his report of events in China was rejected, and Stalin – for whom Roy had a 'sentimental attachment' – refused to see him after the Chinese debacle. As the Plenum proceeded, Roy began to realize not only that his Comintern career was finished, but also that his life might well be in danger.

When he left Moscow some weeks later, Roy travelled clandestinely by plane, occupying a seat reserved for someone else. Nor did he feel safe until the aircraft had put down in Germany.

5 Mao Tse-Tung, the Red Army and the Chinese soviets

Nanchang, Swatow, Hai-lu-feng and the Autumn Harvest Uprising

After the collapse of Stalin's direct interventions in China the Chinese Communist movement found itself fractured into scattered components and uncertain about the proper course. With the departure of Roy, Borodin and other advisers, Ch'en Tu-hsiu was removed from the office of secretary general, and formal leadership came into the hands of a new group. In the countryside, meanwhile, another story began to develop. Over a wide area embracing several provinces a considerable number of small Communist enclaves took shape, and within a few years the foundations of a new power structure started to emerge involving several millions of people and territory as large as many European states.

During these same years the Soviet attitude toward China and the Chinese Communist movement underwent significant evolution. For a brief period during the late summer of 1927 Stalin still clung to the notion of exploiting 'the truly revolutionary elements' of the Kuomintang Left. At the same time, having largely curbed his opposition, the Soviet leader began to advocate a policy which – almost up to the moment – he himself had opposed as heresy, and which Trotsky had championed, namely, the formation of soviets.

But with the passage of time, Stalin and his colleagues became diverted from China, becoming increasingly concerned first, with the exploitation of the world-wide depression of the early thirties, and later with the threat of expanding Japanese influence in Asia and the rise of Nazi Germany.

It was during this 1928–34 period that Mao Tse-tung rose to prominence and the Chinese Communist movement underwent a transformation.

As Roy and Borodin were leaving Hankow in July and early August, 1927, Stalin put forward the next major steps: to replace the reactionary Wuhan hierarchy with a more revolutionary leadership and at the same time to popularize soviets – the establishment of which Trotsky had been urging since spring – 'without rushing ahead of events and without attempting to organize soviets now, by keeping in mind that soviets can be formed only in the situation of a powerful advance . . .'

If Communist efforts at revolutionizing the Kuomintang should fail, the Moscow leadership reasoned, and if the revolution should make a fresh advance, then it would be necessary 'to change the propagandistic slogan of soviets into a slogan of immediate fight and to proceed at once to the organization of workers', peasants' and artisans' soviets.'

To oversee the carrying out of these policies Stalin dispatched two new representatives – Heinz Neumann and Besso Lominadze. In China the influence of these men was felt almost immediately through the 7 August Conference, the Nanchang Uprising, an attack on Swatow, an insurrection in Hai-lu-feng, the Autumn Harvest Uprising, and the Canton Commune.

Neumann, a twenty-six-year-old native of Berlin, was responsible for calling the 7 August Conference of Chinese Communist leaders and for planning the Canton insurrection of the following December. Lominadze, a twenty-nine-year-old Georgian who had attracted the attention of his powerful compatriot Stalin, carried with him plans for an uprising to take place in Nanchang.

The 7 August Conference was called in a second floor room somewhere in the Japanese concession area of Hankow. The Communists who gathered there were afraid of being apprehended by Japanese police, and also of being discovered by Ch'en Tu-hsiu. 'Two square tables were put together . . . The chairman was Ch'ü Ch'iu-pai, who was nervous . . . He wore an open flannel shirt of very loud color which was completely out of harmony with his appearance and age . . . he actually suffered from tuberculosis . . . we could see the swollen veins in his face . . .'

The Conference censured the Central Committee for carrying out 'an opportunistic policy of betrayal' and condemned Ch'en Tu-hsiu and others for restraining the peasantry and 'retreating temporarily in order to retain the alliance with the Kuomintang.'[1] On the other hand, the Conference upheld continuing cooperation with the Kuomintang Left and opposed requiring Communist party members to withdraw from the Kuomintang. Ch'en Tu-hsiu was deposed and Chang Kuo-t'ao, T'an P'ing-shan, Mao Tse-tung and others were demoted. According to some accounts Chou En-lai – a man who has shown remarkable agility in changing from the losing to the winning side at the last possible moment – 'almost got expelled'.

Under Lominadze's direction the Nanchang Uprising was initiated during the night of 1 August by two Communist military officers, Yeh T'ing and Ho Lung, who had been serving in Kuomintang forces. Yeh T'ing was commander of a division in the 11th Kuomintang Army which, along with the 4th Army, comprised the famous Second Army Group, or 'Ironsides', which were commanded by Chang Fa-k'uei and reputed to be the finest troops under the Kuomintang. Ho Lung, who had concealed his Communist affiliation up to this time, was commander-in-chief of the 20th Kuomintang Army. More than 20,000 troops joined in capturing Nanchang, seizing the property of banks, and demanding tribute from local business men – 'under the banner of the Kuomintang Left', according to the Communists.

On 24 September 1927 Yeh T'ing's forces occupied Swatow. The Comintern reported this victory with great enthusiasm and announced that 'a new revolutionary center had been formed', but if such a center existed at all, it did not long survive. Chang Fa-k'uei himself opened attack on the insurrectionary troops and put them to flight. But Stalin was not disheartened. *Pravda*, which had hailed local victories prior to the Swatow defeat as 'a new revolutionary upsurge', now declared that the Kuomintang Left had been 'successfully exploited'. The revolution would soon spread to industrial cities, and then the time would be ripe for establishing soviets of workers', soldiers' and artisans' deputies. The soviet slogan must 'develop from a propaganda slogan into an action slogan'.

After their defeat near Swatow, Yeh T'ing and T'an P'ing-shan fled to Hongkong, while other Communist leaders including Chou

En-lai and Ho Lung withdrew toward the Hai-lu-feng district of Kwangtung Province, where the beginnings of a Communist-led peasant soviet had already taken root under the leadership of a young intellectual named P'eng P'ai. Around mid-October some 800 troops, retreating from Swatow, reached the outlying areas of Hai-lu-feng in a ragged and demoralized state. Later, when morale had been restored, they were organized into the Second Division of the Workers' and Peasants' Revolutionary Army.

The Autumn Harvest Uprising failed as miserably as the attack on Swatow.

Mao Tse-tung, as chief of the Peasant Department of the Wuhan government, had complied with Chinese Communist policy in late May and early June 1927 by checking the peasant rebellion at Changsha and in neighboring areas. After the split between the Communists and the Kuomintang Left in July he had fled to eastern Hunan to organize what became known later as the Autumn Harvest Uprising. A decade after these events Mao described the purposes of the undertaking to Edgar Snow: 1 Severance of the Hunan Communist movement from the Kuomintang. 2 The organization of a revolutionary army of peasants and workers. 3 The confiscation of property belonging to small and middle – as well as big – landlords. 4 The establishment of Communist Party power in Hunan independent of the Kuomintang. 5 The establishment of soviets. At the time, according to Mao, the Comintern had not yet advanced the fifth point, but was actually still opposing it.

Troops for the Autumn Harvest Uprising included Wuhan garrison forces which had defected from the Kuomintang Left, Hanyang miners, and peasant guard forces from Hunan villages. These forces were organized as the First Division of the First Peasants' and Workers' Army.

Mao told Snow subsequently that neither the organization of the army nor the program of the Autumn Harvest Uprising itself were sanctioned by the Central Committee of the Chinese Communist Party. Other sources disagree, and certainly Mao's activities seem to fit the general insurrectionary pattern overseen by Besso Lominadze and Heinz Neumann. On the other hand, when the Autumn Harvest Uprising failed it was Mao who was held primarily responsible, just as other Chinese leaders were censured for the Swatow defeat.

Moving southward through Hunan, the insurrectionary troops fought many battles against Kuomintang troops and suffered many defeats. At one point Mao himself was captured, but succeeded in escaping. Eventually he and his troops withdrew to Chingkangshan, a former bandit stronghold in the mountains of the Hunan–Kiangsi border.

With the collapse of the uprising, Mao was dismissed from the Politburo and relieved of certain other Party functions.

The Canton Commune

In November 1927 the Central Committee of the Chinese Communist Party asserted that a 'decidedly revolutionary situation' existed in China – though victories might not come in weeks or months, but in years. Actually, plans were already underway for a major insurrection in Canton.

By November 1927 power in Canton was shared by two rival generals. Chang Fa-k'uei was still viewed in those days as belonging to the Kuomintang Left, though he later became a staunch Nationalist. Li Chi-shen, on the other hand, belonged to the Kuomintang Right in 1927 – though two decades later, in 1949, he was to serve as one of six vice-chairmen of the Communist-controlled People's Republic of China.

Chang Fa-k'uei, with support from Wang Ching-wei, was preparing to seize full control of the city. But at the same time the Chinese Communists – inspired and instructed by Heinz Neumann – were hoping to exploit the situation for their own purposes. As Chang Fa-k'uei and Wang Ching-wei planned their *coup* in mid-November, the Kwangtung Central Committee laid its own plans for insurrection. According to Heinz Neumann, the Committee was

The execution of Communist rebels after the abortive Canton uprising of December 1927. Jay Calvin Huston, a young American Vice-Consul, who snapped this picture, took his notebook and pocket camera into the midst of the fighting. His efforts, however, were not appreciated by his superiors, who admonished him that such investigation should be undertaken on his own time. 'The execution squads worked fast,' Huston pencilled on this snapshot.

'profoundly convinced that all conditions for victory were joined and that with good technical and political technique victory was assured.'

Specifically, the factional quarrel had drawn many of Chang Fa-k'uei's troops into rural areas, and it was this situation which the Communists hoped to transform into a successful insurrection and a more widespread revolution.

The Communists were relying heavily upon a Kuomintang military training regiment stationed in Canton, where they constituted the major garrison force. Months previously a branch of the Whampoa Military Academy had been established in Wuhan. After Chiang Kai-shek's coup in the spring of 1927 the school was reorganized, however, and the cadets became a training regiment in the Kuomintang Fourth Army under Chang Fa-k'uei. Many were already Communists.

The Communist plan was to coordinate an insurrection in Canton with a general peasant uprising throughout Kwangtung. It was calculated that the peasant revolt would force Li Chi-shen to withdraw part of his forces from the city and thus facilitate its seizure by the Communists. In Moscow the insurrection was perceived as the beginning of a new revolutionary phase. The Chinese Communist Party must abandon entirely all political dependence on the Kuomintang, it was decided at the XV Congress of the Communist Party of the Soviet Union in early December.

Just at that time the Chinese Chief of Police in Canton discovered the conspiracy, however, and ordered the arrest of all Communist labor union members. It was evident that a conflict was about to break, and tension began to rise throughout the city. Frederick W. Hinke, an American Vice-Consul, described it in a report. For three nights the river had been strangely quiet. In the darkness, coolies walked through the streets marking the houses of those considered hostile to the revolution and deserving of execution.

Meanwhile, word was sent by telegraph to the various contingents of Chang Fa-k'uei's 'Ironsides', who set out for Canton post haste. The Communist leadership learned that Chang Fa-k'uei was planning to disarm the training regiment. There was a hasty revision of plans, and the insurrection was set for 11 December at 3.30 a.m. Meanwhile, the Police Department of Canton had continued the arrest of labor union members, and some 2,000 were already jailed.

During the night transport workers placed trucks at the disposal of rebel units, and soon a number of assault squads were moving through the city. Soviet Russian consular officials assumed active leadership and used the consulate as an insurrectionary headquarters. Shooting broke out in the city just before dawn, but it was not yet clear what had taken place. As foreigners on Shameen came out to take their customary Sunday morning stroll they were bewildered by the numbers of cargo boats and sampans massed

Communist casualties during the Canton Commune uprising of December 1927 – a snapshot taken by Jay Calvin Huston.
At Canton the Communist rebels wore red ties and sashes for identification. Later, when they saw that they were losing, the Communists began throwing away these identifying strips of cloth, but the dye had run, and the stains betrayed them.

against the island where the concessions were located. 'When the sampans move out of the canal which separates Shameen from the city of Canton proper,' Hinke observed, 'it is a sure sign of trouble. But on this occasion all the sampans in Canton had sought the protection of the stone sea wall or bund of Shameen. There was an astonishing hush over the sampans which was broken only as they were compelled to move farther and farther away from the Bund of Canton itself.'

The foreigners on Shameen remained largely unperturbed. Tennis went on as usual, and drinks were 'as plentiful as ever'.

But Red Guard troops and rebellious cadets from Chang Fa-k'uei's training regiment soon seized police headquarters, post and telegraph offices, and barracks, and by noon the Communists controlled Canton. A soviet of workers', soldiers', and peasants' deputies was chosen with ten delegates from labor groups and three from each of the other two categories.

Confusion had seized the city. Rebel squads and aimless crowds surged in the streets. The killing was brutal and indiscriminate, but anti-Communist forces were soon to achieve 'an eye-for-an-eye and a tooth-for-a-tooth' revenge.

For purposes of identification the Communists had adopted a red sash and red ties. And since the weather was warm, and as the wearers perspired, the dye discolored their necks. Near the heart of Canton a wildly excited, bobbed haired Chinese girl waved a rifle above her head and harangued the mob.

Communist forces held Canton for two days. Then Chang Fa-k'uei's 'Ironsides' units opened attack. 'The so-called White troops entered the city so quickly that the Russian Vice-Consul and an assistant were caught in front of the Communist headquarters with a red flag on the consulate car. The inmates of the consulate were immediately arrested, and five members, two of whom were peasant organizers of the consulate staff, were shot.'

When the Communists saw that they were losing the fight, they began discarding sashes and ties, but the tell-tale dye stains would not wipe off.

'Execution squads patrolled the streets,' reported Vice-Consul Hinke, 'and on finding a suspect, they questioned him, examined his neck for the tell-tale red. If found, they ordered the victim to open his mouth, thrust a revolver into it, and another coolie came to the end of his Communist venture.'

There seemed to be no end to the killing.

'I, myself, saw a rickshaw stopped, the coolie grabbed by the police, his shirt jerked from his neck disclosing the red stain . . .' Hinke recalled. 'He was rushed to the side of the road, compelled to kneel down, and unceremoniously shot while the crowd of people in the street applauded.'

Everywhere was the odor of fire and corpses . . . One picked one's way carefully . . . Police directed gangs of coolies who were collecting the bodies of the executed into trucks. 'Some of the victims . . . were still quivering.'

Fires broke out in the city. 'The richest shops in Canton were looted, some as many as eighteen times in a single night, until every scrap of goods was removed, together even with the scales, yard sticks, brass cuspidors, and the show cases were smashed.'

The city was terrorized by the senseless killing and by the fires which raged through the night.

'Many private scores were paid off,' according to another American consular officer, Jay Calvin Huston. 'Two lots of 500 and 1,000 men each were taken out and machine gunned. Realizing that this was a waste of ammunition, the soldiers loaded the victims on boats, took them down the river below the city, and pushed them overboard in lots of ten or twelve men tied together. The slaughter continued for four or five days during which some 6,000 people, allegedly Communists, lost their lives in the city of Canton.'

Peasants and Red Army in the Chingkang Mountains

News of the Canton defeat reached Moscow during sessions of the Fifteenth Congress of the CPSU. Victorious over its Trotskyist opposition, the Stalinist leadership passed an optimistic resolution:

'Rattle his bones
Over the stones,
He's only a coolie
Nobody owns.'
Another snapshot taken by
Huston during the
Canton uprising.

the Chinese revolution was alive in spite of its Canton defeat and was gathering forces for a new offensive on all fronts. Two months later, however, the insurrection was subjected to a more critical analysis before the Ninth Plenum of the ECCI. Responsibility for the defeat was assigned to the Chinese Communist Party and to Heinz Neumann and other Comintern representatives on the scene in China. There had been entirely too much unorganized action. 'To *play* with insurrections instead of organizing a mass uprising of workers and peasants,' the Stalinist leadership declared, 'is a sure way of losing the revolution.'

The first revolutionary wave was over, but Stalin and his colleagues saw the Chinese worker and peasant movements moving toward another 'mighty upsurge'.

Meanwhile, cadets of the training regiment and many of the armed workers had retreated from Canton to Hai-lu-feng, where the peasants called a huge mass meeting to welcome them. From this point onward Chinese Communist power tended to be divided between the Central Committee and Politburo, on the one hand, which maintained close liaison with Moscow, and the Red Army and peasant movement of Mao Tse-tung and Chu Teh, which gradually gained cohesion and strength in the countryside. Over subsequent years the relationship between these groups became increasingly antagonistic.

After the defeat at Swatow, troops from the forces of Yeh T'ing and Ho Lung – a few battalions at most – had been reorganized into an important component of the Chinese Workers' and Peasants' Army – later the Red Army. In Hai-lu-feng the cadet regiment was also reorganized and absorbed.

In February Chang Fa-k'uei began a series of attacks against the Hai-lu-feng region. Thousands of peasant soldiers and other troops were killed, and others scattered into the mountains. New fighting broke out intermittently, but eventually P'eng P'ai was assassinated and the troops were dispersed or absorbed into other Communist units.

After the fall of the Hai-lu-feng soviet, Chu Teh led a contingent of surviving Communist troops, including the reorganized training regiment, into the northern regions of Kwangtung and from there to Chingkangshan, the mountain base to which Mao Tse-tung had retreated, after the Autumn Harvest Uprising, with other Communist units.

On reaching Chingkanshan Mao had joined a group of local bandits. With the arrival of Chu Teh's contingent, these various troops were merged into a total force of about ten thousand men. Some months later this army was augmented by a small force from Hunan under P'eng Te-huai.

Life was not easy in the Chingkangshan hideout. Month in and month out the Chu–Mao armies had to fight for barest survival. Constantly vulnerable to attacks from government forces and provincial militia, they were also exposed to the vicissitudes of weather and virtual isolation. Even the peasants of the region tended to be apathetic, frequently hostile. Mao and his troops were hemmed in, also, by an economic blockade which the enemy managed to make increasingly effective.

In the meanwhile, members of the Chinese Communist Central Committee and Comintern leaders in Moscow were still developing official policy. In the latter part of 1928 the Sixth Congress of the Communist International prescribed for China a program of armed insurrection essentially like that which had failed in Canton. This was put forward as 'the sole path to the completion of bourgeois democratic revolution' and the overthrow of the Kuomintang.

The Chinese Communist Party was instructed to 'struggle for the masses' by means of careful organization, strikes, peasant activities, and preparation for the establishment of soviets. At the same time the Sixth Congress of the Chinese Communist Party – held in Moscow concurrently – agreed that the winning over of the masses was synonymous with preparation for armed insurrection.

The foremost Chinese Communist task was to develop a regular revolutionary army of workers and peasants – a Red Army.

Formally, Mao declared his support of Comintern policies, but in practice he worked out his own program as necessity and his own experience dictated. In fact, the Chinese revolutionary situation was not as immediately favorable as it sometimes looked from Moscow – or even as the Chinese Communist leadership in Shanghai often saw it. 'Having fought in various places in the past year,' Mao observed, 'we are keenly aware that the revolutionary upsurge in the country as a whole is subsiding ... Wherever the Red Army goes, it finds the masses cold and reserved; only after propaganda and agitation do they slowly rouse themselves.'[2]

Mao recognized also that the enemy economic blockade was having its effect, especially upon the more well-to-do peasantry. 'The poor peasantry is, comparatively speaking, able to bear such hardships, but the intermediate class will capitulate to the landed gentry the moment it finds them past bearing.' To Mao it was clear that Communist success depended upon disunity in the opposition forces.

But survival in the border areas depended also upon ability to fight.'An independent régime must be an armed one,' Mao Tse-tung wrote at the time. 'Wherever there are no armed forces, or the armed forces are inadequate, or the tactics for dealing with the enemy are wrong, the enemy will immediately come into occupation.'

The anti-Communist forces were undeniably strong and still generally cohesive. 'We have to fight the enemy forces hard whoever they are,' Mao admitted, 'and scarcely any mutiny or uprising has taken place within the enemy forces.' Undoubtedly, the long struggle was not easy to bear. 'We have an acute sense of loneliness and are every moment longing for the end of such a lonely life.' Yet the struggle must be pushed in order to 'turn the revolution into a surging, seething tide all over the country.'

The enemy was able to mass powerful attacks against the Red Army. 'The area in which the Party's Central Committee has instructed us to develop guerrilla warfare,' Mao wrote in November, 1928, 'is too extensive, covering several thousand of *li* in length and breadth; this is probably due to an over-estimation of our strength.'[3] Increasingly, the Red Army was trained not to fight unless confident of victory.

Supplies were short, and the army had neither food nor clothes in sufficient quantities. But they became inured to hardship. 'Furthermore, all alike share the same hardships,' Mao boasted. 'Everybody from the army commander down to the cook lives on a daily fare worth five cents, apart from grain. In the matter of pocket money, if two dimes are allotted, it is two dimes for everybody; if four dimes are allotted, it is four dimes for everybody.'

The number of Red soldiers should exceed the number of rifles by two to one. There was a need for non-belligerents such as packers and political workers, but also '. . . many of the soldiers easily would get ill; without unarmed soldiers the arms of the ill soldiers would be left unshouldered.'

Mao saw clearly the importance of combining guerrilla warfare with class struggle. To succeed, the Red Army must gain the support of poor peasants and alienate no more of the upper class elements than was necessary at any given phase of the long-range conflict. The Red Army sought to recruit above all from among those 'who want revenge upon local bosses and the notorious gentry'; the poorest; those who had already served in the forces of Yeh T'ing and Ho Lung; those who had escaped after the failure of peasant associations in other localities; and those who had taken part in other peasant or revolutionary activities elsewhere.

Wounded prisoners were to be treated with medicine, given money, and 'carried back to the enemy by peasants hired for the purpose' so that they would report 'how wonderful the Red Army was found to be'.

Approximately $50,000 per month was required for the Red Army to function, and funds were raised by demanding 'contributions' from local merchants. Funds were raised also through ransoms from 'local bosses and the notorious gentry' whose families had been captured by Red troops. 'But this is rather difficult to achieve as they often flee before the arrival of the Red Army. An alternate method is to estimate the value of their houses and then send a written demand requiring payment within two days, threatening otherwise the burning of their houses. For example, the demand of one hundred dollars may be made on a ten thousand dollar property. When payment is overdue, the house will be burned down as an example. This is an effective method, and the Red Army now relies on this to solve its financial problems.'

With their own consent, captured enemy soldiers could join the Red Army. 'Otherwise they will be sent away with a farewell party and be given a dollar or two for travelling expenses.' In the farewell speech the Red soldier representative would suggest to the prisoners that they never oppose the Red Army or fight for warlords again, but that they return to fight 'local bosses' and landlords in their villages.

The majority of Red Army soldiers were former mercenaries who had deserted their warlord commanders to join the Red Army, or

Chiang Kai-shek with officers on the battlefield during a Nationalist military campaign. By the early thirties Chiang had developed a well-trained army, but it was not large enough both to destroy Mao's growing Red Army and to deal with the mounting Japanese threat. He had to collaborate with militarist forces and with the Communists.

who had been captured by Communist forces. Mao established a program of political education designed to make these men class conscious and dedicated to the revolutionary struggle.

In spite of these efforts, however, the Chingkang base became increasingly untenable, and in January 1929, Mao and Chu Teh left and fought their way through snow-covered mountains toward the Kwangtung border. P'eng Te-huai was left behind to protect the rear from hostile provincial forces.

Some weeks later, on Chinese New Year's Day, the Red Army troops clashed with a division of anti-Communist forces in a valley between Ningtu and Juichin in southern Kiangsi. With their ammunition giving out, the Communists fought with rifle butts, clubs and stones until the enemy had been routed. Then Mao and Chu Teh called a halt and began establishing a base where they were joined somewhat later by P'eng Te-huai. Other Communist forces were establishing similarly remote bases in several provinces at about the same time. The total Red Army, by now, had shrunk to less than 3,000 men.

The Li Li-san line

While Mao Tse-tung and Chu Teh were building their Red Army and establishing soviets in remote hideouts, Stalinist policy-makers in Moscow and Chinese Communist leaders in Shanghai and elsewhere were searching for ways of facilitating the revolution over larger areas of China by linking the peasant movement on the countryside with labor activities in the major cities. To a considerable extent they were encouraged in the formulation of these plans by the difficulties which the Kuomintang seemed to be facing.

By the late 1920s Chiang Kai-shek was the most powerful military and political leader in China. Peking fell to Kuomintang forces in June 1928, and a new Nationalist constitution was proclaimed the following October. To a degree, China was unified at last. But over the next few years Chiang found himself facing a series of intra-party intrigues, warlord rebellions instigated by Feng Yü-hsiang, Yen Hsi-shan, the Kwangsi militarists, and others, challenges from Wang Ching-wei, and numerous Communist insurrections. As a consequence, the Kuomintang government, with its capital in Nanking, was able to maintain direct control only over those provinces near the mouth of the Yangtze. Elsewhere, Chiang's authority rested upon whatever alliances he could maintain with the very militarists who were continually challenging his power.

These circumstances stood like an open invitation for the Communists to stage insurrections.

Increasingly, after the Sixth Congress in the autumn of 1928, formal leadership of the Chinese Communist Party became identified with Li Li-san, and the militant policy which he tried to implement became notorious in Party annals as the Li Li-san line. How the responsibility should actually be distributed between Li Li-san and his superiors in Moscow is still not clear.

We have already seen how disastrously Stalin misperceived Chinese conditions between 1926 and 1928, and he was to make similar mistakes during and after World War II. Stalin, of course, never in all his life laid eyes upon China, and his conceptions of it were frequently faulty. M. N. Roy once observed, 'When Stalin considered China, he tended to see his own native Georgia writ large.' However that may be, Stalin and his associates were impressed – during 1929 and much of 1930 – by the factional 'small wars' which continually challenged Chiang Kai-shek's leadership in China. Characteristically, they diagnosed these warlord rebellions as Chinese manifestations of worldwide antagonisms among the imperialist powers and as preliminary skirmishes in 'the great war for world leadership' among the United States, Great Britain and Japan. Under these circumstances, it made sense to push the development of soviets and an insurrectionary policy as fast as conditions in China allowed.

But how fast, in fact, did conditions warrant? Communist leaders in Moscow, in Shanghai, and in Mao Tse-tung's mountain hideouts were all watching for a 'revolutionary upsurge'. The question was, how soon could it be expected?

In early 1929, as Mao and Chu Teh were establishing their new base in southern Kiangsi, the ECCI in Moscow had issued a somewhat enigmatic warning to the Chinese Communist Party against over-anxious anticipation of a 'new revolutionary high tide' – and also against failing to keep abreast of the upsurge that was perceived by the Comintern as undoubtedly coming.

Six months later Comintern leaders in Moscow perceived 'many premises' for an upsurge, but warned that a truly revolutionary high tide had not yet emerged. The Chinese Communist Central Committee, in turn, informed all subordinate Party headquarters that the surge of the revolutionary high tide was neither 'imminent' nor 'very remote'. Then, in October 1929, the ECCI suddenly altered its assessment of the situation in China. A new 'fratricidal war' had broken out among 'imperialist-backed' warlord factions; Wang Ching-wei, supported by the military forces of Chang Fa-k'uei, had formed a party demanding reorganization of the Kuomintang and was challenging Chiang Kai-shek; the Nationalist domestic policy was failing. Peasant rebellion in the Chinese countryside was still only a 'side-current' – but a current, nevertheless, 'along which the powerful high tide of the revolutionary movement will grow in the entire country.'

ECCI did not predict how soon the emerging 'national crisis' would be transformed into 'a direct revolutionary situation', but the Chinese Communist task was made explicit: to undertake mass revolutionary preparations for the overthrow of Chiang Kai-shek's government in Nanking and for the establishment of a 'Soviet proletarian-peasant' dictatorship.

The Chinese Politburo formally accepted these Comintern instructions early in January 1930, and asserted that a new revolutionary upsurge was on its way. By March 1930 the Chinese Communist leadership was informing the rank and file that a 'national revolutionary high tide' was close at hand. 'The objective conditions of the revolutionary upsurge are undoubtedly growing riper and riper,' the Central Committee asserted, 'but the subjective power of the Party, on the contrary, reveals great weakness in that it cannot catch up with the development of the revolution, but tends to become the tail of the masses.'[4] There was no time to lose. '. . . the great historical mission – the seizure of national political power – is about to confront us.'

The Chinese Politburo adopted on 11 June 1930 a resolution which emphasized the necessity for coordinating a wide range of struggles, both peasant and proletarian, in order to attack the 'weakest link in the ruling chain of world imperialism' – reactionary China, where a true victory might well touch off a worldwide revolutionary struggle.

Two weeks later Stalin, addressing the Sixteenth Congress of the

CPSU, drew attention to the chain of economic crises that were threatening the whole capitalist world, deepening the destructive antagonisms among the imperialist powers. These economic conflicts could be transformed into political crises enabling the revolutionary mass movement to 'rush forward' and encouraging the proletariat to 'seek remedy' in revolution. On a Russian domestic level, Stalin urged liquidation of the kulaks, the enforced collectivization of agriculture, and the surrender of 'right opportunists' like N. I. Bukharin, who wanted to proceed less militantly.

V. M. Molotov then pressed for similar militancy in China. 'Drawing support from the best provided regions in which the Red Army is active,' he asserted, 'the soviets in China are able to make contact with large industrial centers and form a Soviet workers' and peasants' government under the leadership of the Communist Party.'

On 23 July 1930 the ECCI informed the Chinese Politburo that 'The new upsurge in the Chinese revolutionary movement has become an indisputable fact.'[5]

'The Red Army must be organized and strengthened,' the Comintern declared, 'in order that it may be able to take one or more key cities in the future according to political and military circumstances.' The Comintern concluded by warning the Chinese Communists against either Right (moderate) or Left (radical) deviations – 'with the Right deviation as the main danger'.

Li Li-san's failure and summons to Moscow

In later years Lo Ping-hui, a Communist general, remembered how he and his men took a special oath before setting out to attack Nanchang under the Li Li-san line. 'In order to cooperate with the Communist revolution all over China, we must struggle to win the support of the masses in Hunan and to capture Changsha and Nanchang and then Hankow and Wuchang, and finally carry on down the Yangtze River to Shanghai.'[6]

Lo Ping-hui had once commanded a contingent of *min-t'uan* –

gentry-controlled 'Peace Preservation Corps' or private militia – in Kian, a key city in Kiangsi Province. Later, defecting to the Communists, he had taken many *min-t'uan* with him.

The attack on Nanchang was unsuccessful; so the Communist forces set out for Changsha, hoping to secure it by 1 August in commemoration of the Nanchang Uprising of 1927. 'I was with P'eng Te-huai, Chu Teh and Mao Tse-tung (who was political commissar),' Lo Ping-hui recalled subsequently. 'In the attack on Changsha we experienced our first airplane bombing. A squadron of six airplanes came. At first the Red soldiers didn't know what the planes were and looked up with much interest when they saw something being dropped into the air.'

There was other resistance. 'Five gunboats fired on us from the city,' Lo Ping-hui recalled. 'We thought that all these boats were British, then, as we always expect the British to fire, but maybe some of the gunboats were American – I don't know. Anyway, there were ten gunboats in all at Changsha then, as I recall.'

There were rising expectations among Communists both in China and in Russia as news of the Changsha victory spread. 'In great excitement we made a quick march [from Taowushan] to Changsha, only two days away,' Red Army General Wang Cheng recounted in later years, 'and entered the city while P'eng was still there. The CP ordered all peasants and workers to go to Changsha to help the Red Army. Over 10,000 arrived.'[7]

On 7 August the Comintern organ *International Press Correspondence* carried an enthusiastic account of the victory.

Encouraged by the apparent success of his program, Li Li-san appointed a Central Action Committee to assume responsibility for an attack on Wuhan as the next step toward nationwide insurrection. The capture of Changsha seemed to validate his whole program and augur a series of even greater triumphs. Nor were his plans for seizing the Wuhan cities – Hankow, Wuchang, and Hanyang – unnoted in Moscow: 'The capture of these three sister towns, the largest industrial towns of Central China, is the aim of the Red Army . . . All around Wuhan there already exist soviet districts. The Red Army is endeavoring, with the aid of insurgent peasants, to extend its field of operations more and more to the center and to encircle Wuhan.'[8]

With Changsha seemingly secured, General Lo Ping-hui and his troops were ordered south-eastward into Kiangsi to extend the insurrection. 'After leaving Changsha under the command of Chu and Mao, we captured Kian, though it was strongly defended. My old *min t'uan* were active in the capture of their home base. Kian was the economic center of Kiangsi Province. Its main commercial street was over twenty *li* in length [about 7 miles], and there were many rich merchants and capitalists there. The capture of Kian thus roused the whole province, and the mass movement developed rapidly. The Red Army gained twenty to thirty thousand new troops.'[9]

Despite their fateful experience with the Canton Uprising of December 1927, the Communists seemingly had yet to learn that it was easier to take cities than to hold them. The Red Army contingents, according to Western observers, were well-disciplined and intelligently led, but they were badly armed and inadequately supplied. With the seizure of Changsha, poverty-stricken peasants from rural areas began joining by the thousand. But the working class of Changsha was not at all the powerful force that Li Li-san and his associates had imagined. The workers were insufficiently organized, and the expected proletarian upsurge failed to materialize. Meanwhile, foreign gunboats continued to take a heavy toll from the river, and Nationalist contingents were reported on the way. P'eng Te-huai's troops began withdrawing from the city on 3 August, buildings asmolder and the streets stained by the blood of an estimated 2,000 victims.

'When P'eng Te-huai gave up Changsha . . . ,' Wang Cheng recalled later, 'a part of my Red Vanguards stayed in a near-by village to fight partisan warfare. We had 100 men, all armed with good guns. During those few days some of the partisans acted a little like bandits. They confiscated pretty clothes to wear – for the first time in their lives – and took money from the rich people.'[10]

Attempts to move on Hankow and other cities also failed, as did the Kian seizure and a second attack on Changsha by P'eng Te-huai. Yet neither the Chinese Communist leadership nor Moscow seemed aware, as yet, how colossal a failure had taken place. An *International Press Correspondence* article described the disastrous events as a 'great step forward in the Soviet movement', and *Kommunisticheskii Internatsional* reasserted the key importance of seizing urban industrial centers. Many weeks were to pass before the magnitude of the debacle became apparent.

Not long after the defeat of P'eng Te-huai at Changsha, Moscow sent Ch'ü Ch'iu-pai, who had been in the Soviet Union for some time, and Chou En-lai, who happened to be on a Party mission there, back to China for the Third Plenum, which was scheduled for late September in Lushan, Kiangsi. Subsequently, the Comintern was to charge Ch'ü Ch'iu-pai with duplicity: prior to leaving Moscow, he expressed his opposition to Li Li-san's policies and his support of the Comintern; but once in China he had begun to compromise.

The Third Plenum – under the strong influence of Chou En-lai – raised relatively minor criticisms of Li Li-san and his policies. The Chinese leadership had made incorrect estimates of the speed and extent of revolutionary development, but there had been no fundamental difference between the 'Comintern line' and the 'Li Li-san line'. The errors were tactical rather than strategic.

Moscow itself was not yet clear what the next steps ought to be. Dimitri Manuilsky – as late as 7 November 1930 – was still boasting about the correctness of Soviet predictions and 'the inevitability of the extension and strengthening' of the revolutionary upsurge. 'The Communist Party [of China] is furnishing a living example of the revolutionary–democratic dictatorship in the Soviet districts,' he asserted in *Pravda*, 'and is now rousing millions of Chinese workers and peasants to the struggle for the social and national liberation of China. It is endeavoring to link up the *military struggle with the workers' movement* in the industrial centers of China.'

Against this background the nature of the next Comintern directive to the Chinese Communist Party was all the more remarkable and – to Li Li-san, at least – shattering. 'During an historic movement like this, there arises a grave difference between the Executive Committee of the Comintern and a few comrades of the Politburo on one side, and Comrade Li-san and a few other comrades of the Politburo on the other side . . .' the ECCI told the Chinese Central Committee in a communication which reached China just nine days after Manuilsky's statement in *Pravda*.

The problem was not a matter of minor disagreement, Moscow now asserted, or a difference in timing or tactics. 'It is perfectly clear that we have two political lines of differing principle opposing each other during the most critical moment of the Chinese revolution. These two lines are mutually antagonistic and cannot be coexistant.'

This devastating attack was more than enough to depose Li Li-san, who was soon called to Moscow to answer for his deviations and catastrophic failures. There he was brought before an examining board – presided over by the same Dimitri Manuilsky – and induced to confess his errors in the most abject fashion. Before he was finished, Li Li-san not only condemned himself, but exposed many of his comrades back in China. A decade and a half were to pass before Li Li-san returned to his native land.

6 Kiangsi Soviet and the Long March

Establishment of the Juichin régime

In the spring of 1930 Soviet Russian authorities had appointed the president of Sun Yat-sen University in Moscow, Pavel Mif, as Comintern representative in China. Travelling with him were a group of young men who had been studying in the university and who were referred to subsequently as the 'Returned Student Clique'. The group included Wang Ming (Ch'en Shao-yü), Ch'in Pang-hsien (Po Ku), Chang Wen-t'ien (Lo Fu), and others. 'These fellows were just a group of young students who, needless to say, had done nothing for the Chinese revolution,' a Party defector wrote years later. 'While we were carrying out the revolution, they were taking milk at their mothers' breasts.' Yet these were the young men who were appointed to leadership of the Chinese Communist Party after the fall of Li Li-san and during years when Stalin and his colleagues were beginning to devote somewhat less attention to the Chinese revolution and more to problems of Soviet security.

In responding to Li Li-san's confession, Dimitri Manuilsky had asserted that self-criticism and self-analysis by leading Chinese Communists was not enough. Specifically, he called for a Fourth Plenum of the Chinese Communist Party in order to dig deeper into the underlying issues. Sponsored by Pavel Mif, the Plenum was held in Shanghai during early January 1931, with a total of thirty-nine delegates attending. Before the sessions came to an end, the new Returned Student leadership had obtained confessions of error from Chou En-lai, Ch'ü Ch'iu-pai and other veteran leaders who had been caught, to one degree or another, in Li Li-san's debacle. Ch'ü was sent to work in the soviet areas, but Chou En-lai – characteristically – obtained an important post in the new Central Committee after confessing his 'cowardly rotten opportunism'.

What was the role of Mao Tse-tung during the course of these conflicting and confusing developments? Unfortunately, there is no easy answer.

In 1936 – with possible benefit of hindsight – Mao told Edgar

Mao Tse-tung photographed in Yenan by Nym Wales during 1937. Born in Hunan Province in 1893, Mao drew numbers of fellow Hunanese into positions of leadership as his own power within the Communist leadership grew. Mao came from a well-to-do peasant family, but he graduated from the Hunan Normal School and later attended the Peking National University.

Snow that the defeat of P'eng Te-huai's troops at Changsha may have saved the Red Army from an even more catastrophic set-back at Wuhan. Li Li-san, according to Mao Tse-tung in retrospect, had over-estimated both the military capability of the Red Army and the nature of the revolutionary upsurge. The exhausting war between Chiang Kai-shek and Feng Yü-hsiang had encouraged his belief that the revolutionary potential was approaching a climax and that the Communists could soon achieve power over the whole country.

On the other hand, Mao himself – as early as 5 January 1930 – had criticized comrades who underestimated revolutionary possibilities and had predicted that the revolutionary upsurge would arise soon. But he had been cautious at the same time – more cautious by far than Li Li-san. 'How to interpret the two words "arise soon" in the phrase "a revolutionary upsurge will arise soon" is a common question among many comrades,' Mao had written in his letter of that date entitled *A single spark can start a prairie fire*. 'A Marxist is not a fortune teller: of future developments and changes he should not and cannot mechanically fix the day and the hour.'[1]

In any case, the fall of Li Li-san coincided, roughly, with the Fut'ien Incident of December 1930, when Mao struck down a powerful Party faction which had been formed in opposition to his growing power in the soviet districts – and which he accused of 'Li Li-sanism'.

The Fut'ien Party rebels accused Mao of arbitrarily identifying his personal critics within the Party as members of a reactionary A-B (Anti-Bolshevik) Corps, of presenting false charges and of extracting confessions by torture. Whatever the rights and wrongs of the conflict, and whatever Mao's motives, his own General Front Committee asserted that more than 4,400 members of the A-B League – with their own complex organization and chain of command – were arrested within Red Army units. Also placed under arrest were the leaders of the Kiangsi Provincial Action Committee.

Yet even in the wake of these events Mao's role in the Chinese Communist movement remained uncertain and difficult to define.

Until sometime in 1931 there had been two centers of Communist power in China: the officially recognized Politburo, which headquartered in Shanghai after the 1927 defeats; and the rural base of Mao Tse-tung. During the summer or autumn of 1931, however, the pressures of operating in the Shanghai underground became too great. It is possible, too, that intra-party struggles for power had something to do with the move. If so, the transfer cannot be said to have resolved this difficulty, since the struggle between Mao Tse-tung and the Returned Student leadership continued until after the start of the Long March. In any case, the Politburo seems to have established itself in Juichin by the opening of the First All-China Congress of Soviets on 7 November 1931.

Convened at Juichin, Kiangsi Province, the Congress opened with a Red Army parade and, in the evening, a torch light procession. This Congress established a unified Chinese Soviet Republic and elected Mao chairman of its sixty-one member CEC. A constitution was adopted, together with a political program, a governmental structure, a labor law, a land law, a political program and resolutions on the Red Army.

Over ensuing months, with the drawing together of the many, widely scattered soviet areas, this new government came to embrace some millions of people and an area as large as many European states. Within it, moreover, there developed an hierarchy of institutions, offices and laws that formed the foundations for later Chinese Communist governments – both in north-western China after the Long March, and over the whole mainland with the establishment of the Chinese People's Republic on 1 October 1949.

It should not be inferred from Mao's election to chairmanship of the CEC that he had as yet achieved a preponderance of power within the Party or that he was necessarily a major influence in shaping the new government. The Comintern, of course, had been concerned for years with the establishment of such a régime, and its instructions of 23 July 1930 – just before Changsha – had identified the formation of a central soviet government as a major task. In fact, it was probably the Returned Student leadership which instigated the Congress and formally presided over the installing of the new government. It appears that over the next two or three years the Soviet Republic was to become increasingly an arena of more or less subtle but nonetheless serious struggle between Mao and the Returned Students.

Many aspects of the government and its policies provide partial clues to the Mao–Returned Student conflict – which was partly personal, partly a question of tactics and principles – but disagreements over land policies probably lie close to the heart of the central controversy.

Mao Tse-tung's formal concern with the revolutionary role of the peasant dated back at least to his *Report on an Investigation of the Peasant Movement in Hunan*, written in early 1927. Coming from a peasant background, his feeling for agrarian problems was deep and intuitive. It was probably somewhat later, however, that he began to fit his ideas about the revolutionary role of the peasantry into a more precise Marxist–Leninist conceptual framework.

The Communists and the agrarian revolution

V.I. Lenin had already defined the role of the peasantry with considerable precision. 'We support the peasant movement in so far as it is revolutionary and democratic,' he wrote in 1905. 'We are making ready (making ready at once, immediately) to fight it in so far as it becomes reactionary and anti-proletarian. The whole essence of Marxism lies in this double task . . .'[2] Lenin differentiated the rich peasant, or kulak, from the middle peasant and poor peasant. As a seller of grain and an exploiter of other men's labor, the rich peasant was essentially capitalist in his inclinations. The middle peasant was 'partly a property owner, partly a toiler' and inclined to vacillate. Only the poor peasant – exploited and without property – was a semi-proletarian, the support of the urban working class.

As Lenin saw it in Russian terms, the relationship between the working class and the three main categories of peasantry depended upon the stage of the revolution. First, the urban working class and the Communist Party marched with the 'whole' of the peasantry against the old feudal, medieval régime. In the second stage the revolutionary leadership marched only 'with the poorest peasants, with the semi-proletarians, with all the exploited, against capitalism, including the rural rich, the kulaks, the profiteers.'

Mao Tse-tung had been employing land reform tactics – more or less within a Leninist framework – since his Chingkang Mountain days, but it was under Li Li-san, briefly, and under the Returned Student leadership that much of the codification was accomplished. Differences emerged in general over whose land should be confiscated in a given revolutionary situation; and also over how the confiscated land should be redistributed – who should receive shares of it and who should not.

On the whole, Mao's guidelines tended to be practical in those days rather than doctrinaire. The land problem, as he saw it, lay at the very foundations of revolutionary strategy and tactics, and the role of the rich peasants was crucial. In the Chingkang Mountain period he had identified rich peasant interests as closely interwoven with those of the gentry landlords. Since the greater part of Chinese land belonged to landlords and a few rich peasants, whereas the overwhelming majority of the rural population – and indeed, of the whole population of China – were landless peasants, Mao felt strongly that confiscation and redistribution constituted the key to successful revolution.

Mao saw the agrarian revolution proceeding through three stages: 1 Land confiscation. 2 Land investigation. 3 Land reconstruction. The first phase was appropriate to a region where the agrarian revolution was beginning and lasted until the counter-revolutionaries had been defeated and their property disposed of. The second phase – land investigation – was appropriate to a region where the landlords and rich peasants, though subdued and offering no overt resistance, had hidden themselves among the poor and toiling masses and were claiming a share of redistributed lands or otherwise sabotaging the revolution. By 1933 about eighty per cent of the central soviet area – or more than 2,000,000 people – were perceived as belonging to the 'land investigation' stage.

The land reconstruction, or third stage, was appropriate to an area where redistribution had been essentially completed and consolidated and where a considerable increase in agricultural productivity was at last feasible.

Each step in the procedures was carefully worked out. Money, gold and other valuables confiscated from landlords and rich peasants went to the government for operating expenses, but rice, clothes, and farm implements were distributed among poor peasants on the spot 'so as to encourage them to struggle against the landlords'. It was stipulated specifically that *only local peasant masses* could be assigned goods confiscated from local landlords and rich peasants.

In its undertaking of land confiscation and redistribution the Juichin régime tried to involve the peasant masses as deeply as possible. The aim, indeed, was to facilitate the more or less spontaneous initiation of each phase by the peasants themselves. Trained cadres normally began by entering a village and simply asking questions. 'We must first find out which people are hated by the masses,' a report on the Red Army noted in early 1930. With this information in hand, cadremen were then prepared to raise action slogans – the more specific the better. '. . . . the Red Army seldom uses the slogan "overthrow the local bosses and the notorious gentry" because that is too vague.' It was more effective to name names: 'Down with local bosses and notorious gentry so and so.'

Over the next few years the agrarian program was carried out in conjunction with various mass organizations – especially the Hired Farm Hands Union – and with the active participation of the State Political Security Bureau.

The task of the Hired Farm Hands Union was to consolidate the strength of poor peasants tilling the lands of rich peasants and landlords, to organize them into instruments of class struggle and to teach them how to fight effectively 'for the liberation of the working class'. Selected members of the Hired Farm Hands Union were drawn into the Poor Peasant Corps – specifically, 'those who are activists and carry on resolute struggles against the landlords and rich peasants.'

In June 1933, for example, delegates of the Poor Peasant Corps of eight *hsien* were called to a conference on how to carry on a revolutionary 'land investigation'. In a circular signed by Mao Tse-tung the delegates were directed to gather with their 'rice bowls, chopsticks and unwadded coverlets'.

The purpose was made explicit: '. . . the investigation of land is not by any means another redistribution of land. It is an investigation by the masses themselves of those landlord and rich peasant elements who have disguised themselves as middle peasants and poor peasants. Not until these elements have been discovered and overthrown can the poor and miserable masses be liberated.' The investigation drive was identified as 'a most ruthless class struggle' designed to 'eradicate basically the feudal remnants in the rural districts.'

The State Political Security Bureau was assigned by the Juichin régime a special role in support of the land investigation program instigated by the Hired Farm Hands Union and other poor peasant masses.

Many landlords and rich peasants had buried cash or thrown it into fish ponds for safekeeping. Others had floated down rivers on bamboo or timber rafts with their gold, silver and other valuables aboard. Others had carried their valuables into the mountains and had set themselves up as counter-revolutionary bandits. Security officials in one soviet district were instructed to 'keep strict watch to prevent these escapes' and to maintain as their objective 'the raising of 800,000 silver dollars' by apprehending such fugitives. Security personnel were exhorted to cooperate with the Red Army in the enforcement of curfews and the manning of crossroads inspection stations so that 'not a single landlord, village boss or gentry' should be allowed to escape with his cash into a 'white' area.

The Chinese Communists preferred to organize expropriated landlords and rich peasants into labor corps for re-education and rehabilitation, while reclaiming waste lands and performing other public works. However, those who had previously committed 'counter-revolutionary and anti-soviet acts must be turned over to the poor masses for public trial and executed on the spot in accordance with the wishes and demands of the masses.'

Local officers of the Political Security Bureau, assigned extraordinary power to arrest and try, were specifically absolved from dependence on higher organs if 'arrests have to be delayed until their cases have been reported.' The main thing was to get on with the land investigation. In this connection, those of the populace who exposed landlords to the Party were to be absorbed whenever feasible so as to enlarge the organization.

The soviets, the encirclement campaigns and the Japanese threat

Events outside were not standing still while the new Chinese Soviet Republic established itself at Juichin and tried to extend its power and its revolutionary programs over wider and wider areas. As soon as he was able, Chiang Kai-shek undertook a series of 'extermination campaigns' which used both military force and economic blockades against the Chinese Communists. With the Mukden Incident of 18 September 1931 and subsequent threats from Japan, moreover, the Nationalist leader concluded that he could not oppose a foreign enemy effectively until he had achieved unity at home. So the anti-Communist campaigns were assigned an even higher priority. The Communists reasoned, on the other hand, that Nationalist military forces ought to be fighting the Japanese instead of trying to annihilate the soviets.

Moscow, too, was increasingly affected by events in Asia and elsewhere – and increasingly inclined to concern itself with Russian national interests and Soviet defenses rather than with early adventures in pursuit of world revolution. For soon after Japan began to loom as an imminent threat to the U.S.S.R.'s Asian frontiers, Stalin and his colleagues were forced to take note of Hitler's rise to power in Germany.

In pursuit of Communist annihilation, Chiang Kai-shek – characteristically – was hampered by his dependence, for both political and military capacity, upon constantly shifting coalitions, or alliances between himself and other militarists, in which he sought to maintain a balance of power. If the Japanese threat provided a new stimulus for cohesion, it also opened new possibilities for conflict over priorities, i.e., whether the preponderance of armed force ought to be directed against the invader, or against the domestic Communists, how campaigns in either direction ought to be conducted, and how many resources any given leader needed for maintenance of his personal power. Sooner or later almost everyone got into the controversy – Chiang Kai-shek; Wang Ching-wei; Chang Tso-lin's son, Chang Hsüeh-liang, known also as the 'Young Marshal of Manchuria', and many others.

By the autumn of 1933 Chiang Kai-shek's 'annihilation campaigns' against the Communists were still proving inconclusive. But during subsequent months, with technical assistance from foreign advisers, including the German General von Seeckt, Nationalist forces succeeded in the encirclement of soviet areas with a tight network of block houses and field fortifications. Having drawn a military noose around the Communists, Chiang was in a position to coordinate further offensives with a tight economic blockade.

Meeting in January 1934, the Second All-China Congress of Soviets found the capital city of Juichin seriously endangered.

During the spring and summer Chiang further tightened his encirclement of soviet areas and maneuvered Red Army forces into the substitution of positional warfare for their well-tried guerrilla tactics – a shift in military policy for which Mao would later hold the Returned Students responsible. By early autumn Chinese Communist leaders were beginning to talk about evacuation.

The Japanese threat to China and to the Soviet Union may have

The Second All-Chinese Soviet Congress at Juichin,
Kiangsi in January 1934. During the Congress Mao Tse-tung,
whose influence had been increasing within the Chinese movement,
called for a Red Army of a million men, the
enlargement of the Red Guard and other reserve forces,
and the boosting of agricultural and industrial production.

been a further consideration in planning the Long March. The
Communists had a high stake in the Japanese War – not only
because they were Chinese, and not only because they were against
imperialism, but also because full-scale Chinese prosecution of the
conflict would relieve them of Chiang's annihilation campaigns.
During the summer of 1934 the Returned Student Po Ku (Ch'in
Pang-hsien) disclosed that units of the Red Army might be sent to
fight the Japanese. This statement was soon confirmed by Mao Tse-
tung and Chu Teh, who reported – as part of a broad anti-Japanese

program – that a vanguard of Red Army troops would march northward to fight the invader.

Preparations for the Long March itself were kept secret. 'The first public indication of the idea,' a Party historian told Nym Wales, 'was in an article by Lo Fu [Chang Wen-t'ien] in the newspaper *Red China* on 1 October, telling of the emergency: Only one week was given for mobilizing to leave, though from 120,000 to 130,000 personnel started on the Long March. Personnel were withdrawn from the front and gathered in the rear, and all were given guns. Meetings were held and food supplies organized.'[3]

Only a few top leaders had any inkling of the destination. Besides, everyone was too busy collecting the meagre supplies that were available. 'Many Kiangsi soldiers took money from their families to buy salt and tobacco and other things from districts outside the blockade. During the mobilization week the spirit was good, not passive, and nobody deserted secretly. The original plan was to break through the blockade by surprise . . . We left Juichin, Kiangsi, on 15 October 1934, nearly the whole Red Army moving out of Kiangsi.'

In certain respects, the start of the Long March may be viewed as the beginning of a change in Mao Tse-tung's fortunes. For once the great *anabasis* was underway, it became increasingly difficult for Mao's opponents within the Communist movement to oppose his prestige and leadership.

The Long March

'We marched secretly and only at night,' Hsü Meng-ch'iu, a veteran of the Long March, told Nym Wales some years later, 'because of air bombing we were afraid news of our maneuver would get to the enemy.'[4] He was referring to the first week after Red Army columns left Juichin. Before the Long March was over, Hsü was to suffer the amputation of both legs after exposure to extreme cold.

The main columns of the Long March were under the command of Mao Tse-tung and Lin Piao. Chang Kuo-t'ao and Hsü Hsiang-ch'ien were leading another body of troops along a separate route from the Anhwei–Honan–Hupeh (Oyüwan) soviet area.

During that first week Mao's columns bedded down each morning. 'In the afternoon some of us plaited straw sandals,' another participant recalled years later, 'and others cleaned the rifles. I made the necessary preparations for the coming march and then took a nap.'[5] Later a supper bugle roused the columns. 'I returned the bed plank which I had borrowed from the villagers and hastily swallowed my supper. Then there was a general call to assemble, ready to march off. Soldiers were shouldering rifles, transport personnel were carrying boxes, cooks their kitchen utensils, all rushing to the assembly place. My legs felt as heavy as lead.'

Villagers, young and old, lined the roadway to see the columns off. 'They looked at us wistfully and expectantly as if saying, "Quick to leave and quick to come back! Take care of yourselves in the march. We are waiting for your victory!" '

Political instructors spoke to their units, cheering them. 'Don't think that we are leaving never to return. No, we will come back. We definitely will . . .' Then there was a bugle call from the general headquarters signalling the march. Twilight came, and then darkness. 'Close on each other's heels we proceeded. I set my eyes on the white enamel cup fastened on the back of Lao Tsao in front of me and marched on and on.'

The columns began to climb a mountain. 'The path was crooked, rough, and at times so steep that we had to hold on to the bushes and rocks as we climbed. The marching file was so long, and it was such a dark night that whenever the vanguard came to any obstacles, the men behind piled up. When the obstacles were surmounted the rear had difficulty in maintaining contact with the main column. Whenever we were held up, I would drop into a dream . . . Then someone in front would urge, "Hey, there, don't straggle," and someone behind would push me to move on.'

Elements of the Kwangtung Army attacked during the second week, but the Red Army scattered them successfully. 'We now marched four hours and rested four hours, alternately, both day and night.'[6] Pushing through mountain ranges along the Hunan–Kwangtung border, the Communists were forced to climb at night. 'This was very dangerous, with fighting every day. Hunan troops attacked on one side and Kwangtung troops on the other.'

Over ensuing months the Communist columns marched generally north-westward to the banks of the Yangtze in the direction of Chungking. Then they looped southward toward Kweiyang in central Kweichow, turned westward across a corner of Yunnan into Sikang Province, and then began an incredible journey north-eastward across Szechwan and Kansu Provinces and into far-off Shensi. After interviewing Chinese Communist leaders Edgar Snow calculated that participants in the Long March spent 368 days *en route*, fought almost a skirmish a day, and devoted fifteen days to pitched battles. The mean distance covered daily was nearly twenty-four miles.

According to Snow's classic account in *Red Star Over China*, the Communist columns crossed eighteen mountain ranges, five of them snowcapped the year around, crossed twenty-four rivers, passed through twelve separate provinces, occupied sixty-two cities, forced their way through the enveloping forces of ten local warlords, and eluded or outmaneuvered a series of attempted interceptions by the troops of Chiang Kai-shek.

Even by the time Red Army columns had reached the borders of Kweichow Province – when the Long March had scarcely begun – their numbers had already dwindled by about a third. Later, the number of survivors would become much smaller.

Communist columns approached the Yangtze River at a point somewhat south-west of Chungking. The shortest route to the north-west lay across Szechwan Province, but Chiang Kai-shek was already concentrating thousands of troops in order to prevent a crossing of the Yangtze. Other Nationalist forces were moving into Kweichow toward the Communist rear. The columns seemed to be moving into another noose. 'All crossings were heavily fortified; all ferries were drawn to the northern bank of the river; all roads were blocked; great areas were denuded of grain.'[7] The only way out

At the end of the Long March. Mao stands third
from the left. In *Red Star Over China* Edgar Snow
estimates that Chinese Communist forces crossed five snow-capped mountain
ranges, thirteen lesser ranges, twenty-four rivers and twelve provinces,
and that they occupied sixty-two cities. Probably between 120,000
and 130,000 people undertook the march. Only a fraction survived.

required a wide, sweeping loop south-west into Yunnan which the
columns entered in May 1935, and then north-east through Sikang.

A four days' forced march brought elements of the Red Army
within ten miles of Kunming (Yunnanfu), the Yunnanese capital.
What local warlord forces and Nationalist troops discovered too
late was that the march toward Kunming had been a diversion. The
main columns were heading north-westward toward a huge bend in
the Yangtze where one of the few navigable points on the upper
river was located.

En route, the Red forces captured a messenger from local officials
ordering boats at the crossing to be burned. 'He was treated well
and was won over, and agreed to lead the middle column to the
river bank. Only one boat was left there by now, and this could

carry only ten persons at a time. It took thirty to forty minutes for the boat to cross over and back.'[8]

There was a small tax office on the northern bank where several collectors and about twenty guards were playing mahjongg and smoking opium. 'The [Red] soldiers knocked, and the tax collectors asked who they were. They answered that they were Kuomintang troops and were invited in for tea and cigarettes – they had taken the red star off their caps. Later on the guards were disarmed, but they were not alarmed, because they had already made friends.'[9]

More boats were discovered, but even then it took eight days and nights for the Red troops to complete their crossing.

After marching through a thickly forested wilderness area inhabited by indigenous, non-Chinese Lolo peoples, Red Army columns approached the Tatu River. 'The last part of our march was extremely difficult,' a veteran recalled subsequently. 'It was pitch dark, and there was a continuous drizzle of rain. Our clothes were soaked through, and the biting night wind made us shiver . . .'[10] The vanguard topped a mountain peak early in the evening. 'As we were descending the other side, we heard the roar of the Tatu River below. Halfway down, peering through the misty rain, we saw some straggling lights at the foot of the mountain. It was the Anshunch'ang ferry which we intended to capture.'

The precipitous Tatu gorges were already a fateful place: in the ancient past many warriors had been defeated here, and in the nineteenth century an army of 100,000 men – the last of the Taiping rebels – had been surrounded at Anshunch'ang by Manchu forces and utterly destroyed. Now, under cover of darkness, advance elements of the Red Army prepared to seize the ferry.

Occasionally the moon came out from a break in the clouds, illuminating the whole valley. Then scattered raindrops began falling again. It was morning before the Red Army units were down in the gorge from wet mountain slopes. 'I trotted with the Second Company towards Anshunch'ang. On the way we saw a number of blockhouses, but there was no gunfire . . . It became obvious that the enemy did not expect us so soon . . . We could still hear the strains of Chinese opera, accompanied by a stringed instrument, coming from a house.'

Red Army troops rushed the main guard installation and soon wiped them out. But there was only one boat; the others were on the far bank. '. . . the boatmen had to be natives, since nobody else could navigate the treacherous river. After a time we found sixteen local men, and they took seventeen of our soldiers over in the boat.'[11]

The best machine gunners in the Red Army advance unit covered the opposite bank. 'There was a stone cliff . . . and it was difficult to land the boat . . . The seventeen men had 100 hand grenades which they threw into the enemy trenches. Thus they broke the defense . . .'[12]

Unfortunately, there were only two more boats. The river was swift, and each crossing was difficult. By the end of three days it was taking four hours to move each boatload of men from one side to the other.[13] It would require weeks to get all the columns across. So the main body of Red Army troops began marching along the river bank toward Luting Bridge, fighting enemy troops a large part of the way. 'They climbed a mountain to reach the bridge, which is over a high gorge. When they arrived, they found that the bridge consisted of twelve swaying iron chains, where wooden boards had been stretched across, but all the boards had been taken off by the enemy.'[14] The town of Luting guarded the far side of the bridge.

The Second Company of an advance Red Army unit was designated to secure the cables, the Third Company to cross directly behind and lay new planks. 'The attack began at four in the afternoon,' Yang Cheng-wu recorded later. 'The regimental commander and I directed it from the west end of the bridge. The buglers of the regiment gathered together to sound the charge, and we opened up with every weapon we had. The noise of the bugles, the firing and the shouts of the men reverberated through the valley. The twenty-two heroes, led by Commander Liao, climbed across the swaying bridge chains, in the teeth of intense enemy fire. Each man carried

The Long March

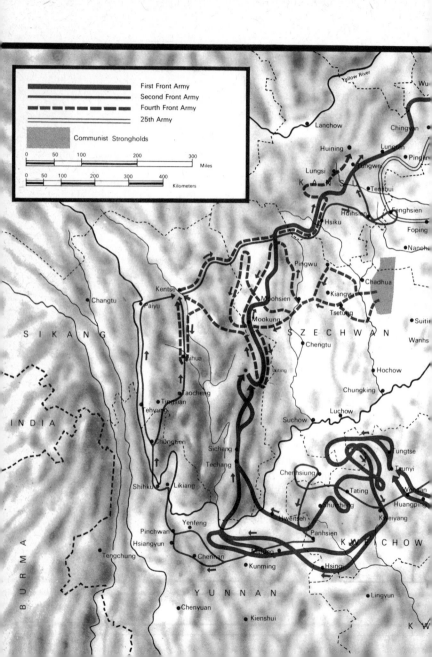

First Front Army
Second Front Army
Fourth Front Army
25th Army

Communist Strongholds

0 50 100 200 300 Miles
0 50 100 200 300 400 Kilometers

Yellow River

Wu

Lanchow

Chingyan

Huining

Lungan

Pingin

Lungsi

Tungwei

KANSU

Tenshui

Fenghsien

Hsiku

Foping

Haihsien

Nanch

Pingwu

Chadhua

Kentse

Moohsien

Kiangyu

Paiyu

Changtu

Tsetung

Suitin

SIKANG

Mookung

SZECHWAN

Wanhs

Chengtu

Huhua

Hochow

Luting

Chungking

Taocheng

Luchow

Tingsian

Tehyung

Suchow

INDIA

Chungtien

Sichang

Tungtse

Techang

Taunyi

Chemhsiung

Tating

Weican

Shihku

Likiang

Shupheng

Huangping

Kweiyang

Yenfeng

Hweitseh

Pinchwan

Panhsien

KWEICHOW

Hsiangyun

Chennan

KWE

Tengchung

Hsingi

Kunming

BURMA

YUNNAN

Lingyun

Chenyuan

Kienshui

KW

a tommy-gun, a broad sword and twelve hand-grenades. Behind them came the officers and men of Third Company, each carrying a plank in addition to full battle gear. They fought and laid planks at the same time.'[15]

Outside Luting's West Gate huge flames shot into the sky as the assault squad reached the far bridgehead. The enemy was trying to throw a fire barrier across the path. The blaze licked at the end of the bridge. 'The outcome of the attack hung by a hair. Our assault squad hesitated for a few seconds and then plunged boldly into the flames. Commander Liao's cap caught fire. He threw it away and fought on. The others also dashed through the flames, closely behind Liao, smashing their way into the city. In the street fighting that followed, the enemy brought their full weight to bear, determined to wipe out our assault squad. Our gallant twenty-two fought until all their bullets and grenades were gone. There was a critical pause as the Third Company came charging to their rescue. Then Regimental Commander Wang and I sped across the bridge with our reinforcements and entered the city.'

The columns were now free to pursue their long journey toward the north-west.

7 Border region governments and the Japanese War

The Mao–Chang conflict

On reaching Shensi Province the Chinese Communists first established their capital in Pao An, where it remained until December 1936. Then, after their occupation of Yenan, they transferred their headquarters to that city. In the meantime, the top Chinese Communist leadership was faced with problems of how to transform new Comintern policies into Chinese terms, and also of how to consolidate their own power – Maoist power – within the broad Chinese Communist movement.

During the Long March, when the main columns reached Tsun-yi, Kweichow Province, in January 1935, a conference had been called and it was during these discussions that Mao Tse-tung successfully attacked the Returned Students and achieved control of the Party. At the conference there developed a new controversy, however, between Mao and Chang Kuo-t'ao, who, as leader of columns marching from the Oyüwan Soviet Area, was in telegraphic communication with Tsun-yi, but not actually present at the conference. Mao, with support from the always adaptable Chou En-lai, asserted that the Returned Students, while wrong in political detail, were primarily in military error. Chang Kuo-t'ao, on the other hand, felt that the Soviet principle itself was inapplicable to China. The debate was rejoined at Mao-erh-k'ai in Szechwan, where the Kiangsi and Oyüwan columns merged in late June. Here a new disagreement emerged. Chang Kuo-t'ao believed that the Long March should proceed into Sinkiang Province, whereas Mao and Chou favoured Shensi which would be accessible to Inner Mongolia and close to a soviet area already established by Kao Kang.

According to Chang Kuo-t'ao, the Chinese Communist leadership re-established contact with Moscow during the Mao-erh-k'ai discussions and referred the issues to Soviet leaders there. It is not clear what the disposition was, however, and the Mao–Chang controversy continued in any case – though with changes in the world situation, as well as in the Chinese environment, the personal conflict became entwined with larger issues.

The Japanese threat

Both the Russian and the Chinese Communist leaderships had been deeply concerned with the Mukden Incident of 18 September 1931, and subsequent evidences of Japanese expansionism. Stalin and his associates had committed themselves to the completion of the first Five Year Plan in four years, however, and were not disposed to commit any more of their energies than was absolutely necessary for countering Japanese moves in Asia. On the other hand, it was evident that the Japanese threats to China offered special opportunities for the Chinese Communists. For if Chiang Kai-shek could be persuaded to mount a full-scale offensive against Japanese forces in Manchuria, Nationalist military pressures against soviet areas would be diverted. Under such circumstances, moreover, the Japanese threat to Soviet Russian frontiers would be diverted and opposed on other military fronts. It was thus in the interests of both Russian and Chinese Communist leaderships to encourage an anti-Japanese united front in China.

In fact, however, the Japanese threat tended to push the Soviet Union and Nationalist – rather than Communist – China closer and closer. The immediate crucial consideration became more and more the stopping of Japanese armies, or the diversion of them from Soviet borders, rather than a Communist victory over the Kuomintang. Under these circumstances Chiang Kai-shek's armies, however 'reactionary', could scarcely be ignored.

With Japanese expansionism, with the rise of Hitler, and especially after the proclamation of the Rome–Berlin Axis, then, the U.S.S.R. became more and more the champion of collective action against aggression. In the League of Nations Maksim Litvinov supported Chinese Nationalist pleas for aid and pointed out again and again how Japan had attacked without a declaration of war, had sent troops into China by the hundreds of thousands, had blockaded Chinese ports and had paralyzed Chinese trade. According to Litvinov the failure of the League to take effective action to stop Japan had encouraged subsequent aggressions by Italy, in Abyssinia

North China

Fighting Red soldiers of China. Mao Tse-tung based
his strategy upon the building of a Communist government,
with all necessary organs, and a Red Army to
protect it and facilitate its expansion. To accomplish this
he had to persuade, cajole or pressure millions of
peasants into regular and reserve military forces.

and by Franco in Spain. And these events, in turn, had encouraged
the Japanese to undertake even larger campaigns in China.

Moscow had established formal diplomatic relations with the
Chiang Kai-shek régime in December, 1932 but interchanges
between the two governments had remained largely suspicious.
Newspapers in Moscow regularly accused Chiang of selling out to
the Japanese, while the Nationalist leadership charged Soviet Russia
with supporting the Chinese Communists. There were also disagreements over disposition of the Russian-built Chinese Eastern Railway in Manchuria which Moscow – intent upon avoiding trouble

Mass meeting of Red troops on the plains of Ninghsia, north-west of Yenan. From their border-region bases Mao and his troops were able to wage successful guerrilla warfare against Japanese army and puppet forces. Later, with the Japanese surrender, Red Army units were able to occupy 'vacuum areas' before Chiang Kai-shek could transport his troops from less advantageously located bases.

on its far eastern borders – sold to Japan in early 1935. And the Nationalist government was less than happy when, on 12 March 1936, the U.S.S.R. issued a protocol which amounted to a defense alliance between Moscow and Outer Mongolia, even though a 1924 Sino-Soviet Agreement had specifically recognized Chinese sovereignty over the Mongolian area. Finally, Chiang Kai-shek and his colleagues were increasingly aware that the U.S.S.R. was extending its influence deep into Sinkiang Province, a region which both Russians and Chinese officially recognized as an integral part of China.

In November 1937 the United States Ambassador to the Soviet Union learned from 'a well-informed colleague' that the U.S.S.R. had agreed to extend 100,000,000 Chinese dollars in credit for the purchase of military supplies *by the Chiang Kai-shek régime*. It was reported, moreover, that actual deliveries had already exceeded that amount. More than two hundred trucks were said to be in operation between the Soviet Union and Nationalist Chinese receiving points. The delivery of 400 Soviet pursuit planes and bombers was nearing completion, and forty Soviet instructors were believed *en route*. Efforts were now being made at a high diplomatic level to work out a better supply route and to facilitate more effective support of the Nationalist régime.

During 1938 and 1939, according to the *China Handbook, 1937–45*, the U.S.S.R. provided Nationalist China with loans totaling $250,000,000 (U.S.). In subsequent phases of the war the United States provided the Nationalists with a much higher level of support. But prior to American involvement, the U.S.S.R. served as a major source of Nationalist funds and equipment. 'With Soviet Russia,' Chiang declared on 2 December 1940, 'there has been no change in her consistent policy of support for Chinese resistance.'

Just as the image of Soviet Russia as a champion of justice and a defender of peace was winning wider and wider acceptance, Moscow prepared for a drastic change in policy. Addressing the Eighteenth Congress of the Soviet Union on 10 March 1939, Stalin reviewed the course of Japanese campaigns in China and emphasized that in some quarters these aggressions had been justified as an anti-Communist crusade. The Western powers, moreover, had apparently decided to leave each nation to fend for itself. In view of these realities, Stalin argued, the U.S.S.R. must depend hereafter upon its own resourcefulness and might, upon the 'moral and political unity' of Soviet society, and upon the Red Army and Navy. For those able to read between the lines – and subsequently, with benefit of hindsight – it was evident that Stalin was preparing for a new course of action. And, indeed, five months later the Soviet Union concluded its pact with Nazi Germany.

The Communists and the Nationalists collaborate again

The Chinese Communist Party, meanwhile, was working toward a new relationship with the Kuomintang – a relationship appropriate to the rapidly changing environment in Asia and in the world. But adjustments to these new circumstances also affected relationships within the Party. To what extent the Chinese leadership acted independently in bringing these changes about and to what extent they were merely responding to decisions already made in Moscow remains controversial.

Mao Tse-tung and his colleagues had decided on an anti-Japanese People's United Front on 1 August 1935 while the Mao-erh-k'ai Conference was still in progress. In Moscow on the following day the Seventh Congress of the Communist International discussed the importance of a worldwide united front policy and 'approved the initiative taken by our courageous brother Party of China in the creation of a most extensive anti-imperialist united front against Japanese imperialism and its Chinese agents . . .' Subsequently, on 20 August, the Comintern passed an important resolution which soon found its way to China. This document demanded a broad united front in colonial and semi-colonial countries, designated the soviets as a rallying point in China, and left the way clear for Chiang Kai-shek to call off his anti-Communist campaigns and participate in the fight against Japan. Thereafter, the Chinese Communists issued a series of invitations to Chiang, but many months passed by before the first attempts at inter-party cooperation were made, and even then the Communist–Kuomintang truce was uneasy and largely ineffective.

The change in Nationalist attitudes came after the kidnapping of Chiang Kai-shek at Sian during December 1936. By that time the Japanese had driven the forces of the 'Young Marshal', Chang Hsüeh-liang, out of Manchuria into Shensi Province. There he and the pacification commissioner of Shensi, Yang Hu-ch'eng, captured Chiang Kai-shek and confronted him with the view that the main war was no longer against the Communists, but against the

Chou En-lai as photographed in Yenan by Nym Wales in 1937. Among top Chinese Communist leaders, Chou and his wife were particularly attractive for foreigners because of their courtesy, charm, and cosmopolitan intelligence and wit. Within the movement, Chou sometimes started out on the losing side of a factional struggle but always managed to align himself with the winners in time.

Japanese. While Chinese soldiers were suffering 'death and bloodshed' at Japanese hands, they argued, 'diplomatic authorities' were still negotiating compromises with the foreign aggressor.

The Chinese Communist role in the Sian affair still remains somewhat unclear. Chou En-lai and others acted as mediators in discussions leading to Chiang Kai-shek's release, but how much influence they may have had on earlier aspects of the incident is not at all certain.

On 7 July 1937 Japanese forces attacked Chinese troops stationed at Marco Polo Bridge, a few miles south-west of Peking. The Central Committee of the Chinese Communist Party issued the next day a manifesto calling upon the whole nation for armed resistance.

The characteristic weakness of Nationalist forces was their dependence upon positional warfare. By contrast, the Communists worked for maximum mobility. 'Geographically, the theatre of the war is so vast that it is possible for us to pursue mobile warfare with the utmost efficiency,' Mao wrote in 1938, 'with a telling effect on a ponderous, slow moving war-machine like Japan's, cautiously feeling its way in the face of fierce actions.' Deep-line concentrations would be a mistake. 'Our strategy and tactics must aim to avoid great decisive battles in the early stages of the war, and gradually break the morale, the fighting spirit and the military efficiency of the living forces of the enemy.'

After months of Communist–Kuomintang negotiations the Nationalist government in September 1937 recognized a Communist garrison area known as the Shensi-Kansu-Ningsia (Shen-Kan-Ning) border region. At about the same time the Red Army was reorganized as the Eighth Route Army. Chu Teh and P'eng Te-huai were appointed commander and vice-commander, respectively, and Ho Lung, Lin Piao and Liu Po-ch'eng were designated division commanders. The Red Army was linked into the Nationalist military command – at least on paper – by the appointment of Chu Teh as deputy commander of the second war zone under the Nationalist general, Wei Li-huang. For the next three years Chiang Kai-shek's government subsidized the Communist Eighth Route Army on the basis of a 45,000 man total strength – although, in fact, the number seems to have been closer to 100,000. The Nationalists also provided a small ammunition allotment. Subsequently, as the Communists extended their control through guerrilla warfare, the Nationalist government also sanctioned establishment of the Shansi-Chahar-Hopeh (Chin-Ch'a-Chi) border region.

As the Communists expanded their military power they established other border region governments operating on a number of different administrative levels. These organisms varied in detail from one region to another, but the general pattern was uniform, and comparison suggests that the Chinese People's Republic established over the mainland in 1949 was largely derived from it.

According to the *Laws and Regulations of the Shensi-Kansu-Ningsia Border Region*, for example, the basic system was composed of a pyramid of people's councils elected by direct, universal and

Red Army artillery. Throughout his long struggle for power over mainland China, Mao Tse-tung had to rely primarily upon whatever weapons and other equipment he could seize or otherwise 'requisition' from his Nationalist, Japanese or other enemies. Even the supplies sent by the Soviet Union during the early phases of the Japanese War were received by the Nationalists and not by the Communists.

secret vote. The structure was held together by 'democratic central-ism': starting from the *hsiang* (town) government at the bottom and proceeding through the *hsien* (county) and on up, each level voted delegates to the next higher echelon – and was required, in turn, to obey its decisions.

Another central feature of the border region government was the 'three-thirds' system whereby the Communist membership of any given administrative organ was limited to one-third of the total, non-Party 'leftist progressives' and 'middle of the roaders' con-

Red Army troops on duty along a stretch of the Great Wall of China. After the fall of Peking on 28 July 1937 the advance of Japanese armies across north China was rapid, and by the end of the year nearly all the important cities were in enemy hands. The Japanese established a puppet government, but many rural districts remained a no-man's-land where Communist forces operated most effectively.

stituting the other two-thirds. Landlords, 'local bullies' and 'bad gentry' were to be kept out. The Communists were crystal clear, moreover, about where the effective power should lie. 'We must ensure the leadership of the Communists in the organs of political power,' Mao Tse-tung wrote in a 6 May 1940 Party directive. 'Therefore the Communists who constitute one-third must possess the best qualities. This condition alone will ensure the Party of its leadership even without a greater representation.'[1] In practice, non-Party elements were included because they were 'linked with the broad masses of the petty bourgeoisie' and the middle-of-the-roaders because they provided access to the 'middle bourgeoisie and the enlightened gentry'. To win over these elements was viewed as an important tactic in 'isolating the die-hards'.

The Communists depended also upon their own cohesiveness and discipline; 'for the practical realization of the leadership of the Party in the "three-thirds" system, the Party relies on ... the unanimity of speech and activity of Party members and Party cadres in the political system and their absolute obedience to Party resolutions; strict Party discipline among Party members and Party cadres in the political system is of grave importance.'[2]

On 28 July 1937 Japanese forces had occupied Peking, and by the end of that year nearly all the major cities of northern China, together with their railway and other communications links, were in Japanese hands. Puppet governments were set up in an effort to preserve order through local Chinese bureaucracies. But, in general, rural areas remained something of a no-man's land where seemingly aimless units of Chinese soldiers, peasants or bandits exchanged occasional blows with Japanese soldiers mopping up or foraging for food. It was into these regions that the Communist Eighth Route Army increasingly expanded its influence.

In September 1937 the Communists defeated two Japanese divisions in eastern Shansi and thus gained badly needed military equipment. According to United States intelligence reports, however, it was from fleeing Nationalist troops that the Communists secured a larger part of their supplies: 'Tens of thousands of rifles were left by fallen and fleeing Chinese soldiers on the battlefields of Shansi, Hopeh, Chahar and Suiyüan. The Chinese Communists collected vast quantities of these abandoned arms and munitions and used them to replenish their own supplies and to arm guerrilla units and local self-defense corps which they organized among the peasants.'[3]

Conflict between Nationalist and Communist forces in the field was frequent, and in January 1941 a disagreement over the demarcation of zones of action led to the notorious New Fourth Army

Chinese Red Banners flying in the province of Ninghsia.
The troopers belonged to the 15th Army Corps, 5th Cavalry Division.
During the Japanese War Communist and Nationalist forces officially
collaborated, with the Kuomintang government regularly subsidising the
Communist Eighth Route Army. In January 1941, however frictions erupted
into the New Fourth Army Incident, a pitched battle lasting eight days.

Incident. Nationalist leaders declared that Communist units,
dispatched against Japanese troops north of the Yangtze, had dis-
obeyed orders in attempts at expanding their own territories southward. The Communists, for their part, charged the Nationalists
with trying to restrict Communist areas unduly and to render the
position of Communist armies ineffectual. More than 2,000 Communist soldiers were killed in the eight-day battle that ensued, and
3,000 were wounded. Nationalist forces were reported to have
suffered nearly 20,000 casualties. By this point it was evident that in
China the 'united front' was more like an armed truce. As the
Japanese War progressed, moreover, and especially after the
United States entered as an active belligerent, the Nationalists and
Chinese Communists devoted more and more of their efforts to
positional maneuvers prior to an anticipated, post-war struggle for
power.

The rights and wrongs of the Communist–Kuomintang relationship were complex and not easy to untangle.

During Communist negotiations with the Kuomintang a new controversy had developed between Chang Kuo-t'ao and Mao Tse-tung. In this instance, Chang – according to his own subsequent account – advocated 'sincere' cooperation with the Kuomintang, whereas Mao insisted that Communist troops should retain their autonomy during the Japanese War, engage only in those campaigns which would advance the Communist position, and press for the eventual defeat of non-Communist groups in the united front as well as for defeat of the Japanese. Mao's overriding objective, according to Chang Kuo-t'ao, was to achieve power without regard for the fate of the Nationalists.

Mao, on the other hand, accused Chang Kuo-t'ao of 'right opportunism', 'retreatism', the disruption of Party discipline, and the development of factional activities.

The Chang–Mao controversy was debated at a conference in Lochuan, and Mao – after arbitrarily cutting off discussions, according to Chang's subsequent assertions – obtained a Party resolution condemning his rival for 'betraying' Communism and the 'cause of the anti-Japanese front' by being too friendly with the Kuomintang, and in Moscow the Comintern supplied its endorsement. Moreover, '. . . as Chang Kuo-t'ao not only persistently refused to correct his mistakes,' Mao charged, 'and resorted to double-dealing, but later on actually betrayed the Party and threw himself in the arms of the Kuomintang, the Party could not but resolutely expel him.'[4]

Cheng-feng – a program of thought reform

While Red Army forces were extending Communist control over wide areas of northern China and providing security for new border region governments, Mao Tse-tung was adapting and developing Marxist–Leninist theories to requirements of the Chinese revolutionary environment and his own achievement of power.

Po Ku, Chou En-lai, Chu Teh and Mao Tse-tung photographed
in Yenan by Nym Wales in 1937. Before the Long March
Po Ku had been prominent in the Returned Students Clique.
Chou had helped organize a group of Chinese Communist students in Paris
as early as 1920. In the early thirties Chu Teh and Mao were
so closely associated that many took them to be a single man called Chu Mao.

Contradictions were at the heart of Maoist – as well as Marxist–Leninist – theory. 'The law of the contradiction in things, that is, the law of the unity of opposites,' Mao declared, paraphrasing Marx, 'is the basic law of nature and society and therefore also the basic law of thought.'[5]

Contradictions were perceived as universal in all things – in physical phenomena, in human relations, and in ways of thinking. No contradiction could possibly disappear except through completion of the process of which it was a part. Some contradictions were antagonistic and some were not. Antagonistic contradictions could be solved only by certain kinds of struggle. 'A bomb, before the explosion,' Mao wrote, 'is an entity in which contradictory things exist because of certain conditions. The explosion takes place only when a new condition (ignition) is present. An analogous situation exists in all natural phenomena when they finally assume the form of open antagonism to solve old contradictions and to produce new things.'[6]

Major contradictions existed among the imperialist powers themselves; between imperialist powers and colonies and semi-colonies (such as China); and between the workers and the capitalists, the exploiters and the exploited.

In a capitalist society, 'where the town under bourgeois rule ruthlessly exploits the countryside' and in Kuomintang-controlled areas of China (exploited by foreign imperialism and native comprador bourgeoisie) the contradiction between town and countryside was extremely antagonistic. But in a socialist country and under the border region governments such contradictions became non-antagonistic, according to Mao. In a truly Communist society the contradiction would disappear.

But there were also contradictions within the Party.

Soviet Russian history revealed that contradictions between the correct ideology of Lenin and Stalin and the erroneous ideologies of Trotsky and Bukharin had developed into acute antagonism. 'A similar case occurred in the history of the Chinese Communist Party,' Mao declared. 'The contradiction between the correct

A farmer and his wife eating a meal while surrounded by water during a Yellow River flood, July 1938. Under normal conditions, the people of China could expect flood and famine as frequent visitors. Revolution, the Japanese invasion, and the subsequent Communist–Nationalist civil war only added to the miseries which millions of Chinese had learned to expect as a matter of course.

ideology of many of our comrades in the Party and the erroneous ideologies of Ch'en Tu-hsiu, Chang Kuo-t'ao and others also in the beginning was not manifested in an antagonistic form, but subsequently developed into antagonism.'[7]

Under these circumstances it was essential to carry on a 'serious struggle against erroneous ideologies' within the Party – but not to push the struggle to excess unless the contradiction became clearly antagonistic.

Referring to Chang Kuo-t'ao's 'serious violation of discipline', Mao underscored the necessity of insisting: 1 That individuals must subordinate themselves to the organization. 2 That the minority must subordinate itself to the majority. 3 That the lower level must subordinate itself to the higher level. 4 That the entire membership must subordinate itself to the Central Committee. If there seemed to be a contradiction between subordination of the minority to the majority, on the one hand, and subordination of 'the entire membership' to the Central Committee, on the other, the concept of democratic centralism tried to resolve it: the entire membership participated, through the delegate system, in selecting the Central Committee, and then subordinated itself to Central Committee decisions. 'He who violates any of these articles of discipline,' Mao warned, 'disrupts the Party's unity.'

In order to defeat foreign and domestic enemies, overcome difficulties and build a new China, the Communist Party needed to expand its organization 'by throwing its door open to the broad masses of workers, peasants and young and active people' who were truly revolutionary, who believed in Party principles, and who were willing to work hard and observe discipline. At the same time, care must be taken lest hidden collaborators, Trotskyites, degenerates and political speculators 'sneak into' the Party in the guise of active people. 'Recruit to the Party boldly,' Mao asserted, 'but never allow a single undesirable person to sneak in – this alone is the correct policy.'[8]

In December 1929 Mao Tse-tung had presented to the Ninth Conference of the Communist Party Organization of the Fourth Army of the Red Army a resolution 'On the Rectification of Incorrect Ideas in the Party.' Because the Red Army recruited from the peasantry, from prisoners of war, from deserters, from warlord armies and even from bandit forces, there were, as Mao put it, 'various non-proletarian ideas' which greatly hindered 'the carrying out of the Party's correct line.' The task was to identify the manifestations of these incorrect, non-proletarian ideas, determine their respective sources, devise methods for rectifying them, and call upon all comrades 'to eliminate them thoroughly'.[9]

For each erroneous tendency Mao listed typical symptoms and techniques for rectification and eradication. Broadly, the cure lay in education – an extremely specialized variety of education based upon the Marxist–Leninist concept of combining theory and practice and involving intense small group discussions, reciprocal criticism of the frankest sort, searching self-criticism, and the testing of all symbolic or verbal concepts through action, especially through 'practical work'. Subsequently, Mao and his colleagues refined these techniques. 'The Red Army is like a furnace,' Mao had written in the Chingkang Mountains, 'in which all captured soldiers are melted down and transformed the moment they come over.'[10] Over the years Mao tried to transform the whole Party membership and – in the 1950s – a considerable portion of the Chinese people by these methods.

Undoubtedly, the Long March was something of a 'furnace'; undoubtedly, the veterans of this incredible *anabasis* had been to one degree or another 'transformed'. But in Yenan, especially with establishment of far-flung border region governments, the war-time expansion of Party membership, and requirements of the united front, there was undoubtedly a strong infiltration of 'incorrect ideas' and 'erroneous tendencies' within the Chinese Communist movement. In order to meet this threat Mao Tse-tung and his colleagues undertook the *Cheng-feng*, or 'ideological remolding movement'.

Cheng-feng was formally inaugurated 1 February 1942 when somewhat over a thousand Party members assembled in a Yenan lecture hall to hear Mao Tse-tung. 'For the complete overthrow of the enemy,' he said, 'our ranks must be in order, we must all march in step, our troops must be seasoned, and our weapons fit. Unless these conditions are fulfilled, the enemy will not be overthrown.' Criticising errors in the Party's style of work and thought, Mao struck out at 'dogmatists', who depended entirely upon theory at the expense of practical experience, and also at 'empiricists' who relied wholly upon experience and were scornful of theory. '. . . there are two kinds of incomplete knowledge,' he said. 'One is knowledge already contained in books, and the other is knowledge which is usually perceptual and partial, and both are one-sided. Only through an integration of the two can excellent and comparatively complete knowledge emerge.' Whatever the source

The Japanese blockade at Tientsin, mid-1939.
The Japanese invaders, through the economic,
political and social destruction they
visited on China, were undoubtedly an
important factor in paving the way for
Chinese Communist victories a decade later.

of this knowledge, moreover, whether from books or from practical experience, it fell completely into two – and only two – basic categories: 'that which concerns the struggle for production and that which concerns the class struggle.' According to Mao, 'The natural and social sciences are the crystalizations of these two kinds of knowledge, and philosophy is the generalization and summary of the knowledge of both nature and society. Is there any other knowledge besides these? No.'[11]

Chinese inhabitants of Kweilin
in Kwangsi Province, read
a wartime news poster on
the occasion of a Chinese
victory over Japanese forces
on the Changsha front.

Mao charged Ch'en Tu-hsiu, Li Li-san, Chang Kuo-t'ao and the Returned Students with grievous errors stemming either from 'dogmatism' or from 'empiricism' and pressed for corrective measures. 'How can we turn these intellectuals who have only bookish knowledge into real intellectuals? The only way is to make them take part in practical work . . .' As for those who depended solely upon practical work, they must learn theory.

Against this background the Party leadership inaugurated a

tightly organized campaign of thought reform which trained more than 30,000 leaders over the next twelve months and also dislodged influential Returned Students and their supporters from crucial positions of authority.

According to Marxist–Leninist theory, human beings are the creatures of their material environments: each human action or attitude is essentially a response to an environmental stimulus. It followed, therefore, that the effective way of reshaping thought and behavior was to manipulate the immediate environment, or milieu. For the most part, small study groups – under strict Party control – provided the milieu which forced individuals to criticize themselves and each other against standards set by *Cheng-feng*. Trained activists took leading roles in guiding and manipulating the study groups, and the personal confession was a major instrument for identifying and excizing erroneous thoughts and tendencies. Confessions were discussed and frequently torn apart by the group, whereupon the writer was called upon to write another, and perhaps a third and a fourth and so on until he had rooted out the offending beliefs and tendencies.

'We must see that the marching order of the entire Party is regular and uniform,' Mao declared, 'and that it struggles toward a common objective.' This meant that harmony must be achieved among various groups and regions, but it also meant subordination of individual interests to Party interests.

A leader in setting Party standards was Liu Shao-ch'i, who – like many increasingly influential Party members – came from Mao's native province of Hunan. 'The interests of the Party above all – this is the highest principle . . .' Liu wrote. 'The Party member should see that he has only the Party and Party interests in mind and no individual purpose. He should see that his own individual interests are identical with Party interests to the extent that they are fused. Where contradictions arise between the interests of the Party and the individual we can, without the slightest hesitation or feeling of compulsion, submit to Party interests and sacrifice the individual.'[12]

Wang Ching-wei, Chinese left-wing revolutionary turned Japanese puppet, 1941. During the mid-twenties Wang emerged as a leader of the Kuomintang Left, which collaborated in the late spring of 1927 with the Communists in opposing Chiang Kai-shek. Subsequently, Wang had a reconciliation with Chiang, but he steered an erratic course in politics and eventually went over to the Japanese.

General Li Yu-tang (*center*), a Chinese Nationalist defender of the Changsha front. A crucial problem for the Chinese during the war was how to secure supplies from the outside. The Soviet Union had sent material overland, but after Pearl Harbor and Japanese expansion throughout the Pacific, nearly everything had to be airlifted from India 'over the Hump'.

The struggle for post-war advantage

Mao Tse-tung's *Cheng-feng* movement was well underway when, in mid-1943, relations between the Kuomintang and the Chinese Communists and also between the Soviet Union and the Nationalist government took a turn for the worse. This change in relations was marked in August of that year by charges which a Russian *Tass* correspondent leveled against 'appeasers, defeatists and capitulators' within the Kuomintang who were resisting Chiang Kai-shek's efforts to reorganize Nationalist armed forces and who preferred negotiating for peace with Japan. These 'anti-democratic and anti-

Chinese Nationalist generals planning moves along the Salween front in defence of China's 'back door', mid-1943. This region along the Burma frontier was particularly important because of the India–Burma–China supply route.

popular forces' were trying to undermine the Communist–Kuomintang united front, weaken China's resistance to foreign aggression, and encourage persecution of the Eighth Route Army. If these destructive elements were to gain power in the Nationalist government, *Tass* charged, a fratricidal war might break out and put an end to the war of liberation. 'Discontent with the Kuomintang's policies is widespread throughout China,' *Tass* declared.

These views were in sharp contrast to prevailing Soviet attitudes, which had remained generally favorable toward the Kuomintang even during the period of the Nazi–Soviet pact.

The *Tass* correspondent's charges were soon echoed by other

Soviet authors and by Communist spokesmen in other countries. Increasingly, moreover, these criticisms were cited by non-Communist commentators in the United States and elsewhere who, being genuinely alarmed by the events in China, were perhaps unduly inclined to accept the *Tass* arguments without considering their somewhat partisan source. Soon the charges were broadened to include Chiang Kai-shek.

How justified were these charges?

Clearly, it was assumed by Communist leaders in Soviet Russia and China alike that collaboration with the Kuomintang was a temporary, purely tactical policy and that one way or another, in due course, a Communist-led government would replace the Nationalist régime. Thus, Communist sources were inevitably biased and fundamentally hostile. On the other hand, it is undeniable that Kuomintang leaders, in confronting the Japanese invasion, had resorted to special measures which many Westerners considered undemocratic and even authoritarian both in spirit and in consequence. Specifically, the New Life movement tried to regenerate some of the more paternalistic and even repressive concepts of earlier neo-Confucianism. The rigidly disciplined San Min Chu I Youth Corps seemed almost as totalitarian in its intent as a Stalinist or Hitlerian youth movement. The granting of extraordinary powers to Chiang Kai-shek was understandable in a wartime context, but many Western observers felt that the Kuomintang had gone unnecessarily far in the arbitrary designation – rather than election – of a portion of the National Congress membership and in the extension of facilities for party purging by means of a party superviser's net. It was becoming painfully evident, moreover, that – apart from whatever else they might accomplish – the new repressive measures were of no consequence whatever in checking wartime inflation, black-marketeering, and the spread of corruption within party and governmental circles.

Marshal Li Chi-shen – the Kwangsi militarist who in late 1927 had shared power in Canton with Chang Fa-k'uei – complained of the 'drift toward dictatorship' and departure from democratic

General Hsueh Yueh, Nationalist officer who in early 1942 scored victories over Japanese forces along the Changsha front. During the late thirties the Soviet Union sent considerable supplies to the Chinese Nationalists, but was forced to discontinue when Hitler invaded the U.S.S.R. After Pearl Harbor, it was the United States which became the major supplier of Nationalist China.

principles. An American military source was even more critical. 'All observers agree that the greatest cause of the poor showing made by the Chungking [Nationalist] forces last year [1944] during their defense against the Japanese was the hostility of the people toward their own army, and the hopeless disunity between the regular Kuomintang or Central Army and the provincial armies.'

This American appraisal appeared in a remarkable document.

During late 1944, the United States Military Intelligence Service undertook an investigation of developments in China, and the report that emerged was in many respects prophetic – though very little attention was paid to it at the time.

Issued by the Chief of Military Intelligence, Brigadier General P. E. Peabody, this report recorded that after the New Fourth Army Incident of January 1941 and increasingly after United States entry

A Japanese regimental flag captured by Nationalist forces on the Changsha front in early 1942.

into the war, both Nationalists and Communists had expended more energy fighting each other than in resisting the Japanese invasion: 'The history of this inter-party struggle, against the background of the war against Japan, presents both the Kuomintang and the Chinese Communists in a most unfavorable light.'[13]

The Peabody report charged the Nationalist régime with concluding what amounted to a truce with Japanese puppet troops and withdrawing their forces from effective contact. 'As a result, practically all the coastal provinces of North China came under either Communist or Japanese control.'[14] The main Nationalist effort went into the blockading of Communist areas and the increasing of Nationalist strength in western China. 'American observers came

Searchlights guarding Chungking against Japanese air raids. While Communist forces waged guerrilla warfare, Kuomintang forces pursued more conventional tactics on a number of fronts. After the U.S. had entered the war, both Communists and Nationalists tended to jockey for positions on the assumption that American, rather than Chinese forces would defeat Japan.

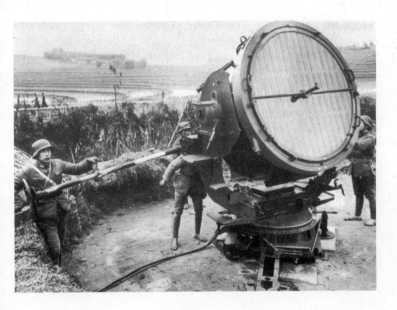

to believe that many leading Chinese Government officials felt that China had done her part in fighting Japan and that it was henceforth up to the United States and Britain to defeat Japan.'

Meanwhile, the Chinese Communists were devoting less and less energy to fighting the Japanese and more and more to the expansion of their own territory. 'From control of about 35,000 square miles with a population of about 1,500,000 people at the beginning of 1937,' the Peabody report estimated, 'the Communists have expanded their control to about 225,000 square miles with a population of some 85,000,000 people.'

The immediate post-war importance of Japanese-held areas – and more particularly the areas held by puppet forces – was not underestimated by either the Kuomintang or the Chinese Communist leaderships. As American forces came closer and closer to a victory over Japan, both Mao Tse-tung and Chiang Kai-shek began preparing for the same contingency. For it was evident to both that whichever party gained control from the defeated Japanese of the major share of railroads, mines, agricultural regions, cities of the Yangtze valley, and port cities, would be well situated for establishing sovereignty over all of China. For months the two sides jockeyed their forces with the hope of achieving a favorable head start – with the consequence that explosions over Hiroshima and Nagasaki sounded in many Chinese ears more like the crack of a starter's pistol than the massively destructive blasts of an era hitherto unknown to mankind. For Mao and Chiang the race for power was on.

8 Communist China in a nuclear world

The Communist bloc, the West, and the emerging nations

The Chinese Communist leadership achieved national power in a world that was undergoing incredibly rapid change. Disintegration of the old empire system had been accelerating for years. China's Manchu Empire had been the first to go, seeming to collapse beneath its own weight in 1911. It was followed into oblivion by the Russian Empire in 1917, and then by the Austro-Hungarian, German and Ottoman Empires. Core parts of each were transformed to one degree or another under new governments, while more peripheral parts achieved independent status or were encompassed by surviving empires. Former German colonies were absorbed by the victors after World War I.

From the chaos of 1917 Russia a new kind of integrating system had emerged – the Communist system. Its true nature became the most controversial issue of an era. Believers hailed it as democratic, anti-imperialist, non-exploiting, and egalitarian. But critics and enemies condemned it as undemocratic, inherently exploitive, non-egalitarian – a new aggressive and dangerous imperialism.

The new system identified the old as an historic and predetermined antagonist and bent every effort to speed its destruction. For Communist leaders, moreover, there was little to distinguish one actor in the old system from another: the tottering Chinese Empire, the British Empire, the French Empire, Kaiser Wilhelm's Germany, Hitler's Germany, the Japanese Empire, the United States – whatever the differences, all were perceived by Communist theoreticians as shaped by similar processes from essentially similar substance, and all were equally doomed to disintegrate.

As history unfolded, spokesmen of the new system appeared correct in their predictions to this extent: the old empires with their vast colonies and spheres of influence found themselves increasingly challenged from within, less and less capable of adapting to the rapidly changing environment and increasingly unable to function effectively.

World War II speeded the disintegration process, and during the first two decades of aftermath the British, French, Dutch, Belgian and Portuguese empires – 'voluntarily' or 'involuntarily' – lost most of their colonies, only a few enclaves remaining. In Asia and Africa there was a rapid fragmentation of the old imperial units, followed by a proliferation of new states. At the same time there was an *integration* of vast areas and large populations into the new – *Communist* – system. The consequence was a world embraced more and more by three different systems: a loose, more or less Western-influenced system; a Communist system stretching from East Germany to China and North Korea; and a third, disparate, un-cohesive 'system' of emerging nations with widely differing potentials and characteristics – full of energy and expectations, but frequently groping for even minimally effective ways of establishing themselves and breaking out of their quandaries and difficulties.

The Western system and Communist system found themselves competing more and more for influence in the third, 'emerging' system. Each of the two tried to adapt its own economic, political and social institutions to meet the needs of these new countries. But more often than not the day-to-day problems there – to say nothing of more long-range requirements – defied the ingenuity of every-body.

If the West discovered that its own most hallowed institutions did not always thrive in remote regions of Asia and Africa, the Communists began somewhat painfully to learn that it is sometimes easier to facilitate *dis*-integration over vast areas and among already disparate peoples than it is to maintain subsequent *in*tegration. Even between a well-established Communist Russia and a newly founded Communist China problems of cooperation became increasingly difficult.

And as if the world did not face problems enough, World War II developments in nuclear weaponry made certain of the basic assumptions and favorite doctrines of everybody – Communist, capitalist, democratic, totalitarian, black, white, rich, poor, young, old, educated and illiterate – crucially inappropriate and obsolete.

Post-war Nationalist dilemmas

Friends of Nationalist China have frequently asserted that Chiang Kai-shek would have succeeded if the United States had not been deterred by its own internal, Communist-inspired subversion, thus falling down on its responsibilities and commitments. These critics of American policy recall the post-war mission of General George C. Marshall, whom President Truman charged with the task of bringing United States influence to bear upon Communist–Kuomintang conflicts in order to achieve a 'unified, democratic and peaceful' China. Why were the negotiations undertaken, they ask, and on what premise was it considered advisable to bring the Communists – under any circumstances at all – into the Nationalist government? In retrospect, it indeed seems doubtful that the Marshall mission enjoyed realistic possibilities of success.

A thorough knowledge of Chinese Communist history – something few Westerners had during World War II – would have made clear that Mao's notion of a China 'independent and free, democratic and united' was not the same thing as General Marshall's concept of a 'unified, democratic and peaceful' China. Moreover, a careful reading of Mao's April 1945 report to the Seventh Congress, *On Coalition Government*, might have revealed that, in using that term, he envisaged a 'coalition' in which the Communists – and not the Nationalists – had maximum power.

But there were further considerations which some of the more vociferous critics of United States policy – as well as some of its champions – tended to overlook.

A long-time observer might have argued that an unreconstructed Nationalist régime was almost certain to remain non-adaptive and dysfunctional, and that even from its beginnings the Kuomintang – as it stood – scarcely had a chance.

In the West, unfortunately, there had been no concept of 'aid for emerging nations' when Sun Yat-sen first approached Great Britain and the United States. Ignored by London and Washington, he had turned to Moscow, which was delighted to oblige – within

Japanese troops storm the ruined walls of a fort on the Lunghai front. The Chinese fought well in many individual engagements, but the country as a whole lacked the cohesion and resources to mount an effective defense. Japanese forces seized major transportation routes in the lowlands, but mountain districts normally remained in Chinese hands, or became part of a vast no-man's-land.

its own strategic and tactical framework. As reshaped by Borodin, the Kuomintang was intended to serve Communist, rather than Nationalist purposes. When Chiang Kai-shek broke away in 1927 he retained as much of the apparatus as seemed useful. But Nationalist success or failure depended essentially upon Chiang's personal capacity for holding together a creaky coalition of party members, financiers (including several members of his own family), a limited number of troops under his own command, and a constantly shifting coterie of regional warlords who were willing to collaborate – sometimes quite temporarily – each for his own purposes.

Under these circumstances the possibilities for success were something less than encouraging.

Whatever its merits or good intentions, the Nationalist government never held even the formality of a national election on the Chinese mainland, nor directly involved more than a comparative handful of the Chinese people, nor accomplished more than token efforts at economic or social reform. Throughout nearly the whole of its tenure, the régime was under attack not only by the Communists, but also by one wing or another of its own party dissidents, by dissatisfied and personally ambitious warlords, and by the Japanese – either directly, or surreptitiously through local militarists. At intervals the régime was also harassed by encroachments of the Soviet Union (especially in Sinkiang), by demands for protection or advantage by Western commercial interests, and by squabbles among the powers who enjoyed political and economic spheres of influence over parts of China.

The usual Chinese droughts, floods and famines were also persistently recurring elements of the picture. It had to be taken for granted, year in year out, that millions of people would die from vast and largely unavoidable catastrophies of nature. Also, it had to be taken for granted that the Chinese population would skyrocket by some 10,000,000 a year.

In view of these factors, it seems questionable whether the jerry-built Nationalist régime was adequate. Whether the Communist

régime will prove equal to the stupendous tasks remains to be seen. In his sober moments, indeed, the sophisticated observer may find himself hard pressed to conjecture *what kind of régime*, over the long haul, can solve the problems of China.

However this may be, the Nationalist government was in a fundamentally disadvantageous position at the close of World War II. With their traditional reliance on conventional methods of warfare, Chiang's troops lacked the mobility and flexibility which had allowed Mao Tse-tung's guerrilla units to range over wide areas and behind Japanese lines. This Nationalist immobility was particularly frustrating when, just before the end of the war, Soviet Russian troops moved into Manchuria. The United States provided the Nationalists with air and water transport, and United States Marines were detailed to hold key railroads, coal mines and other strategic locations for Kuomintang occupation.

In spite of armed clashes with the Communists, Chiang Kai-shek's armies accepted the surrender of a majority of the 1,200,000

Japanese troops in China proper, cleared the Lunghai Railway, and secured control of Peking, Tientsin, and communications to the Manchurian border. At that time the Kuomintang enjoyed an estimated five-to-one advantage in troops, weapons, heavy equipment, transport and air strength. But major north–south trunk lines – crucial for logistic support if the Nationalists were to enter Manchuria – were largely in Communist hands. Chiang thereby faced a dilemma: whether to postpone occupation of Manchuria or, in advancing, to risk over-extension of his transport lines and possible Communist attack from the rear.

Delayed by critical military dilemmas, the régime, meanwhile, was more and more engulfed by economic problems. China had long been plagued by inflation, but during and after the war the value of Nationalist currency dropped lower and lower. At the same time, new influxes of United States material and other assistance encouraged black-marketeering and corruption in many party, governmental and commercial circles. As the régime in power, Chiang Kai-shek and the Kuomintang could not escape responsibility for calamities that would have tried the capacities of whatever kind of government might have found itself in their position.

In the meantime, there were larger forces at work which limited possibilities even further. Undoubtedly the defeat of Japan would upset the whole balance of power in eastern Asia.

The problem was complicated during war years by the question of Soviet Russia's entry into the Pacific conflict. 'It should be remembered that at this time the atomic bomb was anything but an assured reality,' the United States Department of State pointed out in subsequent years; 'the potentialities of the Japanese Kwantung Army in Manchuria seemed large; and the price in American lives in the military campaign up the island ladder to the Japanese islands was assuming ghastly proportions. Obviously military necessity dictated that Russia enter the war against Japan prior to the mounting of Operation Olympic (the assault on Kyushu), roughly scheduled for 1 November 1945, in order to contain

Japanese forces in Manchuria and prevent their transfer to the Japanese home islands.'

After the war it was charged that these estimates were based upon faulty intelligence: in fact, Japanese forces in Manchuria had been depleted by transfers to the Philippines and Okinawa, and in Japan the home front was uncertain and 'full of tensions'. But however the situation may have appeared in retrospect, the widely-shared expectation during the war had been that the Japanese would put up bitter, essentially suicidal resistance both in Manchuria and on the home islands.

After meeting in Cairo, Prime Minister Churchill, President Roosevelt and Generalissimo Chiang Kai-shek had issued a declaration on 1 December 1943 which asserted their determination that Manchuria, the Pescadores and Formosa should be restored to the Republic of China. On 11 February 1945, however, Churchill, Roosevelt and Stalin – without consulting China – signed the Yalta agreement identifying the conditions under which the Soviet Union would enter the war against Japan.

The treaty remained secret until several months after the war was over – though it had been agreed that the decisions concerning Mongolia and the ports and railroads would 'require the concurrence of Generalissimo Chiang Kai-shek.' President Roosevelt was to 'take measures in order to obtain this concurrence on advice from Marshal Stalin.' For its part, the Soviet Union expressed readiness to conclude a pact of friendship and alliance with the National Government of China.

Subsequently, there arose many disputes over the wording of the Yalta agreement and over the propriety of its clauses – particularly those which recognized Soviet Russian rights in Dairen, Port Arthur and the railway zones of Manchuria. Soviet Russian troops were already moving into Manchuria, moreover, when on 15 August 1945 a Treaty of Friendship and Alliance was announced between the U.S.S.R. and Nationalist China.

Despite numerous attempts at negotiation, by late October 1945 fighting between Nationalist and Red Army forces had spread over a large portion of mainland China. In late November 1945 President Truman appointed General George C. Marshall as his Special Envoy to China with the rank of Ambassador. During subsequent months General Marshall served as peace negotiator between the Kuomintang and Communist leaderships, and in January 1946 a cease-fire agreement was achieved. Fighting was soon resumed, however, developing rapidly into a full-scale civil war.

Red Army victories on the Chinese mainland

If Chiang Kai-shek was confronting obstacles, it appears in retrospect that Mao Tse-tung was not entirely without frustrations, either. During most of 1946 Nationalist prospects looked comparatively bright. According to United States estimates, Kuomintang forces had three times more men under arms than the Communists. And by early 1947 Nationalist military potential – with more and more aid coming from the United States – seemed to be approaching a new peak.

Admittedly, there were delays and wastage in delivery of material from the United States. American transport was not always efficient, and many supplies disappeared in the black market and other illicit channels. General Claire Lee Chennault charged subsequently that the United States – in seeking to 'pressure' Chiang Kai-shek into more effective negotiations with the Communists – 'shut off the flow of military supplies.'[1] Also, the Soviet Union was turning over to the Chinese Communists large numbers of Japanese rifles from military stores in Manchuria. Yet, there seems little doubt but that Nationalist military strength – measured in men under arms, number and calibre of weapons, provisions and supplies, mechanical transport and financial resources – considerably over-balanced the resources of the Communists.

Nor does it appear that the Soviet Union was supplying Mao Tse-tung and his colleagues with anything like the support that outsiders frequently imagined at the time. Indeed, in 1948 Stalin admitted that he had been dubious about the capacity of the Chinese Communist movement and its immediate prospects. '. . . after the war,' Stalin was reported as asserting, 'we invited Chinese comrades to come to Moscow and we discussed the situation in China. We told them bluntly that we considered the development of the uprising in China had no prospect, and that the Chinese comrades should seek a *modus vivendi* with Chiang Kaishek, that they should join the Chiang Kai-shek government and dissolve their army. The Chinese comrades agreed here with the views of the Soviet comrades, but went back to China and acted otherwise. They mustered their forces, organized their armies, and now, as we see, they are beating the Chiang Kai-shek army. Now, in the case of China, we admit we were wrong. It proved that the Chinese comrades and not the Soviet comrades were right.'[2]

What, then, were the sources of Nationalist weakness – and of Communist strength?

On 9 July 1947 President Truman dispatched Lieutenant-General Albert C. Wedemeyer on a fact-finding mission to appraise the political, economic, psychological and military situations – 'current

A scene during the battle of Huai-Hai, which opened much of central China to the Communists. The fighting raged from 7 November 1948 until 10 January 1949 and resulted in the routing of an estimated 550,000 Kuomintang soldiers. Shown in the picture are troops, guns and trucks captured by the Communists.

and projected' – in China and Korea. In a report dated 19 September 1947, General Wedemeyer asserted that the bulk of people in China were not disposed toward Communism – though some had become affiliated with it 'in an indignant protest against oppressive police measures, corrupt practices and mal-administration of National officials.'³ While condemning the Communists, bound ideologically to the Soviet Union, General Wedemeyer sharply criticized the Nationalists, 'whose reactionary leadership, repression and corruption' had been responsible for a 'loss of popular faith in the Government.' Meanwhile, moderate groups were finding themselves caught between 'Kuomintang misrule and repression' and ruthless Communism. 'Some have lost all hope for China under existing leadership and turn to the Communists in despair. Some accept a new leadership by mere inertia.' The United States must urge upon Chiang Kai-shek the utter necessity for

Nationalist forces march on Christmas Day, 1948, to
defend Nanking, the Kuomintang capital, from Mao's advancing armies.
Weakened by the Japanese invasion and by post-war monetary
inflation and other disorders, the Nationalist government found it
increasingly difficult to hold back the
rising tide of Communist influence and power.

political and economic reforms if Communism were to be stopped.

The Nationalists did not succeed in achieving effective reforms, however, and increasingly the tide began to turn. More and more the Communists were able to supplement Russian-donated Japanese rifles with more powerful American weapons captured from American-trained and American-equipped Nationalist forces. During November 1948 the United States Embassy in China reported that in four recent battles the Nationalists had lost thirty-three divisions, 300,000 men, and 230,000 rifles. Eight of these divisions had been eighty-five per cent American-equipped and American-trained, and 100,000 of the rifles had been American-made. Less than a month later the United States military attaché in Nanking reported the total loss of 'seventeen originally United States equipped divisions.' And during the last four months of 1948 alone 400,000 rifles and 1,000,000 men were estimated to have been lost by Nationalist armies.

In October 1948 Nationalist military leaders in Manchuria defected to the Communists, taking weapons and other equipment

with them. 'The Nationalist troops in Manchuria were the finest soldiers the Government had,' according to the commander of the United States Advisory Group in China. 'The large majority of the units were United States equipped and many soldiers and junior officers still remained who had received United States training during the war with Japan. I am convinced that had these troops had proper leadership from the top the Communists would have suffered a major defeat.'[4]

Soon the Communists were piling up one victory after another. In January 1949 Peking surrendered without a fight. Red Army forces pushed steadily southward, and Chiang Kai-shek eventually withdrew to Taiwan.

The Chinese new democracy

On 1 October 1949 Mao Tse-tung took his place upon a reviewing stand which had been erected in front of the gate of the former imperial palace. All day long the streets of Peking had been alive with bands and military columns and marching students, and now the great city square in front of the palace was jammed by nearly

Unit of the Red Army, now designated the People's Liberation
Army, enter an unresisting Peking in January 1949. Thereafter
Communist victories followed one another in rapid succession. At this
crucial stage of the struggle Communist forces were welcomed by
many classes of the Chinese people, although many of them
later suffered at the hands of Mao's thoroughgoing revolutionary régime.

200,000 people. There was an audible stir, and then an expectant
silence as the Communist leader prepared to speak.

Nearly thirty years had passed since Lenin told the Communist
International in 1920 that during early phases of the struggle in
colonial and semi-colonial countries the national bourgeoisie would
'march with the revolution' in a temporary four bloc alliance. Over
the decades Soviet Russia had tended to emphasize this collaboration – with the expectation that 'the proletariat', through the local
Communist Party, would achieve more and more influence and
power within the party and governmental coalition. In China, Mao
Tse-tung had accepted Lenin's perception of class structure and
primary class antagonism, but on the basis of his own first-hand
experience, he had refused to place much confidence in national
bourgeois leaders. He wanted reliable Communist control from the
start.

In practice, this Party hegemony had taken the form of the New
Democracy, a governmental instrument for imposing sovereignty
over all the classes and firmly guiding the revolution through its
stages by exercising the power of the Red Army and the whole
Communist movement. Under institutions of the New Democracy
there was assurance that the non-proletarian classes would be
tightly supervised and constrained from seriously endangering
progressive stages of the revolution.

Initially, the People's Republic of China was established under
a tentative Common Program, but subsequently, on 20 September
1954, the First National People's Congress adopted the Constitution of the People's Republic of China. Under Article II of this
document all power in China now belonged to the people.

Under 'new democratic' concepts the 'people' had already been
carefully identified. 'At the present stage in China,' Mao had explained in mid-1949, 'they are the working class, the peasant class,
the petty bourgeoisie, and the national bourgeoisie. Under the
leadership of the working class and the CP, these classes unite together to form their own state and elect their own government [so as
to] carry out a dictatorship over the lackeys of imperialism – the

The Soviet Ambassador to Nationalist China N.V. Roschin (*left*) at Nanking airport on 2 February 1949, *en route* to Canton, designated as the new capital by the retreating Kuomintang. Since the early twenties the U.S.S.R. had tried to maintain diplomatic relations with whichever Chinese government was legal – even while supporting Sun Yat-sen or other revolutionary forces opposing it.

landlord class, the bureaucratic capitalist class, and the KMT reactionaries and their henchmen representing these classes ... These two aspects, namely democracy among the people and dictatorship over the reactionaries, combine to form the people's democratic dictatorship.'[5]

The immediate task, as Mao saw it, was to ensure 'proletarian hegemony' over the new democratic four-class alliance by strengthening the apparatus of the people's state: *the people's army, the people's police, and the people's courts* – the 'tools of the classes for the oppression of classes.'

Thus, in Mao's view, the purpose of the state was to advance the interests of 'the people' as defined at any given revolutionary stage by the Communist Party as the vanguard of the proletariat. There was no concept here of the state as a mediator between different classes or different interests. 'We decidedly do not adopt a benevolent rule toward the reactionary acts of the reactionaries and the reactionary classes,' Mao declared. 'We only adopt a benevolent

Mao Tse-tung proclaims the People's Republic of China in Peking, 1 October 1949. According to Chinese Communist statements the new government belonged to the 'people'. But it made clear that the 'people' did not include everybody. The régime was opposed to the 'lackeys' and 'running dogs' of imperialism – the landlord class, the 'bureaucratic capitalists' and the 'Kuomintang reactionaries and their henchmen'.

administration among the people and not towards the reactionary acts of the reactionaries and the reactionary classes outside the people.'

Implicit was the notion that the 'people' were those who, at any revolutionary stage, would support a class alliance – and its policies – as defined by the Communist régime according to Marxist–Leninist theory. Thus, as the revolution progressed over succeeding years, class after class would 'go over to the enemy' and would thus be excluded from 'the people' – though the state stood ready to 're-educate' individual members of any class into a 'proletarian viewpoint' and accept them as 'people'. The government of the New Democracy, then, was at the same time an instrument for imposing sovereignty – under Communist Party hegemony – over all the classes, a nationwide institution for thought reform, and a systematic program for guiding the revolution, phase by phase, toward its objective.

The primary long-range intent was to overtake the West as

rapidly as possible by transforming China into a modern industrial state. Peking hoped to build a first-rate socialist régime by 1973. To achieve this objective the Chinese leadership had to devise procedures and techniques for raising vast amounts of capital as a foundation for building industry and promoting twentieth century technology. Within an environment like that of China much of this capital had to be squeezed out of the agricultural economy or raised at the expense of consumers – including the vast masses of the peasantry.

By 1949 Mao Tse-tung had accumulated vast experience – in the soviets of Kiangsi and elsewhere, and in the border region governments. The Kiangsi régime of the Chinese Communists, under Returned Student leadership, had frequently attacked the rich peasants as well as the landlords. Subsequently, the policy shifted with changes in leadership and also with changes in circumstance. During the Japanese War Mao Tse-tung and his colleagues tried to win rich peasant support – a policy that was consistent with the united front and designed, also, to encourage maximum agricultural production. But after V-J day the official attitude hardened, the focus having shifted back from international war to domestic revolution. The Red Army needed mass peasant support and participation to defeat the Kuomintang, and land, including that of the rich peasants, was used as a stimulus for poor peasant revolt.

After the establishment of the People's Republic, however, the policy changed again. 'The war has fundamentally ended on the mainland,' Mao Tse-tung told the Central Committee on 6 June 1950, 'and the situation is entirely different from that between 1946 and 1948, when the People's Liberation Army was locked in a life and death struggle with the Kuomintang reactionaries and the issue had not been decided. Now the government is able to help the poor peasants solve their difficulties by means of loans to balance up the disadvantage of having less land.'[6] In order to facilitate the early restoration of agricultural production in rural areas, it was desirable to preserve a rich peasant economy once again and concentrate on elimination of the landlord.

Under a 1950 Agrarian Reform Law the landlord was singled out as a target of class struggle: his land, farm implements, surplus grain and draft animals must be confiscated and either nationalized, thus becoming state property, or assigned to the *hsiang* peasant associations [embracing several villages] for distribution 'in a unified, equitable and rational manner' to poor peasants with little or no land and to other categories who lacked means of production. It was stipulated, however, that former landlords were to receive an equal share of the redistributed property so that they might 'reform themselves through labor' and thus learn to make a living through their own industry in place of the 'exploitation' of others.

The basic institution for ensuring implementation of these processes was stipulated in the Agrarian Reform Law. 'A people's tribunal shall be set up in every *hsien* in the course of agrarian reform to ensure that it is carried out. This tribunal shall travel to different places and try and punish, according to law, hated despotic elements who have committed heinous crimes, whom the masses of the people demand to be brought to justice, and all such persons who resist or violate the provisions of the Agrarian Reform Laws and decrees.'[7]

These tribunals were empowered to arrest and detain suspects, to try cases, and to pass sentences including confiscation of property, imprisonment and death.

Mao had made clear in *On the New Democracy* that big banks, big industries, big commercial establishments and all foreign enterprises would be owned by the state. In view of the backwardness of China's economy, however, it would be advantageous to use capitalist production techniques as long as they functioned under 'new democratic' control and thus facilitated the people's livelihood. In the long run, state-controlled private enterprise would join with cooperative enterprise and state enterprise to destroy both foreign and domestic capitalism.

Mao drew sharp distinctions between the 'new democratic' and 'socialist' stages of the Chinese revolution. 'The idea of some people who think it possible to bring about an early elimination of capitalism and to introduce socialism,' he told the Central Committee in mid-1950, 'is wrong and unsuitable to the conditions of the country.'[8]

'In China, which is backward in industry,' the new Minister of Heavy Industry, Ch'en Yün, declared, 'it will be progressive and beneficial to the country and the people for the national capitalists to develop industry and make investments in it for a long time.'[9]

While fostering 'limited capitalism', however, the new régime made unmistakably clear that it would deal harshly with 'war criminals', 'feudal landlords', 'bureaucratic capitalists', and 'other leading incorrigible counter-revolutionary elements who collaborate with imperialism, commit treason against the fatherland, and oppose the people's democracy.'

'If you do not cooperate with the Communists,' Mao Tse-tung had asserted in *On the New Democracy*, 'then you must oppose them.'[10] In this spirit the Government Administrative Council and the Supreme People's Court in Peking issued a joint directive in July 1950 which provided the death sentence for the leaders of gangs 'who take up arms against the people's government' and stipulated that no appeal would be available to those who had received a death sentence under this decree.

Some months later the Supreme People's Court and its regional branches repudiated the 'boundless magnanimity' which was asserted to have been practised until then. Law, under the New Democracy, was defined as 'a tool in the hands of the ruling class to control the ruled class', and 'boundless magnanimity' was denounced as 'harmful to the people'. And on 21 February 1951 the 'Regulations of the People's Republic of China for Counter-Revolutionaries' stipulated 'vigorous and timely' suppression of counter-revolutionary activities. Under this law spying, plotting, spreading of counter-revolutionary propaganda, crossing state frontiers for counter-revolutionary purposes, organizing jail breaks and similar activities were punishable by imprisonment, life imprisonment or death.

'This much is certain,' Mao had warned in *On the New Democracy*, 'whoever wants to oppose Communism must prepare to be smashed to pieces.'[11] In Peking on 20 May 1951 a Chinese Communist journal, in identifying various modes of punishment, offered the following definition: 'Execution means fundamental physical elimination of counter-revolutionaries and is, of course, the most thorough and severe measure of depriving counter-revolutionaries of their conditions for counter-revolutionary activities.'

During early 1952 the Peking régime undertook a '3-Anti's Campaign' against 'corruption, decay and bureaucracy' with Party and governmental officials as the main targets. 'The following shall be accomplished during the present campaign . . .' announced Kao Kang to a high-level cadre meeting, 'Purge all departments of corruption, waste and bureaucracy. The cases of corruption and waste should be given penalties ranging from dismissal, prison terms, labor reform to death sentence.'

At about the same time Mao and his colleagues also launched a '5-Anti' struggle against tax evasion, bribery, theft of state assets, cheating and theft of state economic secrets. Now the major targets were 'lawbreaking merchants'. In this struggle against 'corrupt bourgeoisie' the régime identified five categories of punishment – surveillance by government organs, reform through labor, imprisonment for a fixed period, life imprisonment, and death. Cases were ranked both according to the seriousness of the crime and the willingness of the accused to confess and submit himself to reform.

The confiscation of landlord and rich peasant land and its redistribution to the poor peasants was scarcely completed before the Peking régime started a program of collectivization. '. . . some of our comrades are tottering along like a woman with bound feet,' Mao declared in a speech on 31 July 1955, 'always complaining that others are going too fast.' This was all wrong, he said. Socialist industrialization depended upon cooperative, as distinct from private agriculture, and thus the redistribution of land from gentry to peasants was only a first step. Unless China could leap from small-scale farming with animal-drawn implements to large-scale farming with machinery, the achievement of socialist industrialization would be impossible. In switching from handicraft production to mass production, China must change from private ownership to common ownership. The social revolution and the technological revolution were thus interlinked. During 1955 and 1956 the peasants were organized into producers' cooperatives at a rapid rate. By the end of that period something like ninety percent of the peasantry were said to have been absorbed into cooperative organizations – 110 million households, according to Liu Shao-ch'i, drawn into more than one million cooperatives.

Mao pointed out, however, that most of the agricultural cooperatives established so far remained semi-private in nature, thus restricting productive forces in the opinion of the régime. Now the time had come to transform these elementary cooperatives into collectively managed organizations in which all the means of production would be owned jointly. 'When the ties hampering the forces of production are thus loosened,' Mao declared, 'production will develop much more rapidly.'

Meanwhile, the régime had been pressing a massive 'bootstrap' program for economic and technical development. The goal was to transform China into a modern, industrialized state as rapidly as possible. But Mao warned the people that it would be a long pull to industrialization and full socialism. 'To win country-wide victory is only the first step in a long march of ten thousand *li*,' he declared. China must not only free itself from remnants of the old order. In time the new Chinese society must surpass the imperialists and replace them. Under the leadership of the Communist Party, however, every kind of miracle could be performed. 'We believe that revolution can change everything,' Mao had asserted some years back, 'and that before long there will arise a new China with a big population and a great wealth of products, where life will be abundant and culture will flourish.' Now the Chinese Communist leader proposed to demonstrate before the whole world the feasibility of his earlier forecast.

Chinese peasants terracing previously desolate and unproductive hills in the north-west, March 1961. China must not only feed its rapidly increasing number of people, but must somehow squeeze out of its soil a large part of the surplus capital needed to build an industrial base. No régime, whatever its ideology, could escape this basic task.

At the Eighth Congress of the Chinese Communist Party in September 1956 the leadership estimated that three five-year plans would be needed for achievement of industrialization in China. According to official predictions, the heavy industry goals of the First Five-Year Plan would be over-fulfilled by its termination date in 1957.

The First Five-Year Plan had been formally initiated early in 1953 – though a detailed text was not made public until mid-1955.

Preliminary targets of a Second Five-Year Plan were announced before the Eighth Congress, and in 1958 the Plan was inaugurated virtually on schedule. There were five major objectives: 1 industrial construction with increased emphasis upon development of heavy industry. 2 ideological indoctrination, thought reform, social transformations, and 'remoulding of individuals'. 3 agricultural, industrial and handicraft production, commerce and transportation. 4 the training of technical and scientific specialists

Back-yard furnaces built by the Chinese Communists in the hope of boosting steel production. During the Great Leap Forward the Peking régime relied heavily upon experimentation and spectacular short-cuts to achieve 'twenty years' progress in a day'. Many of these measures, including the back-yard furnaces, failed to achieve the results that had been hoped for.

and the abolition of illiteracy. 5 the achievement of higher levels of both material and cultural life within the People's Republic.

For a time it seemed that Communist China was making unprecedented progress in raising itself from economic backwardness toward modern industrialization. The slogan was 'twenty years in a day', and the régime began boasting that it would overtake Great Britain within a decade or so.

Early in 1958 Peking inaugurated the 'Great Leap Forward' in economic and technical development. The program included the communization of the peasantry and the building of 'back-yard' furnaces for producing pig iron in rural areas. Previously-set production targets were put aside in favor of unprecedented new goals: more than 700,000 collective farms were to be transformed into 26,000 rural communes during the course of a few months.

By the summer of 1959 it became clear, however, that the Chinese Communists had over-reached themselves. During August the Peking régime began a series of admissions that 1958 production reports had been grossly exaggerated, and government planners undertook drastic reductions in 1959 output goals.

On returning to Peking from a tour of the country in September, Mao reported progress toward industrial goals and commented on the tremendous energy of the Chinese people. But the crucial efforts in iron and steel, he admitted, left much to be desired. 'There are still a few comrades who are unwilling to undertake a large-scale mass movement in the industrial sphere. They call the mass movement on the industrial front "irregular" and disparage it as "a rural style of work" and a guerrilla habit. This is obviously incorrect.' He urged a redoubling of effort in the iron and steel sectors, but warned at the same time against sacrificing agriculture. 'The 1959 task in agriculture,' he declared, 'is to achieve a leap forward even greater than that of 1958.' The system of people's communes must be extended.

This was easier to urge than to achieve, however. In the field sheer necessity forced peasants and Party administrators alike to make adjustments in the commune program according to local require-

ments, with the consequence that arrangements in many regions bore slight resemblance to the highly disciplined communal models the régime had initially enforced.

In the meantime, mainland China was plagued by more of the floods and droughts that have characterized generations in Chinese history. Undoubtedly the Communist régime was unique among Chinese governments of the nineteenth and twentieth centuries with respect to the efforts it made toward alleviating the inevitable mass suffering that accompanied these catastrophes. But the efforts were seldom sufficient. However spectacular China's progress, it did not approach the levels of accomplishment which Party leaders had predicted, nor did it approach what was desperately needed, especially in view of the country's exploding population growth.

Traditional Marxist–Leninist doctrine asserts that a country is over-populated only because there is a gap between the technological level of the society and the appropriateness and effectiveness of the political and economic systems. Any population problem in a capitalist society is thus viewed by Marxist–Leninists as a consequence of the conflict between the economic system and the productive, that is, the labor force. This clash between capital and labor gives rise inevitably to relative over-population and under-employment. The solution, of course, is the seizure of state power by the proletariat and the reorganization of the society into a socialist, and hence, a more productive and equitably organized economic and political system.

The Bolshevik revolution in Russia offered no test of Marxist–Leninist population theory. Even today the vast spaces and natural resources of Soviet Russia are being used by only a little more than 200 million people, and the problem is shortage of man-power rather than over-population. It was the establishment of Communist power in China that put Marxist–Leninist population theory to empirical test.

'We have a population of more than 600 million,' Liu Shao-ch'i told the Eighth Congress of the Chinese Communist Party in May 1958, 'and our Party has ties of flesh and blood with this vast population. By relying on this great force we can, or soon can, do anything within the realms of human possibility.' The huge population was not a liability, but an asset. And Chinese man need not limit his numbers. Chinese man could do anything.

Subsequently, these optimistic attitudes were altered, however. With the faltering of the Great Leap Forward, the Peking régime turned to a 'campaign against early marriages' and the official discouragement of too many children in the early years as oblique attacks on the problem of birth control. Later marriages were encouraged, and unmarried young people were warned against premature unions motivated by 'bourgeois affection' and like emotions rather than by the requirements of society. In view of the total problem, however, these measures seemed scarcely adequate to many outside observers.

All in all, the Great Leap Forward was more remarkable for its failures, perhaps, than for its undeniable accomplishments. In retrospect it appears that the program may have been conceived by planners who were Party leaders rather than trained scientists and technicians – by men who, in terms used increasingly by the leadership, were more 'Red' than 'expert'.

Red and expert, or expert and Red?

A major problem faced by the Chinese Communists was how to press the anti-imperialist struggle against those who had been most thoroughly exposed to foreign influences – the intellectuals – and at the same time to employ the rare and crucially important skills and talents which this group – and only this group – possessed.

According to Mao, the imperialist powers, in carving up China, had extended their invasions by supplying Chinese 'reactionaries' with large supplies of arms and ammunition and a host of advisers. 'Besides,' he said, 'the imperialist powers have never slackened their efforts to poison the minds of the Chinese people, that is, to carry out a policy of cultural aggression. Carrying on missionary activities, establishing hospitals and schools, publishing newspapers, and enticing Chinese students to study abroad, are the ways this policy is implemented. Their aim is to train intellectuals to serve their interests and to fool the great masses of the Chinese people.'[12]

Thus, as Mao saw it, the struggle against imperialism had to be pressed on many fronts, both foreign and domestic, and even in the minds and social and cultural habits of the Chinese people.

In early days of the new régime large numbers of intellectuals had supported the Communists as an alternative to the inadequacies and confusions of the Kuomintang. But the '3-Anti', '5-Anti' and other campaigns had alienated much of this early support.

The Peking régime was in deperate need of engineers, scientists, writers and other specialists. But large numbers of these professional men and women had been trained in Europe or the United States or in missionary schools and colleges in China itself. Most were ignorant of Marxism–Leninism; many were antagonistic. The crucial question arose, therefore, to what degree the intellectual must become 'Red' as well as 'expert' to take part in planning and implementing the march toward industrialization.

As far back as 1939 Mao Tse-tung had presented the Central Committee with a resolution which revealed the difficulty faced by the Communists. 'Without the participation of the intellectuals,' he warned, 'the revolution cannot achieve victory.'[13] Yet Party and Red Army authorities were frequently afraid of the intellectuals and unwilling to admit them. This was an error. Care had to be taken, of course, to reject intellectual elements 'sent by the enemy or the bourgeois political parties'. But others should be encouraged. '. . . we should educate them, steel them in war and work, and enable them to serve the army, the government, and the masses . . .'

The problem was to transform the intellectual, and Mao, recalling his student and early revolutionary days, saw his own change in attitude as a model. At first it had seemed that the intellectuals were 'the only clean persons in the world', while the workers and peasants were dirty beside them. But later, 'Having become a revolutionary, I found myself in the same ranks as the workers, peasants and soldiers of the revolutionary army . . . It was then and only then that a fundamental change occurred in the bourgeois and petty-bourgeois feelings implanted in me by bourgeois schools. I came to feel that it was those unremolded intellectuals who were unclean as compared with the workers and peasants, while the workers and peasants are after all the cleanest persons, cleaner than both the bourgeois and petty-bourgeois intellectuals, even though their hands are soiled and their feet smeared with cow dung. This is what is meant by having one's feelings transformed, changed from those of one class into those of another.'[14]

Without such remoulding and transformation, Mao Tse-tung believed, the intellectual could 'do nothing well' and would be ill-adapted to any kind of useful work. Over succeeding years the Chinese Communist transformation program became a major effort – though modifications were made during the 'Hundred Flowers' period of 1956, and again in 1961.

Mao made clear that the Party should use no more than the minimal amount of force necessary to achieve the transformation. The intent was 'to cure the patient but not to kill him'.

With their establishment of the People's Republic, Mao Tse-tung and his colleagues started a 'mass study movement' throughout the mainland. Every effort was made to involve the whole population – children, workers, peasants, professors, housewives, old men and women, technicians, and the unemployed. Existing schools and universities were commandeered into service, and new, specialized revolutionary schools and universities were established.

By manipulating the immediate milieu through small study groups and group study brigades, Chinese thought reform cadres brought to bear upon their subjects a series of social and sometimes physical pressures and deprivations – at the same time allowing the individual only a very limited set of beliefs and actions. These pressures (and/or deprivations) – whether purely social and psychological, or partly physical – were eased at appropriate moments and then applied and eased again. Under these circumstances many subjects – on the subconscious as well as the conscious level – saw no choice other than to reshape themselves in order to survive politically, socially and psychologically.

From this conditioning and enfoldment of the subject within the study group the Chinese Communist thought reformers tried to mold a new personality – 'bold', 'selfless', 'disciplined', 'determined', 'loyal', 'sincere'. Such a man, according to Liu Shao-ch'i, 'bears the sorrow of the world now for the sake of later happiness. In the Party he toils now for the sake of later satisfaction.'[15] He can work independently, without supervision, and have nothing to fear from subsequent investigation. His mistakes – if he makes them – are 'public as an eclipse'. He can 'love men or hate them' and treat 'humanity's parasites' with the 'greatest determination'. He is sincere, straightforward and content. 'Being right, he is strong.'

The collective pressures – social and psychological – that were brought to bear upon the individual were calculated to be irresistible. 'It took us ten days [to complete the thought conclusions],' a student recalled later, '. . . in the course of which we did not even have a recess on Sunday. During this period, the students were engaged in meditation and writing day and night, each person endeavouring to scrape out, to expose, to analyze, and to criticize his personal history and thought. If there was any part of the ugly

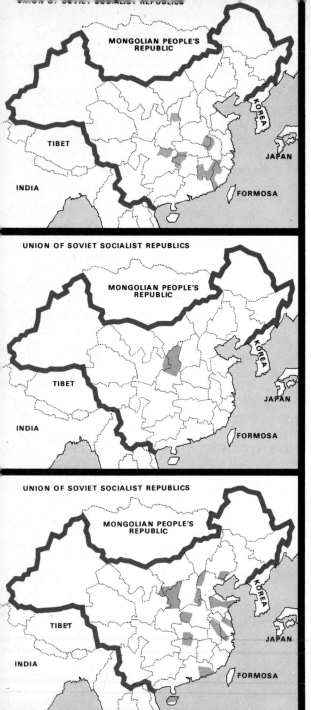

The balance of forces in China, October 1934. Chiang Kai-shek and his Nationalist Government controlled most of central China. Nominally, autonomous provincial warlords held south-western and southern parts and Sinkiang; Japanese forces occupied Manchuria. The Chinese Communists controlled isolated enclaves in central China but Chiang Kai-shek's 'encirclement campaigns' were drawing the nooses tighter.

Chiang Kai-shek's expanding influence, December 1936. As the Japanese threat became more immediate, Chiang was able to draw recalcitrant provincial warlords into closer association. The Communists, having completed the Long March, were consolidating their power in the environs of Yenan. The Japanese had not yet begun their major drive southward. To the west, Sinkiang was still essentially autonomous, but Soviet Russian influence was growing.

The pattern of Japanese control, August 1945. The Japanese had cut off the eastern approach to China, so that Nationalist forces had to be supplied from India 'over the Hump'. The Communists had penetrated the western flank of the Japanese.

Chinese Communist forces, July 1947. With the Russian withdrawal from Manchuria in 1946 Chinese Communist troops began moving in. Using Japanese rifles supplied by the Russians and American equipment acquired in the black market or from the Nationalists, Mao's forces pressed southward against Chiang's armies. The Nationalists maintained control over Mukden, however, and other key cities in northern China.

The Nationalist–Communist see-saw, November 1948. On paper Chiang Kai-shek still commanded the bigger armies, possessed the larger share of weapons and equipment, and controlled the wider territory. But Chiang's sovereignty over much of the country was nominal. Week by week the Communists pushed their way southward along major transportation routes, and in places Nationalist forces began defecting, whole regiments and even divisions at a time.

The Communists poised for take-over, April 1949. In early 1949 Communist victories followed each other rapidly: Tientsin fell on 15 January; Peking surrendered; Shanghai fell in May. The Nationalists moved to Canton, but on 15 October that city too capitulated.

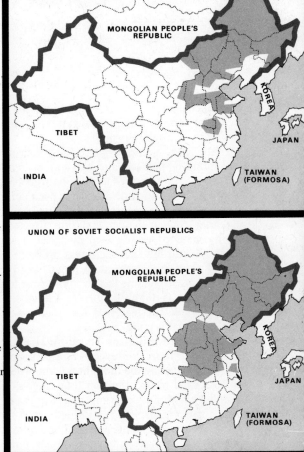

past which had not been brought into the open, here was the last chance to report to the organization . . . in order to complete the final and thorough reform.'[16]

'*I surrender to the people*,' one intellectual pleaded after confessing that he had lied and had sought to alienate the people from the Party. '. . . my ugly face as a bourgeois Rightist and an opponent of the Party and socialism has been completely unmasked.' He went on to describe the state of mind which had induced him to surrender. 'When the whole nation directed its solemn criticism to me, I began to see my own mistakes. I suffered intense anguish within me and felt that there was no more place for me. Each day when the postman comrade brought newspapers and letters to my door, I was too ashamed to go to the door to get them. Week before last when I was ill and had to see a doctor, I did not dare give him my true name for fear that the doctor would identify me as the Rightist Chu An-p'ing.'[17]

According to Professor Theodore H. E. Chen, who has examined a hundred or more confessions and personal testimonies written by intellectuals during the thought reform of 1951–2, pro Americanism was accorded more attention than any other variety of 'incorrect thought' which the program sought to eradicate. A corollary error was a hostile or suspicious attitude toward the Soviet Union.

Chinese scholars confessed to 'blind admiration of America', the use of American laboratory techniques and equipment, reliance on American teaching methods, profession of Darwinism rather than the theories of Michurin, the exchange of specimens with American scholars, and so forth. 'I failed to realize that botanical resources were a matter of great value to the imperialists in their exploitation of colonial and semi-colonial countries,' a professor of biology confessed. 'I not only did not feel ashamed of serving the cause of imperialism; I was even proud of it.'[18]

Many Chinese intellectuals found difficulty in submitting to other demands of a collective society. 'I was deeply in love with my wife and we never parted in twenty years of married life . . .' a professor of Chinese literature confessed. 'The more children I had, the more

I loved them . . . I used to say to my wife, "We live for our children." My whole life was dominated by individualism.'[19]

By the end of 1955 it had become evident, however, that the transformation program was not winning sufficient support and participation from intellectuals in the push toward industrialization. A new, relatively 'soft' policy seemed appropriate. Hereafter, the Communists proposed to 'Let A Hundred Flowers Bloom and A Hundred Schools of Thought Contend' – a program based upon grossly inaccurate estimates of the Party's strength and of spontaneous support for it among students, intellectuals and professional people.

The Peking régime could scarcely have anticipated the response of Chinese intellectuals to this invitation. The comments were cautious, at first, but during May 1957 Chinese intellectuals began speaking out with a volume and intensity that caught the leadership wholly unprepared. Not only the Communist Party, but even Mao himself, was bitterly criticized. By June the Communist leadership was making it clear that the right to 'bloom and contend' was not unqualified – that freedom of criticism must further, and in no way damage, 'socialist construction'.

Later, however, with the faltering of the Great Leap Forward, it again became evident that the talents and loyalty of the intelligentsia remained indispensable, and in mid-1960 a new invitation was issued. This time the Party proceeded with more realism, laying down sharp criteria for differentiating academic discussion from ideological contention. Free speech and criticism must unite the people, not divide them, and facilitate socialist transformation at every step. Within these boundaries the flowers were encouraged to bloom again and the various schools of thought to resume contending. But if the régime had learned a lesson, so had the intellectuals: this time their response was much more circumspect.

The problem of performing technical and scientific functions became even more trying when the Soviet Union withdrew its technicians from China in mid-1960.

Meanwhile, in their efforts to replace the discredited bourgeois intellectual, Party leaders pushed the notion of training 'worker-inventors' and 'worker-scientists' in a variety of techniques and making specialized roles interchangeable. Being 'Red' was judged more functional than being 'expert', even in science and technology, and a good Communist was asserted to be capable of doing virtually anything. Indeed, it was within this climate of official opinion that the Great Leap Forward was initiated.

Chinese Communism in a world of cataclysmic change

When Mao Tse-tung and his colleagues achieved power over main-land China they found themselves caught almost immediately in an international turbulence that had been increasing rapidly since the post World War I founding of the Chinese Communist Party. A less confident leadership might have moved into world affairs with greater caution, but these men had dynamism and motivation and purpose and boldness that was both Communist and Chinese, a fusion of cultural, historical, social, economic and psychological drives – compelling, almost irresistible.

Thus impelled, the Chinese Communists wanted to move fast internationally as well as domestically, and they were soon making it clear that in both spheres they considered the 'Chinese way' unique, effective and right. At first they found themselves in conflict with their more or less natural enemies, the 'imperialists' who had penetrated China so effectively, making the country and its people economically and to a considerable degree politically subservient. But soon the Chinese leaders were also in conflict with their Soviet Russian comrades, competing with them for influence within the international Communist movement and in the world at large.

A major purpose of the Chinese Communist leadership was to build the power and prestige of their régime and re-establish China as a great power – perhaps *the* great power – among the nations.

In order to achieve this status quickly, the new régime relied heavily upon assistance from the Soviet Union. But relations between the Russian and Chinese Communist leaderships had never been entirely satisfying, and in some respects the acquisition of power over the mainland by Mao Tse-tung and his colleagues made collaboration more difficult than ever. The world Communist movement found itself with two major capitals, for one thing; two strong and ambitious centers of doctrine and influence. Then the death of Stalin in 1953 raised a new leadership in Moscow, and for Mao Tse-tung and his colleagues the adjustment to this change was not easy.

During Stalin's lifetime, Mao Tse-tung and his colleagues had tended to pay lip service to the Soviet dictator's authority and omniscience, but then to proceed with problems in China as they themselves saw fit. And, at the time of his death, Peking hailed Stalin as the 'greatest genius of the present age' and asserted that his 'contribution to our era through his theoretical and practical work' was beyond estimation. His development of Marxism–Leninism was described by the Chinese as epoch-making. But the Chinese left it clear that Mao enjoyed somewhat comparable stature as a theoretician and innovator.

As far back as 1946, Liu Shao-ch'i, who in 1959 succeeded Mao as Chairman of the Chinese People's Republic, told an American journalist, Anna Louise Strong, that Mao had transformed Marxism from a European to an Asiatic form. 'The basic principles of Marxism are undoubtedly adaptable to all countries,' Liu declared, 'but to apply their general truth to concrete revolutionary practices in China is a difficult task. Mao Tse-tung is Chinese; he analyses Chinese problems and guides the Chinese people in their struggle to victory. He uses Marxist–Leninist principles to explain Chinese history and the practical problems of China. He is the first that has succeeded in doing so.'[20] Increasingly the Chinese Communists seemed to feel that the Maoist pattern for revolution in the 'colonies and semi-colonies' of Asia, Africa and Latin America offered greater possibilities than whatever the Soviet Russians could contribute.

With the initiation of Khrushchev's 'de-Stalinization' program,

Liu Shao-ch'i, Party veteran and fellow Hunanese, who succeeded Mao Tse-tung as Chairman of the People's Republic on 27 April 1959. 'The interests of the Party above all – this is the highest principle,' wrote Liu, a leading Party theoretician. 'The Party member should see that he has only the Party and Party interests in mind and no individual purpose.'

Opposite: Mao Tse-tung pays a call on the First Secretary of the Central Committee of the Soviet Union, N.S. Khrushchev, 4 November 1957. Mao told a group of Chinese students at Moscow University that 'the east wind prevails over the west wind, that is, the strength of socialism exceeds the strength of imperialism.' Many observers believe that Mao was influenced by successful tests of the Soviet ICBM the previous August.

Chinese leaders conceded that the Soviet dictator had made serious mistakes – mistakes which Mao had successfully avoided. Particularly, having won 'high honor among the people both at home and abroad by the correct application of the Leninist line', Stalin had begun to exaggerate his own role and to counterpose his individual authority to the collective leadership.

Chinese Communist leaders emphasized, however, that there were two ways of criticizing Stalin's works – the Marxist way and the doctrinaire way. As far back as the period from 1927 to 1936 some Chinese comrades – obviously Mao's Party opponents – had crudely persisted in trying to apply certain of Stalin's mistaken ideas in China. Indeed, the major errors committed during the development of the Chinese revolution, according to Peking, had occurred when Moscow – not Mao – was shaping Chinese Communist policy. Since the Tsun-yi Conference of January 1935, however, no serious mistakes had been committed by the Chinese central leadership. This was because Mao, unlike Stalin, had kept in close touch with the people and had avoided the error of a 'cult of the personality'.

On the other hand, according to the Chinese Communists, it

was an error on the part of 'western', i.e. Russian, Communists – and indeed one more manifestation of the same tendency toward overrating the individual – to account for Stalin's misdeeds in terms of personal character flaws. Rather, the Soviet Union as a nation had allowed 'non-antagonistic' contradictions, appropriate for a socialist state, to get out of hand and develop into inappropriate and destructively hostile antagonisms.

'Some people consider that Stalin was wrong in everything,' the Chinese Communists charged. 'This is a grave misconception. Stalin was a great Marxist–Leninist, yet at the same time a Marxist–Leninist who committed several gross errors without realizing that they were errors.' The correct Marxist–Leninist approach was to make a proper, all-round historical analysis to see where Stalin was right and where he was wrong and to draw useful lessons therefrom.

Essentially, the Chinese Communists seemed to be declaring their ideological independence from the Soviet Russians and putting their own revolutionary record forward as a more sucessful and correctly Marxist–Leninist undertaking. In any case, the whole de-Stalinization episode produced a stubborn paradox.

For Khrushchev, without prior consultation, had demanded that other Communist parties of the world join in the demolishing of Stalin's heroic image; but once 'the greatest genius of our era' had been rejected, the question was inevitably raised in Peking and elsewhere upon what authority Khrushchev could now base his attempt to issue instructions to other Communist parties and make demands.

Meanwhile, however, both Moscow and Peking remained in confrontation with a common antagonist – the West with its newly developed nuclear capacity – and for a time the two leaderships gave the impression to outsiders of hand-in-glove achievement.

During the first decade of Chinese Communist power over the mainland the People's Republic and the U.S.S.R. concluded a series of agreements which returned Dairen, Port Arthur and the Chinese Changchun Railway to China and also provided vast quantities of economic and technical assistance to the Peking régime. In retrospect it became evident, however, that relations had not been as satisfactory as had appeared on the surface. By the early 1960s Peking was claiming further areas which the Russians had no intention of giving up. And as late as 1959 Doak Barnett could write that the Soviet Union had 'not given Communist China a single free grant for economic development, as far as is known on the public record, and even the volume of Soviet loans and credits for economic purposes has been small in relation to China's needs.'

Chinese Communist relations with the West had developed from misunderstanding and friction, meanwhile, to outright bloodshed. Months of negotiation were required before Great Britain and the People's Republic achieved official – but cool – diplomatic relations. And the United States, while withholding recognition, became a champion of Chiang Kai-shek's government on Taiwan and a leader in blocking Chinese Communist admittance to the United Nations.

On 25 June 1950 the Korean War broke out, and within three days Russian-trained and equipped North Korean troops were in possession of Seoul, the South Korean capital. In an *Aide Memoire* of 27 June the United States informed the Nationalist Chinese Government on Taiwan that President Truman had ordered the United States Seventh Fleet to prevent any Chinese attack on Taiwan and to ensure that the Nationalist government ceased all sea and air operations against the mainland. The presence of United States naval units made Chinese Communist hopes for the seizure of Taiwan frustratingly unfeasible.

By early October 1950, Communist Chinese troops were entering Korea – a state once tributary to the Chinese Empire – as 'People's Volunteers'. Peking's motivations have never been clearly determined. According to one view, the move had been ordered by Stalin; other observers suggest that the Chinese may have acted through fear that the United States was preparing to invade Manchuria. Possibly the motivation was complex, with these elements and others – conscious and unconscious – all contributing.

In any case, the war was largely indecisive – and too costly and frustrating for either side to continue indefinitely. In October 1953 the Peking régime agreed to begin discussions at Panmunjom toward ending it. In subsequent years the Chinese Communists proclaimed their determination to 'liberate' Taiwan, and there were conflicts such as the bombardment of Nationalist-held Quemoy in 1954 and the Quemoy–Matsu crisis of August–October, 1958, but the régime drew back from action that might trigger a full-scale military confrontation.

After the Korean War it appeared that Peking had entered a new phase of 'peaceful coexistence' with its neighbors. In 1955 at the Asian–African Conference in Bandung, Indonesia, Chou En-lai recalled the *Panch Shila*, or 'Five Principles' which he and Prime Minister Nehru of India had proclaimed a year previously: 1 mutual respect for each other's sovereignty and integrity. 2 non-aggression. 3 non-interference in each other's domestic affairs. 4 equality and mutual benefit. 5 peaceful coexistence. To these Chou En-lai now added recognition of the equality of races; and respect for the right of the people of all nations to choose their own way of life and their own political and economic systems.

China incorporates Tibet. In a 1950 New Year's message the
Chinese People's Republic declared that Tibet was rightfully a part
of 'continental China', and in October Chinese Communist forces invaded
the country and established military and administrative headquarters. In the
spring of 1951, delegates from the 'local government of Tibet'
signed an agreement with the Chinese as shown here.

But there were at least two factors which made it difficult for the People's Republic to maintain relationships with certain states – especially neighboring ones – on this level of mutual respect and good will. Boundary problems constituted the first of these, and the second was the Chinese conviction that 'the people' of all developing nations, if allowed to choose freely and without coercion, would prefer the 'Chinese way over all Western alternatives – and even over Soviet-style possibilities'. This was a view which Chinese representatives began promulgating in other parts of Asia and in Africa and Latin America.

Ever since the Opium War and the Taiping Rebellion Chinese leaders of differing beliefs and political persuasions had tended to be more or less at one in their hostility toward the West – even though many of them also admired Europe and the United States for economic, political and technological accomplishments. Under the Old Empire, during its latter years, the 'barbarian' and the 'foreign devil' were castigated. A generation later the imperialist and his Chinese 'running dogs' had become the major targets. Now, with a dynamic leadership and expectations of unprecedented economic and technological developments, the Peking régime began paying more and more attention to frontier areas which were perceived as having been unjustly appropriated from China by various foreign powers.

Sun Yat-sen had identified all the major treaty ports as Chinese territory lost to foreigners. 'In addition,' he wrote, 'there are those small countries which at one time paid tribute to China – the Loochoo [Ryukyu] Islands, Siam, Borneo, the Sulu Archipelago, Java, Ceylon, Nepal, Bhutan.' But these were only a part of what had been taken away. China had also lost Korea, Taiwan (Formosa), and the Pescadores, according to Sun. 'Still further back in the century we lost Burma and Annam . . . as soon as Annam was ceded to France, England occupied Burma, and China did not dare protest.'

To Russia, moreover, China had lost '. . . the Amur and Ussuri river basins and before that the area north of the Ili, Khokand and

Amur rivers . . . all of which China gave over with folded hands to the foreigner without so much as a question.'[21]

Sun also claimed certain regions south of the Himalayas as belonging to China rather than India.

Both Chiang Kai-shek and Mao Tse-tung identified the same vast territories as historically Chinese; this was one of the relatively few issues upon which they agreed.

In October 1950 Chinese Communist forces 'liberated' Tibet and established military and administrative headquarters. From that point on there were recurring reports of systematic Chinese extensions of influence into Nepal, Afghanistan, Bhutan, Sikkim, and India. Concurrently, there were also accounts of Chinese support of Viet Minh forces in Indo-China and of the establishment in Yunnan Province, near Burma–Thailand–Indochina borders, of a Thai People's Republic. And Peking soon found itself embroiled in a border dispute with Burma.

In consolidating their domestic control, the Peking régime frequently faced opposition by non-Chinese minorities: by Mongol groups in Inner Mongolia; by Kazakhs and Uighurs in Sinkiang; by Thai and other minorities in Yunnan; and elsewhere. In 1958, while putting down a revolt of dissident elements in Tibet, the Chinese found themselves involved in a border dispute with India.

For years there were border clashes, and in October 1962 a series of full-blown military engagements were fought between Chinese Communist and Indian Army contingents.

The Sino-Soviet controversy

In the meantime, differences in Soviet and Chinese Communist attitudes on a variety of issues had been developing into a major controversy. Undoubtedly, the Chinese still smarted from Khrushchev's failure to consult with them before unleashing his de-Stalinization program before the Twentieth Congress of the Communist Party of the Soviet Union in February 1956. But there were many other aspects.

The substantive issues separating Chinese and Russian Communist leaders were perhaps basic – disagreements about their own common frontiers and about rights and wrongs of the Sino-Indian border dispute; differing views about how the Soviet ICBM capacity ought to be used; divergent predispositions with respect to inter-state and inter-party relations and the exercise of authority within the Communist bloc; and so forth. But as the controversy developed, those aspects of it exposed to public view became more and more doctrinal. How should a Communist party achieve power in a former colony or semi-colony – and how should a party do so in an advanced industrial state? How should the transition be accomplished from the dictatorship of a bloc of revolutionary classes to a socialist state? Was the peaceful coexistence of states with differing social systems relatively feasible or infeasible? How inevitable or avoidable in the contemporary era was an 'imperialist war'? What were the possibilities for peaceful revolutions and for the avoidance of local as well as large-scale wars? These and other questions cut deep into the heart of Marxist–Leninist theory.

The dispute over Sino-Soviet boundaries was slow to emerge into the public view, but it was also bitter. Peking listed nine treaties between the two countries which Mao and his colleagues considered 'unequal' and not permanent. Three of these instruments – the Treaty of Aigun (1858), the Treaty of Peking (1860), and the Treaty of Ili (1881) – had ceded Chinese territory to Czarist Russia. Soviet areas claimed by China stretched from south of Alma Ata in Kzakhstan, nearly to Irkutsk; and from Vladivostok north to Nicolaevsk and west in the direction of Skovorodino and the Aldan Plateau. At some points along the long border there were armed clashes between the Russians and the Chinese.

Soviet attitudes during the Sino-Indian border struggle of October 1962 were also deeply galling for the Chinese. Indeed, Moscow had scarcely bothered to temper even for public view its fundamental sympathy for India during this crisis.

Disagreements with respect to the proper use of Soviet ICBM capacity dated as far back as Moscow's Twentieth Congress in February 1956. At that time Khrushchev and his Russian colleagues made clear that advances in nuclear weaponry rendered large-scale warfare unfeasible, with the consequence that the triumph of world Communism must be achieved without recourse to massive violence. There was, of course, a Marxist–Leninist precept that wars are inevitable as long as imperialism exists. According to Khrushchev, however, 'This precept was evolved at a time when 1 imperialism was an all-embracing world system, and 2 the social and political forces which did not want war were weak, poorly organized, and hence unable to compel the imperialists to renounce war.' Now a socialist encirclement of capitalism was replacing the old capitalist encirclement of socialism, and world wars had ceased to be fatalistically inevitable.

Mao and his colleagues maintained, on the other hand, that the imperialist threat was essentially the same, that the fundamental nature of imperialism had not changed. But in the long run China had nothing to fear from imperialism, as Mao saw it, nor was the nuclear threat to China as serious as some people seemed to think.

'The First World War was followed by the birth of the Soviet Union with a population of 200 million,' Mao asserted in his essay

The Paper Tiger, a cartoon from a collection devoted to the idea that history, in the long run, is on the side of Communism. Chinese Communist leaders concede, however, that for the immediate future the U.S. must be viewed as a real tiger. Many Western observers take the reverse view, arguing that the world Communist system has passed through its period of maximum cohesion.

On the Correct Handling of Contradictions Among the People. 'The Second World War was followed by the emergence of the Socialist camp with a combined population of 900 million. If the imperialists should insist on launching a third world war it is certain that several hundred million more will turn to socialism. Then there will not be much room left in the world for the imperialists, while it is quite likely that the whole structure of imperialism will utterly collapse.'[22]

The West (particularly the United States) was an immediate menace, but only a 'paper tiger' over the long haul. The economic, political and social forces of history were on the side of revolutionary socialism, and capitalism had no future. 'I consider that the present world situation has reached a new turning point,' Mao told a group of Chinese students at Moscow University in November 1957. 'There are now two winds in the world: the east wind and the west wind. There is a saying in China: "If the east wind does not prevail over the west wind, then the west wind will prevail over the east wind." I think the characteristic of the current situation is that the east wind prevails over the west wind, that is, the strength of socialism exceeds the strength of imperialism.'[23]

The Chinese Communists were openly critical of what they perceived as Soviet Russian caution and disappointed that Moscow was not using its own missile and nuclear capability more aggressively – not only in its own interests, but in the service of world revolution. Under these circumstances it was not surprising that

Communist leaders in Peking became deeply disturbed during the late 1950s and early 1960s by what they perceived as Soviet–American attempts to achieve a *détente* while leaving the People's Republic of China out in the cold. Negotiations pursued in the 'spirit of Camp David' – both during and after Khrushchev's conversations with Eisenhower in the American president's retreat – and photographs of the Soviet dictator cheerily banqueting with prominent members of the San Francisco bourgeoisie could scarcely be expected to stir enthusiasm in Communist China.

Meanwhile the Chinese and Russian leaderships each castigated the other for 'undermining the unity of the socialist camp'. And whatever else might be said for it, the controversy left an impression among outside observers that the Communist bloc, and indeed the Communist movement throughout the world, was undergoing strain, torment, and what might turn out to be a crucial rearrangement of its component parts and forces.

In the western world there was a widely-shared conclusion that the Sino-Soviet controversy and many of its outcomes were the consequence of *national* interests in China, Soviet Russia, and elsewhere taking more and more precedence over *Communist* interests – especially international Communist interests. Even more, perhaps, it was perceived as the consequence of a desire on the part of the Chinese and others to assert their independence of policies that were essentially in the Russian national interest, but which the Stalinist leadership had tried to invoke and sustain as universally Communist. In short, now that Stalin was dead, Mao Tse-tung and other Communist leaders were less willing to pay even lip service to the notion that what was good for Soviet Russia was necessarily good for them, too, or for the world Communist movement.

During the 1950s Mao Tse-tung and his colleagues seemed to have developed the view that the Soviet Union should refrain from interference in the domestic affairs of other Communist states which, in turn, should be consulted on issues of general concern. On the other hand, Peking had appeared to concede that the Soviet Union should enjoy a certain primacy in the formulation and execution of common policies. In line with this viewpoint, Communist China had bitterly condemned Tito for seeking a neutral position for Yugoslavia somewhere between the western and Communist camps, and, when Moscow seemed to hesitate, had urged a ruthless suppression of the 1956 Hungarian uprising. It was also in line with this predisposition, however, that Peking had supported Gomulka during the 1956 Polish revolt and had counseled Moscow to refrain from military action. For in the Hungarian case, the Communist party had lost control of the uprising, and there was real danger that the country might escape from the Communist camp. But the Polish revolt, by contrast, remained under Party control, and there was no intention of breaking away from the Communist camp or demanding more than the right to pursue a 'liberalized' and more distinctly Polish 'road to socialism'.

By the early 1960s, however, the recriminations tended to obscure the issues, and it was difficult to judge where the Chinese, Russian and other leaderships stood. A Pandora's box had been opened, and no one seemed capable of getting it shut.

Perspectives

Time was slipping away, meanwhile, and the top men in both Peking and Moscow were getting visibly older. Who would take their places, and how would these new leaderships respond to each other, to third nations, and to the rapidly changing environment? In October 1964 there occured two events which looked as though they might mark important turning points. In Moscow, Nikita Khrushchev was deposed from leadership, and in Communist China a team of scientists and technicians succeeded in exploding a nuclear device. Men and women throughout the world watched carefully for omens. The new leaders in Moscow were younger and bore the mark of industrial managers rather than old-line Party politicians or revolutionists. As for the nuclear

device, it was judged to be relatively small – less a weapon in its own right than a signal-fire announcing new status for the country that had set it off.

Many people in western nations expressed the hope that Soviet Russia had settled down after its revolutionary past and would be increasingly easy to deal with over the years. There were also feelings that Communist China ought to be drawn into nuclear negotiations, and that the Peking régime, now that it enjoyed a certain nuclear capacity, would grow more respectful of modern weaponry and its awesome implications.

In some of the newly emerging nations of Africa and Asia, on the other hand, the admiration for Communist China's achievements was enhanced. The feeling was that Chinese failures, almost gleefully underscored by the west, could not have been so dismal after all in view of the country's advance to nuclear status in less than a generation.

Where these matters actually stood, and what the trends were, only passing time could reveal, but it seemed safe to predict that China, the other Communist countries, and probably the whole world were already launched in a new, fast-moving and largely unprecedented era.

Chronology

1644	The Ch'ing, a foreign, Manchu dynasty, establishes rule over China.
1793	Earl of Macartney heads British Embassy to Chinese Court. Great Britain and other Western countries develop increasing interest in trade with China.
1839	Expansion of British commerce with China – particularly opium trade – leads to first Anglo-Chinese war; Imperial Chinese forces consistently defeated.
1842 August	Chinese Empire cedes to Great Britain island of Hong Kong. Treaty of Nanking also opens Canton, Amoy, Foochow, Ningpo and Shanghai to foreign residence.
1851	Local unrest and disorder in Kwangsi Province give rise to Taiping Rebellion; lasts ten years and costs estimated 10,000,000 Chinese lives.
1853 March	Taiping rebel armies under Hung Hsiü-ch'uan capture Nanking, make preparations for Northern Expedition against Manchu capital in Peking.
1856	Having failed to capture Peking, Taiping forces withdraw; revolutionary tide begins to recede. British, French, Russian and other foreign interests now free to expand throughout large areas of an exhausted China.
1858	Through series of treaties France, Great Britain, Russia and U.S. gain advantages of trade, residence, travel, and missionary activity in China. Treaties extended during 1859–60 to provide even further advantage for foreigners.
	Through Treaty of Aigun, Russia obtains from China territory extending east from Amur and Ussuri rivers to Pacific seaboard.
1860	Anglo-French forces occupy Peking. Tsarist Russia, acting as intermediary, promises to 'secure' for China a withdrawal which occupying powers have already planned. As a consequence Russia, through Convention of Peking, acquires title to large portions of Manchuria.

1864 19 July	Manchu troops, with support from Great Britain and other European interests, capture Nanking, Taiping capital.
1871	Russian troops occupy Ili territory of Chinese Turkestan to safeguard trade routes.
1879	Treaty of Livadavia cedes to Russia western part of Ili, together with mountain passes in Tien Shan ranges.
1881	Through Treaty of St Petersburg China re-acquires from Russia some of Turkestan territory lost by Treaty of Livadavia.
1894 1 August	Japan declares war on China, which is quickly defeated.
1895	China cedes Formosa, Pescadores Islands and Liaotung peninsula in Manchuria to Japan. Other Powers scramble for leases and concessions.
	Russia completes construction of first stage of Trans-Siberian Railway.
1896	Russia and China sign contract for construction of Chinese Eastern Railway across Manchuria, to be jointly operated.
1898	Tsarist Russian Government obtains from China 25-year lease of Dairen and Port Arthur areas for naval base; arrangements made for spur line to connect Dairen with Chinese Eastern Railway.
March	Port of Tsingtao leased to Germany for 99 years, German mining and railway concessions in Shantung Province assured. France obtains 99-year lease to Kwangchowan in Kwangtung. Great Britain acquires Wei-hai-wei for as long as Port Arthur is occupied by Russia.
1905	Sun Yat-sen organizes the T'ung-meng Hui, or Alliance Society, to overthrow Manchus, regenerate China, establish republic, and equalize land ownership. Organization forerunner of Kuomintang.

1911 9 October	Explosion in headquarters of Chinese revolutionary group in Wuchang touches off revolution which topples Manchu Dynasty.
1912 January	Having assumed Provisional Presidency of China, Sun Yat-sen finds himself powerless; presents office to Yüan Shih-K'ai, commander of Imperial forces, in exchange for securing Manchu abdication.
1914 August	Outbreak of World War I opens door for Japanese expansion in Asia, and offers to restless colonial peoples first possibilities for extensive organization and revolutionary intrigue against leading imperial powers.
1915	Kiakhta Agreement between China and Russia labels Outer Mongolia Chinese vassal state; actually transforms it into Tsarist protectorate.
	Taking advantage of World War I chaos, Japan presents China with Twenty-one Demands which extend Japanese political and economic encroachments over large areas of country.
1916	With death of Yüan Shih-k'ai prolonged struggle for power breaks out among Chinese provincial governors and other regional 'warlords'. Lacking own army, Sun Yat-sen forced to rely upon uneasy alliances with local military leaders.
1919 4 May	Japanese support of certain Chinese warlord leaders gives rise to outburst of student demonstrations.
25 July	In special declaration L. M. Karakhan of Soviet Union offers to abrogate Russian claims to Chinese Eastern Railway and other Soviet interests in China; subsequent negotiations prove frustrating to both sides.
1920	Local warlord Ch'en Ch'iung-ming occupies Canton, makes himself governor of Kwangtung Province, and invites Sun Yat-sen to establish Nationalist government there; now two Chinese governments – legal government in Peking, dubiously manned by shifting warlord combinations, and Sun's nationalist revolutionary government in Canton.

July–August	Lenin and M.N.Roy hammer out program for exploiting revolutionary nationalism in 'colonies and semi-colonies' of Asia, Africa and other parts of globe and for harnessing discontent against landowning and other privileged groups.
1921 July	Small group of Chinese intellectuals meet in Shanghai to found Chinese Communist Party.
August or Sept.	Sun Yat-sen confers with Henricus Sneevliet (Maring), delegate of Communist International to CCP.
	Young student-turned-Communist, Mao Tse-tung, helps organize mine workers near Hankow; Li Li-san establishes workers' school nearby.
1922 16 June	Ch'en Ch'iung-ming turns against Sun Yat-sen in sudden *coup*; Nationalist leader escapes to Shanghai.
August	Soviet Union sends A.A.Joffe to negotiate treaty relations with Peking; discussions drag on for nearly three years.
1923 January	After negotiations with legal Chinese government in Peking, Soviet representative Joffe concludes in Shanghai the Sun–Joffe Declaration with Sun Yat-sen which records Russian willingness to support Kuomintang struggle for 'national unification and independence'. Individual Chinese Communists begin joining Kuomintang.
21 February	Sun Yat-sen recovers Canton from Ch'en Ch'iung-ming with aid of rival combination of local militarists.
Summer	Sun Yat-sen sends Chiang Kai-shek for brief period of study with Red Army in Soviet Russia.
September	Soviet Union sends Michael Borodin to China as Comintern adviser to help reorganize Kuomintang.
1924 January	Under Borodin's influence, First Congress of Kuomintang reinterprets Sun Yat-sen's Three Principles of Nationalism, Democracy and the People's Livelihood.
May	Borodin and Soviet Military Adviser Galen (V.K.Blücher) supervise establishment of Whampoa Military Academy to train Kuomintang Army officers.

24 May	Soviet Union and legal Chinese government in Peking conclude Sino-Russian Agreement – Soviet officials simultaneously arranging funds, weapons and advisers for Sun Yat-sen's revolutionary nationalist movement in Canton.
18 June	Five members of Kuomintang Central Advisory Committee submit petition for impeachment of Communists working within Kuomintang.
7 October	First shipment of Soviet supplies reaches Canton as Kuomintang is threatened by private militia forces organized by local merchants.
1925 12 March	Sun Yat-sen dies in Peking. Factional disputes intensify within Kuomintang leadership. Left, Center and Right Wing groups become discernible. With support of Borodin and other Soviet advisers, Chiang Kai-shek achieves increasing military and political power.
1926 18 March	*Chung-shan* gunboat incident; Chiang Kai-shek strikes out against Chinese Communists and his Soviet advisers; relations soon patched up again.
6 July	Chiang Kai-shek elected Chairman of Standing Committee of Kuomintang Central Executive.
9 July	Chiang Kai-shek launches Northern Expedition against Peking Government; Soviet Union and CCP provide militant support; Chiang also dependent upon collaboration with various other military leaders.
Summer	Two opposition groups develop within CCP, one favouring withdrawal from Kuomintang, other urging a struggle to seize Kuomintang leadership; Party Central Committee condemns both proposals and requires continuing support for Chiang Kai-shek.
Autumn	Victorious sweep of Chiang Kai-shek's Northern Expedition brings Chinese Communists into direct touch with peasant masses ready to rebel against landlord class, which includes many Kuomintang leaders supported by Communists.

October   Fearing the peasant revolutionary groundswell may threaten Communist–Kuomintang alliance, Stalin wires Chinese Communists to restrain rebellious Chinese peasantry. Trotsky later uses this decision and others like it to criticize Stalin's leadership.

November   Seventh Plenum of Communist International, meeting in Moscow, urges policy of peasant revolt in China coupled with continuing Communist support for Kuomintang.

December   M. N. Roy leaves Moscow as Stalin's personal emissary charged with transforming Kuomintang into a 'real people's party – a solid revolutionary bloc of the proletariat, peasantry, urban petty bourgeoisie and other oppressed and exploited strata'.

1927
January   Tensions mount between Chiang Kai-shek and increasingly vocal Kuomintang Left Wing over allocation of supplies and money, location of party and governmental headquarters, and feasibility of a south-eastern campaign against Nanking and Shanghai.

7 March   Chiang Kai-shek issues public criticism of Borodin and other Soviet advisers, but reaffirms friendship for Soviet Union; Communists, both Russian and Chinese, increasingly divided over issue of continuing support for Chiang.

17 March   Stalin denies possibility that Chiang Kai-shek may turn against Communists in immediate future; re-asserts policy of supporting the Kuomintang. In the meanwhile, Communist underground forces in Shanghai storing weapons for possible use against Chiang's approaching forces.

22 March   Nationalist forces capture Shanghai, though Chiang Kai-shek himself still some distance off. Rumored that Communists are planning an attack.

24 March   Nationalist forces seize Nanking.

26 March   Chiang Kai-shek approaches Shanghai aboard gunboat; walks ashore without opposition, Communist underground forces having been ordered to bury all insurrectionary arms

and ammunition; Chiang reported to have established contact with alternate sources of funds in order to be no longer dependent on Moscow.

12 April   Shanghai Communists and their labor pickets systematically rounded up by Nationalist forces and all but annihilated.

Now a clear break between Chiang Kai-shek and Kuomintang Right on the one hand, and Kuomintang Left and their Communist collaborators.

21 April   Defending Stalinist policies in China, Communist press in Moscow and elsewhere asserts 'treachery' of Chiang Kai-shek not unexpected, but that it had been better to avoid battle than to be forcefully disarmed.

27 April   At Fifth Congress of CCP in Hankow, Borodin, M. N. Roy and various Chinese revolutionary leaders disagree over major issues; particularly divisive being continuing problem of how to support peasants without antagonizing Chinese military leaders of Kuomintang Left.

18 May   Hsia Tou-yin, commander of Kuomintang Left's Fourteenth Division, suddenly strikes out against Left régime and seeks to overthrow it.

21 May   Hsü Ke-hsiang and other officers of revolutionary forces also change sides, stage *coup d'état* in Changsha, and overthrow local governmental and party organs of Kuomintang Left. More than 20,000 peasants counter-attack under local Communist and Kuomintang Left leaders; checked by top Chinese Communist leaders in order to avoid antagonizing other military commanders of Left.

1 June   Borodin, Roy and other Comintern agents in Hankow receive telegram from Stalin urging organization of army under Communist and reliable pro-Communist officers. Roy shows telegram to Wang Ching-wei; Wang perceives it as threat, immediately strikes out against Communists.

27 July   Leaders of Kuomintang Left speed Borodin on return journey to Soviet Union; many Chinese Communists exe-

cuted in streets as Roy and other Comintern agents also leave Hankow; military and political leaders of Left already undertaking cautious negotiations with Chiang Kai-shek.

1 August   Communist officers Yeh T'ing and Ho Lung initiate uprising in Nanchang under direction of new Stalinist representative in China, Besso Lominadze; uprising achieves no lasting consequence.

7 August   Special conference of CCP, under Soviet pressure, condemns Ch'en Tu-hsiu and other top Chinese Communist leaders for restraining peasantry and 'retreating' in order to maintain alliance with Kuomintang Left.

24 September   Yeh T'ing's Communist forces occupy Swatow; soon put to flight by Kuomintang troops under General Chang Fa-k'uei.

October   After leading peasant contingents in abortive Autumn Harvest Uprising, Mao Tse-tung gathers together scattered Communist units; joins group of bandits in hide-out on Chingkan mountain. Survivors of Nanchang, Swatow and other engagements take refuge there.

11 December   Communist forces in Canton stage insurrection under supervision of young Stalinist agent Heinz Neumann; Soviet of Workers', Soldiers' and Peasants' Deputies established. Two days later uprising put down by General Chang Fa-k'uei; surviving Communist units eventually reach Mao Tse-tung's hide-out.

Mid-December   News of Canton defeat reaches Moscow. Victorious over Trotskyist opposition, Stalinist leadership asserts that Chinese revolution is gathering forces for new offensive on all fronts.

1928 February   Under Stalin's control Ninth Plenum of Communist International rejects Roy's defence of mission to China; responsibility for Canton defeat assigned to CCP, Heinz Neumann and other Comintern representatives in China.

After pitched battles in Hai-lu-feng region, Chu Teh and

contingent of Communist troops retreat before Chang Fa-k'uei's forces; join Mao Tse-tung and army at Ching-kanshan.

June   With Kuomintang capture of Peking, Chiang Kai-shek emerges as most powerful figure in China; Nationalist régime soon recognized by most foreign nations as legal government.

Spring and Summer   Mao Tse-tung, Chu Teh and other Communist leaders at Chingkanshan hold Red Army contingents together in struggle for survival.

Autumn   Moscow prescribes for China a program of armed insurrection essentially like that which failed in Canton.

After Sixth Congress of the CCP, held in Moscow, formal Party leadership identified with Li Li-san and militant policy he tries to implement; Mao Tse-tung's formal position in Party hierarchy ambiguous.

November   After months of patching together Red Army in Chingkanshan hide-out, Mao Tse-tung records that Central Committee expects to pursue guerrilla warfare over too large an area; supplies short, and base under frequent attack by Nationalist and local warlord forces.

1929
January   Mao Tse-tung and his Red Army units fight their way out of Chingkanshan into safer territory along Kwangtung border; finally establish new base around Juichin in southern Kiangsi.

Moscow warns CCP against over-anxious anticipation of a 'new revolutionary high tide', and also against failing to keep abreast of coming upsurge.

August   Mao Tse-tung and Chu Teh establish soviet régime in Kiangsi Province.

1930
11 June   Chinese Politburo resolves to coordinate peasant and proletarian struggles in order to attack Nationalist régime, perhaps touch off world-wide revolutionary struggle; Mao

Tse-tung's attitude toward Li Li-san policies not entirely clear.

1 August — Chinese Communists attack Changsha and seize city despite heavy fire from foreign gunboats; two days later begin to withdraw as expected proletarian uprising fails to materialize.

7 August — Publications of Communist International report Communist victory at Changsha.

September — Chinese Communist Third Plenum criticizes Li Li-san but asserts that his errors have been tactical rather than strategic.

November — Chiang Kai-shek undertakes first 'encirclement' campaign against soviet areas in Kiangsi Province.

7 November — Soviet leader Dimitri Manuilsky boasts about correctness of Soviet predictions and inevitability of growth of revolutionary upsurge in China; no indication of fundamental strategic difference between 'Moscow line' and 'Li Li-san line'.

16 November — Chinese Communist Central Committee receives from Moscow devastating attack on Li Li-san and policies; Li Li-san called to Moscow for explanation of failure.

December — Mao Tse-tung strikes down large number of opponents during Fut'ien Incident, but formal party leadership bestowed elsewhere.

1931
January — In China, Fourth Plenum installs new 'Returned Student' leadership sponsored by Soviet Union; in Moscow Li Li-san required to answer for failures.

May — Chiang Kai-shek launches second encirclement campaign.

July — Beginning of third encirclement campaign.

18 September — So-called Mukden Incident marks beginning of Japanese military aggressions in China. Chinese Communists soon undertake intensive campaign to deflect Nationalist hostilities away from soviet areas and against Japanese invaders.

7 November	First All-China Congress of Soviets convenes at Juichin, Kiangsi, establishes unified Chinese Soviet Republic; Communists now have own territory and government.
1932 April	Chinese Soviet Republic issues declaration of war against Japan.
May	Nationalists conclude armistice with Japan.
June	Initiation of fourth encirclement campaign.
1933 June	Delegates from Poor Peasant Corps called to conference on how to carry out revolutionary 'land investigation'.
October	Chiang Kai-shek launches fifth encirclement campaign.
Autumn	Though still inconclusive, encirclement campaigns begin to take economic and military toll of Chinese soviet areas; Communists condemn Chiang for not concentrating military power against Japanese forces in Manchuria.
1934 January	Second All-China Congress of Soviets finds Communist capital city of Juichin seriously endangered by Nationalist encirclement.
1 October	Juichin régime announces state of grave emergency, allows one week of mobilization for Long March from Kiangsi to North-west.
15 October	Main column of Long March leaves Juichin on year-long journey across vast reaches of China.
1935 January	Reaching Tsun-yi in Kweichow Province, main column of Long March halts for few days' rest and consultation; many sources date Mao Tse-tung's achievement of Party power from these meetings.
May	Long March enters Yunnan Province.
June	Main columns of Long March converge at Mao-erh-kai in western Szechuan Province; controversy erupts between Mao Tse-tung and Chang Kuo-t'ao, main rival for leadership.
1 August	From Mao-erh-kai Chinese Communists proclaim anti-

Japanese People's United Front; urge all classes to fight against Japan

2 August	Soviet Russian leaders proclaim world-wide united front policy against Axis powers.
October	After 368 days *en route*, main columns of Long March converge on Paoan in Shensi Province; provisional capital established; later, capital moved to Yenan.
1936 December	In Sian Chiang Kai-shek captured by non-Communist Chinese military leaders who urge that main war effort should be directed against Japanese; Communist role in Sian incident never fully clarified.
1937 March	Kuomintang, while asserting that it will continue to 'uproot the Communists', present formal proposals for an understanding; Chinese Communists agree to most of Nationalist proposals; an uneasy truce is achieved.
7 July	Japanese forces attack Chinese troops few miles south-west of Peking; Nationalists and Communists step-up cautious negotiations.
28 July	Japanese forces occupy Peking.
September	Nationalist government recognizes Communist garrison area in north-west known as Shensi-Kansu-Ningsia Border Region; Communists, in turn, declare willingness to abandon soviet government in favour of 'democracy based on the people's rights' and to reorganize troops into National Revolutionary Army under Nationalist government.
December	By this date nearly all major cities of northern China have fallen into Japanese hands.
1938 October.	In a report entitled *On the New Stage* Mao Tse-tung provides theoretical justification for Communist–Kuomintang collaboration.
1939 30 January	Chiang Kai-shek approves new Shansi-Chahar-Hopeh Border Region Government replacing Chinese soviet régime.

23 August	U.S.S.R. and Germany subscribe to Nazi–Soviet Pact.
30 September	Seemingly in line with Nazi–Soviet Pact, Mao Tse-tung describes World War II as another imperialist war in which *both sides* seek nothing but redivision of colonies and semi-colonies to their best advantage and spread of imperialism and fascism in one form or another.
October	Mao tells Party colleagues that without armed struggle, and especially guerrilla warfare, there would be no place for the working class, the Party, or the people – and no victory.
December	Mao publishes *The Chinese Revolution and the Chinese Communist Party* and *On the New Democracy* which take more critical view of Communist–Kuomintang relations and provide guidelines for post-war Party policy.
1940 February	Published as special article for wide Party circulation, extract from *On the New Democracy* asserts that there is only imperialist way and anti-imperialist way.
1941 January	Nationalist and Chinese Communist troops clash during so-called New Fourth Army Incident; heavy casualties on both sides.
1942 1 February	In Yenan, Mao Tse-tung inaugurates the *Cheng Feng*, or ideological remolding movement to train and indoctrinate Party membership down to lowest units; this helps to eliminate last vestiges within Party of opposition to Mao's leadership.
1943 Summer	Relations between Kuomintang and Chinese Communists and also between Soviet Union and Nationalist government worsen.
1 December	Meeting in Cairo, Churchill, Roosevelt and Chiang Kai-shek assert determination that Manchuria, Pescadores and Formosa be restored to Republic of China.
1944 Autumn	U.S. Military Intelligence issues report charging both Nationalist and Chinese Communist camps with expending more energy struggling against each other than in fighting Japanese.

1945 11 February	Churchill, Roosevelt and Stalin, without consulting China, sign Yalta Agreement identifying conditions under which Soviet Union will enter war against Japan.
14 August	Soviet Russian troops are moving into Manchuria as Japan, after Nagasaki and Hiroshima, proclaims readiness to surrender; subsequently, Soviet Union turns over to Chinese Communists large quantities of Japanese rifles seized during Manchurian occupation.
15 August	Soviet Union and Nationalist China conclude Treaty of Friendship and Alliance; proclamation well received in Nationalist China; enthusiasm cools when publication of agreements reached at Yalta suggest major terms of treaty formulated in advance.
October	Fighting between Nationalist and Communist forces begins to spread over large areas of mainland China; Nationalist-controlled areas seriously debilitated by inflation, black-market activities and governmental corruption; Communist guerrilla experience facilitates rapid movement of Mao's troops into many key areas.
November	President Truman appoints General Marshall to negotiate between Nationalist and Chinese Communist leaderships; situation, already complex, further confused by presence of Soviet troops in Manchuria, stripping of Manchurian industry by Russian forces, and well-founded Nationalist fears that whenever Russians leave, Chinese Communists will flow into vacuum.
1946 January	Chinese Communists and Nationalists achieve short-lived cease-fire agreement.
15 April	As remaining Russian units begin evacuating Manchuria, Chinese Communist troops attack and seize city of Chang-chun in direct violation of agreement previously concluded with Nationalists; Chiang, having over-extended lines to enter Manchuria, presents particularly vulnerable target.
1947 January– February	Despite evidence of Communist strength in northern China, Nationalists, with U.S. assistance, appear to be achieving

peak of military successes and territorial expansion; but Chinese Communist generals beginning to bring superior forces to bear precisely at points of Kuomintang over-extension.

30 May   U.S. Consul-General at Mukden reports that 'apathy, resentment and defeatism are spreading fast in Nationalist ranks causing surrenders and desertions'.

9 July   President Truman dispatches Lieutenant-General Wedemeyer on fact-finding mission to appraise economic, psychological and military situations in China and Korea.

19 September   In report condemning Chinese Communists, General Wedemeyer also criticizes 'reactionary leadership, re-pression and corruption' of Nationalist régime.

Autumn   Communist forces cut off important Nationalist garrisons in Manchuria.

1948 October   Numbers of Nationalist military leaders in Manchuria begin defecting to Communists, taking U.S.-supplied weapons and other equipment with them; estimated that third of a million men surrender or defect.

1949
January   Peking surrenders to Communists without a fight.

April   Communist forces cross Yangtze.

May   Shanghai falls to Communists.

1 October   In Peking Mao Tse-tung proclaims People's Republic of China; Chiang Kai-shek's headquarters already moved to Formosa.

8 December   Kuomintang régime declares Taipei in Formosa to be national capital.

1950 6 June   Mao Tse-tung tells Central Committee that in order to improve economic situation in China nation-wide agrarian reform must be completed, economies observed in govern-ment spending, and readjustments effected between com-merce and industry.

25 June	War breaks out between North Korean forces, Russian-trained and equipped, and South Korea.
July	Peking régime provides death sentence for counter-revolutionaries.
October	Chinese Communist troops begin entering Korea as 'People's Volunteers'.
	Chinese Communist forces enter Tibet, establish military and administrative headquarters.
1951 21 February	Mao Tse-tung demands imprisonment, life imprisonment or death for those guilty of counter-revolutionary activities.
1952 10 January	'3-Anti Campaign', initiated against 'corruption, decay and bureaucracy', followed by '5-Anti' struggle against bribery, tax evasion, theft of state assets and theft of state economic secrets.
1953 January	Inauguration of First Five-Year Plan.
October	Peking régime agrees to begin discussions at Panmunjom toward ending Korean War.
1954 28 June	Nehru and Chou En-lai issue *Panch Shila* ('Five Principles') to guide relations between two states.
September	Communists undertake first bombardment of Quemoy, but meet stubborn resistance.
1955 April	Asian–African conference in Indonesia, deeply influenced by Communist China, gives rise to 'Bandung Spirit' in relations between Peking and other nations, including India and Burma; this era of good feeling soon damaged, particularly by bitter disputes between Communist China and India.
1956 14 January	Khrushchev develops controversial thesis concerning 'the peaceful co-existence of the two systems'.
February	Chinese Communist leadership initiates 'Hundred Flowers Movement' in attempt to regain cooperation of intellectuals.

September	Mao Tse-tung and colleagues estimate three five-year plans needed for industrialization of China; Second Five-Year Plan proclaimed as program for pushing China into competition with West and well along toward 'pure' Communism.
1957 June	Communist leadership warns that right to 'bloom and contend' does not permit criticism in any way damaging to socialist construction.
August	U.S.S.R. demonstrates capacity to deliver nuclear warheads by long-range missile.
November	Mao Tse-tung tells group of Chinese students at Moscow University that the 'east wind prevails over the west wind, that is, the strength of socialism exceeds the strength of imperialism'.
1958 January–February	Peking régime inaugurates 'Great Leap Forward' in economic and technical development under slogan 'twenty years in a day'.
10 March	Armed rebellion breaks out against Chinese Communist régime in Tibet; soon put down.
May	General Liu Ya-lou, Commander of Communist Chinese Air Force, predicts that China will produce nuclear weapons and rockets 'in the not-distant future'.
August–October	Chinese Communists undertake second major bombardment of Quemoy and neighboring island of Matsu; again Nationalist resistance stubborn. Close observers become increasingly aware of differences between Soviet and Chinese Communist attitudes in crisis and in other spheres of mutual concern.
September	Mao Tse-tung urges creation of people's communes.
1959 Spring and Summer	Peking accuses India of supporting Tibetan revolt; lays claim to nearly 40,000 square miles of territory inside Indian borders.
Summer	Peking régime strengthens military concentrations along Tibetan–Indian frontiers.

26 August	Chinese Communist leaders admit 1958 production figures seriously exaggerated; drastic reductions being made in 1959 output goals.
4 September	In Moscow *Tass* news agency publishes first public attack in Sino-Soviet controversy with severe criticism of Peking's position in Sino-Indian border dispute.
26 October	Ministry of Foreign Affairs in Peking, asserts that considerable territory inside India's northern frontier 'has always been Chinese territory'.
1960	Mao Tse-tung begins issuing series of public statements denouncing 'imperialists' and assuring Chinese support for peoples of Asia, Africa and Latin America.
16 April	In editorial entitled 'Long Live Leninism' Chinese Communist leadership launches detailed and bitter attack against 'revisionists' who 'whitewash the war preparations of the imperialists'.
May–September	Soviet Union starts withdrawing thousands of technicians from China.
1962 October	Chinese Communist troops invade India along Himalayan frontier – and as suddenly withdraw.
1964 October	Communist China explodes nuclear device; Khrushchev deposed from leadership in Soviet Union.

Biographical register

A. Albrecht. One of three young Soviet representatives in China, highly critical of Stalinist policies there during the winter and spring of 1927; co-author of the 'Letter from Shanghai'.

V. K. Blücher (Galen). Soviet military adviser to the Kuomintang who supervised the establishment of the Whampoa Military Academy.

Michael Borodin (Gruzenberg). Agent of the Communist International in China (1924–7) and adviser to the Kuomintang.

N. I. Bukharin. Soviet leader and major theoretician who helped shape Soviet policies toward China, but was purged by Stalin in the 1930s.

Chang Fa-k'uei. Commander of the Kuomintang 'Ironsides' division who supported the Kuomintang Left in 1927, but later switched allegiance to Chiang Kai-shek; a major figure in the suppression of the Canton Commune in December 1927.

Chang Hsueh-liang. Son of Chang Tso-lin, known as the 'Young Marshal of Manchuria'; one of the kidnappers of Chiang Kai-shek at Sian during December 1946.

Chang Kuo-t'ao. A founder of the Chinese Communist Party who was Mao Tse-tung's major rival for leadership in the Chinese Communist movement during the 1930s.

Chang Tso-lin. Warlord in Manchuria who vied with Wu P'ei-fu and other warlords of northern China for control of the official government in Peking during the 1920s.

Chang Tsung-ch'ang. Warlord whose power centered in the region around Shantung.

Chang Wen-t'ien (Lo Fu). An influential member of the 'Returned Student Clique' who was active in Chinese Communist leadership during the 1930s.

Ch'en Ch'iung-ming. A warlord whose power was based in Kwangtung.

Ch'en Kung-po. A founder of the Chinese Communist Party in July 1921.

Ch'en Shao-yu. See *Wang Ming.*

Ch'en T'an-ch'iu. A founder of the Chinese Communist Party who wrote an account of the meetings many years in retrospect.

Ch'en Tu-hsiu. Intellectual and revolutionary leader, virtually the father of the Chinese Communist movement, later dismissed from leadership for alleged errors and deviations.

Theodore H. E. Chen. American scholar who has examined confessions and other documents written by Chinese intellectuals during the reform of 1951–2.

Chiang Kai-shek. Commandant of the Kuomintang's Whampoa Military

Academy during the early 1920s and heir to Sun Yat-sen's leadership of the Kuomintang.

G.V.Chicherin. People's Commissar of Foreign Affairs in the Soviet Union during the early 1920s.

Ch'in Pang-hsien (Po Ku). An influential member of the 'Returned Student Clique' who was active in Chinese Communist leadership during the 1930s.

Chou En-lai. Veteran Communist leader and Premier of the Chinese People's Republic.

Chou Fu-hai. One of the founders of the Chinese Communist Party in July 1921

Ch'ü Ch'iu-pai. A Communist leader who was prominent in the 7 August 1927 conference, and was later charged by the Comintern with duplicity with respect to attitudes toward Li Li-san.

Chu Teh. Veteran Communist general who joined with Mao Tse-tung in founding the Chinese Red Army and establishing the Soviet government in Kiangsi during the late 1920s and early 1930s.

Feng Yü-hsiang. Known also as the 'Christian General', whose power was based in Honan and Shensi and who collaborated with the Soviet Russians during the mid-1920s.

N.Fokine. One of three young Soviet representatives in China, highly critical of Stalinist policies there during the winter and spring of 1927; co-author of the 'Letter from Shanghai'.

Galen. See *Blücher*.

Gruzenberg. See *Borodin*.

Frederick W.Hinke. American Vice-Consul who reported details of the Canton insurrection of December 1927.

Ho Lung. Veteran Communist general influential in early years of the Chinese Red Army.

Hsia Tou-yin. Commander of the Kuomintang Fourteenth Division who rebelled against the Kuomintang Left on 18 May 1927.

Hsü K'e-hsiang. A Kuomintang general who staged a *coup d'état* against the Kuomintang Left in Changsha on 21 May 1927 – just after Hsia Tou-yin's revolt.

Hsü Meng-ch'iu. A veteran of the Long March interviewed subsequently by Nym Wales.

Hung Hsiu-ch'üan. The titular head of the Taiping movement which rebelled against the empire in the 1850s.

Jay Calvin Huston. American Vice-Consul who reported details of the Canton insurrection of December 1927.

A.A.Joffe. Soviet diplomat who negotiated with the Chinese government in Peking and also with Sun Yat-sen during the early 1920s.

L.M.Karakhan. Soviet diplomat and author of the Karakhan Declaration of 1919 who negotiated with the Chinese government authorities in the early 1920s.

Liao Chung-k'ai. Leader of the Kuomintang Left, mysteriously assassinated 20 August 1925.

Li Chi-shen. Kuomintang general who belonged to the Right in 1927 but served as one of six vice-chairmen of the People's Republic of China after 1949; a major figure in the suppression of the Canton Commune in December 1927.

Li Han-chün. A founder of the Chinese Communist Party, executed by counter-revolutionary forces in 1923.

Li Li-san. Controversial leader of the Chinese Communist Party, deposed after the failure of his policies during 1930 but partially reinstated after World War II.

Lin Piao. Veteran Chinese Red Army general who commanded a column during the Long March.

Lin Tse-hsü. Imperial High Commissioner and director of the Chinese Emperor's War Board who negotiated with the British at the time of the Opium War in 1839.

Li Pao-chang. A northern military leader who became commander of the Eighth Nationalist Army in 1927.

Li Ta-chao. Chinese intellectual and revolutionary who influenced early phases of the Chinese Communist movement.

Liu Jen-ch'ing. A founder of the Chinese Communist Party in July 1921, denounced a decade later as a Trotskyite.

Liu Po-ch'eng. Veteran Chinese Red Army General.

Liu Shao-ch'i. Veteran Communist leader and Party theoretician from Hunan who is believed to be ranked second only to Mao Tse-tung since the establishment of the People's Republic.

Besso Lominadze. A young Georgian Communist, protegé of Joseph Stalin, who planned the Nanchang Uprising of 1 August 1927.

Lo Fu. See *Chang Wen-t'ien.*

Lo Ping-hui. A Chinese Red Army general who participated in major engagements while the policies of Li Li-san were in force during 1930.

Dimitri Z. Manuilsky. Soviet leader and theoretician who predicted in 1926 that the United States, Japan and Great Britain would fight a major war in the Pacific.

Mao Tse-tung. A founder of the Chinese Communist Party in July 1921 who rose to top leadership of the Party and of the People's Republic of China.

Maring. See *Henricus Sneevliet.*

General George C. Marshall. Distinguished American military officer charged by President Truman after World War II with the task of bringing United States influence to bear upon Communist–Kuomintang conflicts.

Pavel Mif. Soviet theoretician who wrote extensively about China and installed the so-called 'Returned Student' leadership over the Chinese Communist movement in late 1930.

N. Nassonov. One of three young Soviet representatives in China highly critical of Stalinist policy there during the winter and spring of 1927; co-author of the 'Letter from Shanghai'.

Heinz Neumann. A young German Communist who called the 7 August 1927 conference of Chinese Communist leaders and planned the Canton insurrection of the following December.

Pao Hui-sheng. A founder of the Chinese Communist Party who later defected to the Kuomintang.

Brigadier General P. E. Peabody. Chief of United States Military Intelligence who reported in detail on political and military conditions in China during World War II.

P'eng P'ai. A young intellectual who founded the Hai-lu-feng Soviet in the early 1920s.

P'eng Te-huai. Veteran Communist general who helped Mao Tse-tung and Chu Teh in organizing the Red Army and devoted his life to Chinese Communist military affairs.

Po Ku. See *Pang-hsien.*

M. N. Roy. Indian revolutionary nationalist who joined the Communist movement in 1920 and represented Stalin in China during the spring of 1927.

Henricus Sneevliet (Maring). A Hollander representing the Communist International in China during the early 1920s.

Edgar Snow. American correspondent, author of the enduring volume *Red Star Over China*, who interviewed Mao Tse-tung after the Long March.

George Sokolsky. American correspondent who reported revolutionary events in China – particularly the struggle between Chiang Kai-shek and the Communists during the mid-1920s.

Sun Ch'uan-fang. A warlord whose power was centered in the eastern provinces of China with Shanghai as a major base.

Sun Yat-sen. Founder of the Kuomintang and father of the Chinese revolution of the early twentieth century.

Tai Chi-t'ao. Veteran Kuomintang leader and anti-Communist theoretician.

T'ang Sheng-chih. A warlord in Hunan who supported the Kuomintang Left in late 1926 and early 1927.

T'an P'ing-shan. Chinese Communist leader who held important positions in the government of the Kuomintang Left during the winter and spring of 1927.

Ts'ai Ho-shen. Veteran Communist and Party historian who wrote a valuable account of Communist–Kuomintang relations during 1926 and 1927.

G.N. Voitinsky. Comintern representative in China during the mid-1920s.

Nym Wales. Pseudonym for Mrs Helen Snow, author of *Red Dust*, who interviewed Chinese Communist leaders after the Long March.

Wang Cheng. A Chinese Red Army general who participated in major engagements while the policies of Li Li-san were in force during 1930.

Wang Ching-wei. Leader of the Kuomintang Left during 1926–27, who collaborated with the Japanese during the late 1930s.

Wang Ming (Ch'en Shao-yü). A member of the 'Returned Students Clique' who was an important influence in the Chinese Communist Party during the 1930's.

Lieutenant General Albert C. Wedemeyer. An American officer dispatched by President Truman on 9 July 1947 to appraise the political, economic, psychological and military situations in China and Korea.

Wei Li-huang. Nationalist general during World War II.

Wu P'ei-fu. Northern Chinese warlord who contended with Chang Tso-lin and other warlords for control of the official Chinese government in Peking during the 1920s.

Yang Cheng-wu. A veteran of the Long March who wrote an account of the Luting Bridge crossings many years later.

Yang Hu-ch'eng. 'Pacification Commissioner' of Shensi who, together with Chang Hsüeh-liang, kidnapped Chiang Kai-shek at Sian in December 1936.

Yeh T'ing. An early Chinese Communist general who played an important role in formative phases of the Chinese Red Army.

Yen Hsi-shan. A warlord with power in Shansi.

Yüan Shih-k'ai. A general in the Imperial Chinese Army who was invited by Sun Yat-sen to be the first president of republican China.

Bibliography and notes

If a book has been published both in the United States and in Britain both publishers are listed, the American one being named first. Dates are of first publication.

1 China and the challenge of the West

BIBLIOGRAPHY

For traditional Chinese views of the Empire see J. K. Fairbank and S. Y. Teng, 'On the Ch'ing Tributary System', *Harvard Journal of Asiatic Studies*, VI, No. 4 (June 1941), 138–9; and M. C. Wright, *The Last Stand of Chinese Conservatism*, Stanford University Press/O.U.P., 1957. English translations of Lin's letters are in *The Chinese Repository* (*1832–51*), edited by E. C. Bridgman and S. Wells Williams, the former a missionary and the latter United States Chargé d'Affairs in Canton. Editorially, *The Repository* tended to be hostile toward the opium trade and sympathetic with the Chinese. Documents are also available in P. C. Kuo, *A Critical Study of the First Anglo-Chinese War*, Stechert/Kegan Paul, 1935; and see D. E. Owen, *British Opium Policy in China and India*, Yale University Press/O.U.P., 1934. For critical commentary consult Arthur Waley, *The Opium War Through Chinese Eyes*, Macmillan/Allen and Unwin, 1958. General sources for China's relations with other powers in the nineteenth and early twentieth centuries include H. B. Morse, *The International Relations of the Chinese Empire*, Longmans, New York and London, 1910; E. T. Backhouse and J. O. P. Bland, *Annals and Memoirs of the Court of Peking*, Houghton Mifflin/Heinemann. 1914; W. W. Rockhill, *Treaties and Conventions With or Concerning China and Korea, 1894–1904*, Government Printing Office, Washington, 1904; T. W. Overlach, *Foreign Financial Control in China*, Macmillan, New York and London, 1919; W. W. Willoughby and C. G. Fenwick, *Types of Restricted Sovereignty and of Colonial Autonomy*, Government Printing Office, Washington, 1919. For the Taiping Rebellion see J. C. Cheng, *Chinese Sources for the Taiping Rebellion, 1850–64*, Hong Kong University Press, 1964; and E. P. Boardman, *Christian Influence Upon the Ideology of the Taiping Rebellion, 1851–64*, University of Wisconsin Press, 1952. Differing views of the 1911 revolution are found in C. T. Hsueh, *Huang Hsing and the Chinese Revolution*, Stanford University Press, 1961; R. L. Powell, *The Rise of Chinese Military Power, 1895–1912*, Princeton University Press/O.U.P., 1955; H. F. MacNair, *Modern Chinese History: Selected Readings*, Stechert, New York, 1923; F. Farjenel, *Through the Chinese Revoloution*, Stokes, New York, 1916;

A. J. Brown, *The Chinese Revolution*, Student Volunteer Movement, New York, 1912; Editorial, *The Chinese Recorder and Missionary Journal*, XLII, No. 11 (November 1911), 614.

Attitudes of intellectuals after the 1911 revolution will be found in T. C. Wang, *The Youth Movement in China*, New Republic, New York, 1927, and Chow Tse-tsung, *The May Fourth Movement*, Harvard University Press/O.U.P., 1960. Mao Tse-tung's recollections of the period are in E. Snow, *Red Star Over China*, Random House/Gollancz, 1944, pp. 136–8. The First Congress can be reconstructed from Chen Pan-tsu (Ch'en T'an-ch'iu), 'Reminiscences of the First Congress of the Communist Party of China', *Communist International* (October 1936), pp. 1361–3; C. M. Wilbur (ed.), *The Communist Movement in China*, East Asia Institute of Columbia University, 1960; and Nym Wales, *Red Dust*, Stanford University Press/ O.U.P., 1952, pp. 39–40.

NOTES

1 *Repository*, III, No. 7, 423
2 Backhouse and Bland, 325–6
3 Boardman, 34
4 *Repository*, VIII, No. 10, 497–503
5 *Repository*, VIII, No. 1, 9–12
6 Kuo, 250–1
7 *Repository*, VIII, No. 9, 489–93
8 *Chinese Recorder*, XLII, No. 11, 614
9 Chen Pan-tsu, 1362–3

2 The great empires and their disintegration

BIBLIOGRAPHY

German imperial aspirations and policies are scattered through many sources. Those used in this chapter include *Memoirs of Prince von Bulow*, Vol. I, Little Brown, Boston, 1931; and annotations by Kaiser Wilhelm II in M. Montgelas and W. Schücking (edd.), *Outbreak of the War: German Documents Collected by Karl Kautsky*, Carnegie Endowment for International Peace, New York, 1924, p. 350. Imperial plans for disrupting the British Empire can be found in United States of America vs. Franz Bopp, *et al.*, *Reporter's Transcript*, Vols. 1–40, 6–75, 6133 India Office Manuscript No. MSS. Eu. C. 138; in General Records of the United States Department of Justice, File No. 193424, Section I; and in India, Sedition Committee,

Report, Calcutta, Superintendent Government Printing, India, 1918; see also G. T. Brown, *The Hindu Conspiracy and the Neutrality of the United States, 1914–17*, M.A. Thesis, University of California, 1914.

Woodrow Wilson's concepts of self-determination and his hopes for a post-war world appear in R. S. Baker and W. E. Dodd (edd.), *War and Peace: Presidential Messages, Addresses and Public Papers (1917–24) by Woodrow Wilson*, Harper, New York, 1927, Vol. I, p. 63; Vol. II, pp. 5, 11.

For attitudes of Mao Tse-tung see Emi Siao, *Mao Tse-tung, His Childhood and Youth*, People's Publishing House, Bombay, 1955; and Mao Tse-tung, 'The New Democracy', in *The Strategy and Tactics of World Communism*, Supplement III, 'Communism in China', Government Printing Office, Washington, 1949. The post-war disillusion of many Chinese intellectuals is described by Chow Tse-tung, *op. cit.*, W. H. Kiang, *The Chinese Student Movement*, King's Crown Press/O.U.P., 1948; *New Youth*, I, No. 1 (September 1915) as quoted in T. C. Wang, op. cit. p. 99.

J. T. Murphy, *New Horizons*, Bodley Head, London, 1941, provides recollections of the Second Congress. For proceedings consult – but use with care – *The Second Congress of the Communist International*, Moscow, 1920; for a more complete and reliable source, use *Vtoroi Kongress Kominterna, iiul-avgust, 1920g*, Moscow, 1934, pp. 490–6; for ready reference, see X. J. Eudin and R. C. North, *Soviet Russia and the East*, Stanford University Press/O.U.P., 1957.

NOTES

 1 von Bulow, 224
 2 United States vs. Franz Bopp
 3 Kautsky, 350
 4 Baker and Dodd, I, 63; also II, 5, 11
 5 *Radical Humanist*, XVIII, No. 23, 270; and No. 24, 283–4
 6 Siao, 112
 7 Wang, 99
 8 *Ibid.*, 161–2
 9 Mao, 'New Democracy', *Strategy and Tactics*, III, 86
10 Murphy, 104
11 *Vtoroi Kongress*, 490–6
12 Eudin and North, 64–5
13 *Vtoroi Kongress*, 499 ff.
14 Eudin and North, 66

3 The Communist–Nationalist collaboration

BIBLIOGRAPHY

Early Soviet Russian relations with groups in China are analysed in A. S. Whiting, *Soviet Policies in China, 1917–24*, Columbia University Press/ O.U.P., 1954; and Eudin and North, *Soviet Russia and the East*, cited for chapter 2, which also contains documents.

The period from 1911 until the mid-1920s is a difficult one, and reliable documentation is not plentiful. For the succession of warlord governments in Peking, see H. F. MacNair, *China in Revolution*, University of Chicago Press/C.U.P., 1931. Early phases of the Kuomintang are discussed in L. S. L. Hsü, *Sun Yat-sen, His Political and Social Ideals*, University of Southern California Press, 1933; *The China Year Book, 1924–25*; *The China Year Book, 1928*; T. C. Woo, *The Kuomintang and the Future of the Chinese Revolution*, Allen and Unwin, London, 1928; and A. N. Holcombe, *The Chinese Revolution*, Harvard University Press/O.U.P., 1930. Kuomintang leftist views are presented in Tang Leang-li, *The Inner History of the Chinese Revolution*, Dutton/Routledge, 1930. Observations of an American correspondent appear in G. Sokolsky, *The Tinder Box of Asia*, Doubleday/Allen & Unwin, 1932, p. 336.

Standard books, monographs and documentary collections on Sino-Soviet relations during the 1920s include C. Brandt, *Stalin's Failure in China, 1924–27*, Harvard University Press/O.U.P., 1958; H. R. Issacs, *The Tragedy of the Chinese Revolution*, 2nd revised edition, Stanford University Press, 1961; R. C. North, *Moscow and Chinese Communism*, 2nd edition, Stanford University Press, 1963; B. Schwartz, *Chinese Communism and the Rise of Mao*, Harvard University Press/O.U.P., 1951; C. Brandt, B. Schwartz and J. K. Fairbank, *A Documentary History of Chinese Communism*, Harvard University Press/Allen & Unwin, 1952; and C. M. Wilbur and J. L. Y. How, *Documents on Communism, Nationalism, and Soviet Advisers in China, 1918–27*, Columbia University Press/O.U.P., 1956.

Comintern and Soviet sources include *International Press Correspondence* (cf. English, French, Russian and German editions); *Kommunisticheskii International v dokumentakh*, Moscow, 1933; and G. Kara-Murza and P. Mif, *Strategiia i taktika Kominterna v natsionalno-kolonialnoi revoliutsii na primere Kitaia*, Moscow, 1934.

NOTES
1   Wilbur and How, 85
2   Isaacs, 63

242

3 Mitarevsky, 130
4 Brandt, Schwartz and Fairbank, 72
5 Woo, 253
6 Wilbur and How, 186–99
7 *Ibid.*, 255
8 *Ibid.*, 264
9 *Ibid.*, 411
10 *Ibid.*, 418

4 The Communist–Nationalist split

BIBLIOGRAPHY

Soviet and Comintern materials for 1926 and 1927 relations with revolutionary events in China include most of those listed for chapter 3. Other sources are D. Z. Manuilsky, in *International Press Correspondence*, 30 December 1926, pp. 1592–7; *Puti mirovoi revoliutsii*, Moscow, 1927; J. Stalin, *International Press Correspondence*, 23 December 1926, pp. 1581–4; and also Stalin's *Marxism and the National and Colonial Question*, International Publishers/Lawrence & Wishart, 1935; N. I. Bucharin, 'Tekushchii moment kitaiskoi revoliutsii', *Pravda*, No. 145, 30 June 1927; and P. Mif, *Kitaiskaia Kommunisticheskaia Partiia v kriticheskie dni*, Gosizdat, Moscow, 1928.

Criticisms from Stalin's opposition in Moscow and from Comintern agents in China are in L. Trotsky, *Problems of the Chinese Revolution*, Pioneer Publishers, New York, 1932, especially Vuyo Vuyovich at the Eighth Plenum and 'The Letter from Shanghai'. Another excellent critical source is H. Isaacs, *The Tragedy of the Chinese Revolution*, cited for the previous chapter. 'Minutes of the Chinese Sub-Committee of the ECCI', *The New Militant*, New York, 8 February 1936, is a third critical source. The role of M. N. Roy is documented in R. C. North and X. J. Eudin, *M. N. Roy's Mission to China*, University of California Press/C.U.P., 1963; and also M. N. Roy, *Revolution and Counter-Revolution in China*, Renaissance Publishers, Calcutta, 1946, p. 517. Other data will be found in the Wilbur and How volume and in Ts'ai Ho-shen, *Problemy Kitaia*, No. 1, Moscow, 1929. A translation of Mao Tse-tung's 'Investigation of the Peasant Movement' is in Brandt, Schwartz and Fairbank, *A Documentary History*, pp. 80–9; Chiang Kai-shek's address to the Kuomintang, 19 February 1927, is in P. Leon Wieger, *et al.*, *Chine Moderne*, 2nd edition, Vol. VIII (n.d.), 1920–34, pp. 23–4; and for a participant's recollections of the

Hsü K'e-Hsiang *coup*, see Wang Cheng to Nym Wales, *Red Dust*, pp. 92–3.

NOTES

1   IPC, 30 December 1926, 1592–7
2   *Ibid.*, 23 December 1926, 1581–4
3   Text in *M. N. Roy's Mission*, 131–45
4   IPC, 23 December 1926, 1584
5   Trotsky, 403
6   *Ibid.*, 407
7   *Ibid.*, 406
8   Wieger, 23–4
9   Wilbur and How, 388; also *North China Herald*, 2 April 1928, 28
10 Trotsky, 389
11 *China Year Book, 1928*, 1360
12 Trotsky, 411
13 *New York Times*, 3 April 1927
14 IPC, 14 April 1927, 493
15 Trotsky, 431
16 *M. N. Roy's Mission*, 199
17 Mif, 45–6
18 *M. N. Roy's Mission*, 82
19 *Ibid.*, 101
20 *Revolution and Counter-Revolution*, 551
21 *New Militant*, 8 February 1936
22 *Marxism and the National and Colonial Question*, 249
23 Ts'ai Ho-shen, 50
24 Bucharin, *Pravda*, 30 June 1927

5 Mao Tse-tung, the Red Army and the Chinese soviets

BIBLIOGRAPHY

Until recently Chinese Communist events between 1927 and 1934 have remained obscure, and even now the sources are largely in Chinese – available only in a few research collections.

The August Plenum is partially documented in Brandt, Schwartz and Fairbank, *op. cit.* and in other works already listed. For recollections of the Nanchang Uprising see Lo Ping-hui, Hsiao K'e, Cheng Tzu-hua and Nieh Ho-t'ing to Nym Wales in *Red Dust*. J. Guillermaz, 'The Nanchang Uprising', *The China Quarterly*, No. 11, July–September 1962, pp. 161–8, provides historical analysis.

The Hai-lu-feng soviet is discussed by S. Eto, 'Hai-lu-feng: The First Chinese Soviet Government', *The China Quarterly*, No. 8. October–December 1961, pp. 161–83, and No. 9, January–March 1962, pp. 149–81.

Sources for the Canton Uprising are A. Neuberg (H. Neumann), *L'Insurrection Armée*, Bureau d'editions, Paris, 1931; Teng Chen-hsia, 'The Canton Commune and the Tactics of the Communist Party', and F. W. Hinke, 'The Communist Coup d'État at Canton', in the J. C. Huston Collection, Hoover Institution, Stanford, California; and *Räte China, Dokumente der Chinesischen Revolution*, Moscow–Leningrad, 1934, pp. 139–65.

For a Red Army general's recollections see Hsü Hsiang-ch'ien to Nym Wales, *Red Dust*, 150.

English language sources for the Chingkangshan and Kiangsi periods include Mao's *Selected Works*, Vols. I and II, International Publishers/Lawrence & Wishart, 1954; T. L. Hsiao, *Power Relations within the Chinese Communist Movement, 1930–34*, University of Washington Press, 1961; E. Snow, *op. cit.*, 'The VI World Congress . . .', *International Press Correspondence*, 12 December 1928, p. 1672; Chou En-lai, 'Report on the Third Plenum', in Brandt, Schwartz and Fairbank, *op. cit.*, pp. 200–8.

For Sino-Soviet relations during the 1930s see – in addition to sources already listed – C. McLane, *Soviet Policy and the Chinese Communists, 1931–46*, Columbia University Press/O.U.P., 1958.

NOTES

1   *Documentary History*, 102–18
2   Mao, *Selected Works*, I, 99
3   *Ibid.*, 85
4   *Ibid.*, 116, 121
5   IPC, 17 July 1930, 589, 595
6   *Red Dust*, 123–4
7   *Ibid.*, 97–8
8   IPC, 7 August 1930, 698
9   *Red Dust*, 124
10 *Ibid.*, 98

6 Kiangsi Soviet and the Long March

BIBLIOGRAPHY

The most useful English language bibliographies of Chinese sources for this generally obscure period are C. T. Hsüeh, *The Chinese Communist Movement, 1921–37*, and *The Chinese Communist Movement, 1937–49*, Hoover Institution, Stanford, California, 1960 and 1962.

The peasantry is discussed in V. I. Lenin, *Selected Works*, III, pp. 145–6, and in *Sochinenia* (Gosudarstvennoe izdatel'stvo), XXIV, p. 314; also VII, pp. 190–1, and VIII; Mao, 'The Struggle in the Chingkang Mountains', *Selected Works*, I, pp. 87–8; and in Chinese documents available in the Hoover Institution, Stanford University and in a few other repositories. For an analytical treatment of many of these materials see T. L. Hsiao, *Power Relations within the Chinese Communist Movement, 1930–34*, cited in the previous chapter. Descriptions of the Long March include E. Snow's classic account in *Red Star Over China*; interviews with survivors in Nym Wales, *Red Dust*; and *The Long March, Eyewitness Accounts*, Foreign Languages Press, Peking, 1963.

NOTES

 1 Mao, *Selected Works*, I, 128
 2 Lenin, *Selected Works*, III, 145–6
 3 *Red Dust*, 64–5
 4 *Ibid.*
 5 *Eyewitness Accounts*, 1
 6 *Red Dust*, 65
 7 Snow, 197–8
 8 *Red Dust*, 69
 9 *Ibid.*
10 *Eyewitness Accounts*, 82
11 *Red Dust*, 72
12 *Ibid.*
13 Snow, 205
14 *Red Dust*, 72
15 *Eyewitness Accounts*, 107

7 Border region governments and the Japanese War

BIBLIOGRAPHY

Communist political developments in the Border Regions are documented in Mao's *Selected Works*. Care must be used, however, since documents of the time were sometimes altered before their inclusion in either the Chinese or English editions of Mao's works. Material for the *Cheng Feng* movement has been translated in B. Compton, *Mao's China: Party Reform Documents, 1942–44*, University of Washington Press, 1952. An impression of the Chinese Communist governments in the northwest can be derived from *Laws and Regulations of the Shensi-Kansu-Ninghsia Border Region* (n.p., n.d.), p. 17. An excellent analysis of the period is provided by C. A. Johnson, *Peasant Nationalism and Communist Power: The Emergence of Revolutionary China, 1937–45*, Stanford University Press/O.U.P., 1962.

Nationalist policies are stated in *Collected Wartime Messages of Generalissimo Chiang Kai-shek, 1937–45*, John Day, New York, 1946. For analyses from a perceptive American viewpoint consult 'Chinese Communist Movement', Washington, D.C.: Military Intelligence Division, War Department, 1945, reproduced by the United States Senate, Committee on the Judiciary, *Institute of Pacific Relations, Hearings Before the Sub-committee to Investigate the Administration of the Internal Security Act and Other Security Laws*, Part 7A, Appendix II, United States Government Printing Office, Washington, 1952, cited hereafter as *Hearings*.

Soviet influences in Sinkiang are examined by A. S. Whiting in *Sinkiang: Pawn or Pivot*, Michigan State University Press, 1958.

NOTES

 1 Mao, *Selected Works*, III, 190
 2 Compton, 168–70
 3 *Hearings*, 2333
 4 Mao, *Selected Works*, II, 257
 5 *Ibid.*, 52
 6 *Ibid.*, 50
 7 *Ibid.*, 51
 8 *Ibid.*, 249
 9 Mao, *Selected Works*, I, 105
10 *Ibid.*, 83
11 Mao, *Selected Works*, IV, 28–45
12 Compton, 109–10
13 *Hearings*, 2305
14 *Ibid.*, 2354

8 Communist China in a nuclear world

BIBLIOGRAPHY

Books and monographs on the Chinese People's Republic include A. D.

Barnett, *Communist China and Asia*, Harper/O.U.P., 1960; and *Communist Economic Strategy: The Rise of Mainland China*, National Planning Association/O.U.P., 1959; R. G. Boyd, *Communist China's Foreign Policy*, Praeger/Pall Mall, 1962; K. C. Chao, *Agrarian Policy of the Chinese Communist Party*, Asia Publishihg House, Bombay, 1960; I. Gluckstein, *Mao's China: Economic and Political Survey*, Beacon Press/Allen & Unwin, 1957; A. L. Hsieh, *Communist China's Strategy in the Nuclear Age*, Prentice-Hall, Englewood Cliffs, New Jersey, 1962; J. W. Lewis, *Leadership in Communist China*, Cornell University Press, 1963; and *Major Doctrines of Communist China*, Norton, New York, 1964; C. M. Li, *Economic Development of Communist China*, University of California Press/C.U.P., 1959; S. R. Schram *The Political Thought of Mao Tse-tung*, Praeger/Pall Mall, 1963; S. H. Tang, *Communist China Today*, Vols. I and II, Praeger, New York, 1957 and 1958; R. Walker, *China Under Communism, the First Five Years*, Yale University Press/Allen & Unwin, 1955; Y. L. Wu, *An Economic Survey of Communist China*, Bookman Associates/Constable, 1956.

Among sources for the Sino–Soviet controversy are A. D. Barnett, *Communist Strategies in Asia*, Praeger/Pall Mall, 1963; G. F. Hudson, R. Lowenthal and R. MacFarquhar, *The Sino–Soviet Dispute*, Praeger, New York, 1961; K. London, *Unity and Contradiction*, Praeger, New York, 1962; and D. Zagoria, *The Sino–Soviet Conflict, 1956–61*, Princeton University Press/O.U.P., 1962. English language sources for the People's Republic are *Current Background*, *Survey of the China Mainland Press*, and *Survey of China Mainland Magazines*, all issued by the United States Consulate General, Hong Kong; documents issued by Union Research, Kowloon; and New China News Agency (N C N A), the official news service of the Peking régime.

For American policies prior to Communist control of China consult *United States Relations with China*, White Paper, No. 20549, Washington, Department of State, 1949; see also *Hearings . . .* cited in the previous chapter.

China's entry into the Korean war is analysed by A. S. Whiting in *China Crosses the Yalu*, Macmillan, New York and London, 1960; *On the Correct Handling of Contradictions Among the People*, New Century Publishers, New York, 1957, and *Imperialists and All Reactionaries are Paper Tigers*, Foreign Languages Press, Peking, 1958, both by Mao, are valuable sources for Chinese Communist theory.

The thought reform movement is documented by B. Compton in *Mao's*

China, cited in the previous chapter, and T. H. E. Chen, *Thought Reform of the Chinese Intellectuals*, Hong Kong University Press/O.U.P., 1960. Analyses of thought reform techniques are provided by the American psychiatrist R. J. Lifton in *Thought Reform and the Psychology of Totalism*, Norton/Gollancz, 1961, and by E. Schein, *et al.*, *Coercive Persuasion: A Socio-Psychological Analysis of the Brainwashing of American Civilian Prisoners by the Chinese Communists*, Norton, New York, 1961. For an analysis of 'The Hundred Flowers', see Dennis J. Doulin, *Communist China, The Politics of Student Opposition*, The Hoover Institution on War, Revolution and Peace, Stanford, 1964.

NOTES

1 *Hearings*, 605–9
2 Vladimir Dedijer, *Tito*, Simon and Schuster, New York, 1953, p. 322
3 *Hearings*, 255
4 *Ibid.*, 357
5 'On the People's Democratic Dictatorship', NCNA, 9 July 1949
6 *Current Background*, 13 June 1950, 3
7 *Ibid.*, 10 January 1952, 1, 4–6
8 *Ibid.*, 13 June 1950, 4
9 *Ibid.*, Supplement 2, 20 June 1950, 5
10 Mao, *Selected Works*, III, 136
11 *Ibid.*, 137
12 *Ibid.*, 80
13 *Ibid.*, 69
14 Mao, *Selected Works*, IV, 67–8
15 Compton, 109–10
16 Chen, 19
17 *Ibid.*, 187–8
18 *Ibid.*, 64
19 *Ibid.*, 66
20 Anna Louise Strong, *Amerasia*, XI, No. 6, June 1947, 161–74
21 *San Min Chu I*, 35
22 Mao, *On the Correct Handling*, 27
23 Mao, *Imperialists and All Reactionaries*, 28

Acknowledgments

The writing of this book has entailed the support and also the forbearance of many people, but I am particularly indebted to Dr James Doulin and Dr Eugene Wu for their suggestions and constructive criticisms, and to Mrs Helen Grace for her dedicated assistance and eagle-sharp eye. For all errors of omission and commission, however, I am solely responsible.

The Hoover Institution of Stanford University and Mrs Helen Snow have been most generous in supplying photographs. I am also grateful to my wife and children for many hours that belonged rightly to them. The maps were designed by T. Stalker-Miller.

Acknowledgment is due to the following for the illustrations (the number refers to the page on which the illustration appears). Frontispiece, 148, 178, 180, 183, 189, 202, 203, 207, 213 Camera Press Ltd; 6, 17, 24, 27, 56, 70 History Today; 10, 20, 21, 46, 52, 53 Radio Times Hulton Picture Library; 11 Peter Quennell; 13, 14 Mansell Collection; 39, 121, 146, 153 Nym Wales; 55, 110 China Publishing Co.; 67 Whittlesey House, New York; 83, 155, 158, 159, 161, 162, 163, 165, 166, 173, 174, 179 Keystone Press Agency; 100, 102, 105 Huston; 129, 142, 143, 149, 151 *Daily Herald*; 133 New China News Agency; 167, 182 Associated Press; 191 John Hillelson, photo H. Cartier-Bresson; 210 Cultural Press, Peking.

R.C.N.

Index

World University Library

Some books published or in preparation

Economics and Social Studies

The World Cities
Peter Hall, *London*

The Economics of Underdeveloped Countries
Jagdish Bhagwati, *Delhi*

Development Planning
Jan Tinbergen, *Rotterdam*

Leadership in New Nations
T. B. Bottomore, *Vancouver*

Key Issues in Criminology
Roger Hood, *Durham*

The Sociology of Communication
J. L. Aranguren, *Madrid*

Education in the Modern World
John Vaizey, *Oxford*

History

Ancient Egypt
Werner Kaiser, *Berlin*

The Emergence of Greek Democracy
W. G. Forrest, *Oxford*

Mahomet and the Great Arabian Conquests
Francesco Gabrieli, *Rome*

The Crusades
G. Widengren, *Uppsala*

The Medieval Economy
Georges Duby, *Aix-en-Provence*

The Ottoman Empire
Halil Inalcik, *Ankara*

The Rise of Toleration
Henry Kamen, *Edinburgh*

The Left in Europe
David Caute, *Oxford*

Chinese Communism
Robert C. North, *Stanford*

History and Sociology of Religion

History of the Christian Church
W. O. Chadwick, *Cambridge*

Monasticism
Dom David Knowles, *London*

Judaism
Rabbi J. Soetendorp, *Amsterdam*

The Modern Papacy
K. O. von Aretin, *Göttingen*

Sects
Bryan Wilson, *Oxford*

Language and Literature

A Model of Language
E. M. Uhlenbeck, *Leyden*

French Literature
Raymond Picard, *Sorbonne*

Russian Literature
Ronald Hingley, *Oxford*

Satire
Matthew Hodgart, *Sussex*

The Arts

Primitive Art
Eike Haberland, *Mainz*

The Language of Modern Art
Ulf Linde, *Stockholm*

Aesthetic Theories since 1850
J. F. Revel, *Paris*

Art Nouveau
S. T. Madsen, *Oslo*

Academic Painting
Gerald Ackerman, *Stanford*

Palaeolithic Art
P. J. Ucko and A. Rosenfeld, *London*

Modern Drama
Peter Szondi, *Göttingen*

Psyc
Human Biology

Eye and Brain
R. L. Gregory, *Cambridge*

The Ear and the Brain
Edward Carterette, *U.C.L.A.*

The Variety of Man
J. P. Garlick, *London*

The Biology of Work
O. G. Edholm, *London*

Bioengineering
H. S. Wolff, *London*

Psychoses
H. J. Bochnik, *Hamburg*

Child Development
Philippe Muller, *Neuchâtel*

Man and Disease
Gernot Rath, *Göttingen*

Zoology and Botany

Animal Communication
N. Tinbergen and J. M. Cullen, *Oxford*

Mimicry
Wolfgang Wickler, *Starnberg*

Migration
Gustaf Rudebeck, *Stockholm*

The World of an Insect
Remy Chauvin, *Sorbonne*

Biological Rhythms
Janet Harker, *Cambridge*

Lower Animals
Martin Wells, *Cambridge*

Physical Science and Mathematics

Mathematics in Science and Daily Life
H. Freudenthal, *Utrecht*

The Physics of Low Temperatures
K. A. G. Mendelssohn, *Oxford*

Particles and Accelerators
Robert Gouiran, *C.E.R.N., Geneva*

Optics
A. C. S. van Heel, *Delft*

Waves and Corpuscles
J. A. E. Silva and G. Lochak, *Paris*
Introduction by Louis de Broglie

Earth Sciences and Astronomy

Anatomy of the Earth
André de Cayeux, *Sorbonne*

The Electrical Earth
J. Sayers, *Birmingham*

Climate and Weather
H. Flohn, *Bonn*

The Structure of the Universe
E. L. Schatzman, *Sorbonne*

Applied Science

Words and Waves
A. H. Beck, *Cambridge*

Operational Research
A. Kaufmann, *Sorbonne*